Joseph Deharbe, John Fander

A Full Catechism Of The Catholic Religion

Joseph Deharbe, John Fander

A Full Catechism Of The Catholic Religion

ISBN/EAN: 9783742856746

Manufactured in Europe, USA, Canada, Australia, Japa

Cover: Foto ©Lupo / pixelio.de

Manufactured and distributed by brebook publishing software (www.brebook.com)

Joseph Deharbe, John Fander

A Full Catechism Of The Catholic Religion

A

FULL CATECHISM

OF THE

CATHOLIC RELIGION;

PRECEDED BY A

SHORT HISTORY OF RELIGION

FROM THE

CREATION OF THE WORLD TO THE PRESENT TIME,

WITH

QUESTIONS FOR EXAMINATION.

TRANSLATED FROM THE GERMAN OF THE
REV. JOSEPH DEHARBE, S.J.,
BY THE
REV. JOHN FANDER.

Permissu Superiorum.

LONDON:
THE CATHOLIC PUBLISHING AND BOOKSELLING COMPANY,
LIMITED,
53, LATE 61, NEW BOND STREET.

1863.

Entered at Stationers' Hall.

Imprimatur.

WESTMON. 29 JUL. 1862.

N. CARD. WISEMAN.

Google

TRANSLATOR'S PREFACE.

The original of this Catechism was first published in Germany in 1847, and met with such general favour that, in 1853, it numbered twenty-one Editions. It has been approved by all the Archbishops and Bishops of Bavaria, and by nearly all those of the other countries in Germany, and by those of Switzerland. It has been reprinted, with the approbation of Archbishop Purcell, in the United States of America, and has been introduced there into the German Schools; in a word, it has superseded nearly all the various Catechisms previously used in the Dioceses of those countries, and is now almost the only authorized and standard Catechism of the whole German nation.

This Catechism is founded on History, not only on the History of the Old and New Testament, but on the History of Religion from the Creation of the world to the present time. It clearly shows how our Faith originated and spread, what blessings it produced, how it confounded Infidelity and Heresy, and triumphed over all sorts of obstacles and persecutions in every age down to this day. It thus shows how the predictions of the Prophets, and especially those of the Eternal Son of God, with regard to His Church, have been fulfilled at all times, and, consequently, which among the numberless Societies that claim Christ for their Founder, professes the True and Divine Religion really established by Him. In this, it carries out the advice of St. Augustine, who admonishes Catechists, "to give a brief account to the ignorant of the whole History from the Creation to the present time of the Church,[*] and to adduce the causes of the various events." How much is it not to be regretted that this advice of the great Doctor has been so sadly neglected in the course of time! Why are Protestants so much prejudiced against the Catholic Church, and why is it so difficult to convert them? It is, because they impress upon the minds of their children a false view of the History of their Religion, a Religion that dates only from the beginning of the sixteenth century. Why should not Catholics equally, nay, more confirm their children in their attachment to the Church, by showing them how to trace her to the times of the Apostles, and even to the Creation of the world? Is it not, then, of the greatest importance to teach them, together with their Catechism, the History of their Religion? History is a safeguard against internal doubts, and a bulwark against all external attacks. He who has, by this means, been fully strengthened in his conviction that the Catholic Church is from God, and that she is the Only True Church, cannot but love her, and submit his intellect to her doctrine and his heart to her precepts, and thus remain all his life-time faithful to her.

After it has been proved by History that the Catholic Religion is *Divine*, the Catechism begins, and teaches that we must submit to its doctrine; namely, that we

---

[*] Usque ad præsentia tempora Ecclesiæ. (De Catechiz. Rudibus, C. 3. & 6.)

must 1. *Believe* what it teaches; 2. That we must also *practise*, that is, *do the will of God;* and 3. That we can neither believe, nor do the will of God, without His grace, which we receive by means of the *Sacraments* and of *Prayer*. This division is not only dictated by reason, but it embraces also every particular part of the Christian Doctrine; for instance: as *Sin* is the voluntary breaking of the Commandments, and *Virtue* the opposite of sin, these two heads belong to the Second Part. It is, moreover, the only way in which the Catechism should be learnt; for a child cannot even go to Confession, unless he be instructed in the First and Second Part; namely, upon the *Creed*, the *Commandments of God and the Church, Sin* and *Virtue*. Finally, it is the easiest division of all; and a child, with the help of a teacher, may get, in less than a quarter of an hour, such a clear view of all the general and particular parts of the Christian Doctrine, that he will never forget them in after-life. But, as there is a logical connection in the general parts, so there is one also between the questions and answers throughout each particular treatise. One question and answer leads to the following question and answer, and these again to the next, and thus the whole treatise forms, as it were, one coherent conversation; and certainly, these are not to be considered as unimportant advantages.

The dogmatical and moral explanation of the Christian Doctrine itself is comprehensive and plain, and is adapted to the present wants of youth, being proved in full from Holy Scripture, Tradition, and the General Councils. It is at the same time controversial, inasmuch as the objections made against it by Infidels, Heretics, and Innovators, are *solidly* refuted; and, therefore, it may justly be called a *full* Catechism of the Catholic Religion.

This Catechism, however, is not intended for children and Elementary Schools, but more particularly for Colleges, Teachers, and Private Instruction. There are two Abridgments of it for Schools, with the same wording, and made by the Author himself, which have been equally approved of throughout all Germany; and, should this Translation, which is made from the last improved Edition of 1861, meet with the approbation of the Catholic body in this country, Translations of the two Abridgments will soon follow.

THE "SHORT HISTORY OF RELIGION FROM THE CREATION OF THE WORLD TO THE PRESENT TIME," which stands at the head of the Catechism, was edited with a great many Alterations and Additions by the Rev. Dr. Fergusson in 1854. The Translator, who was in no way responsible for those changes, has now carefully revised his first Translation, and most faithfully expressed in it the sense of the Original Text. Here and there, however, he has made a few, but very short, Additions, which he has either translated or compiled from Writers of highly approved authority. These Additions are notified at the end of the History.

OCTAVE OF ST. STEPHEN,
    January 2nd

THE ROSARY,

As it is said in Germany, where the Mysteries, on which we meditate, are expressed in the middle of each *Hail Mary*, immediately after the name of JESUS. All the rest is the same as in other countries.
(See Pages 326 & 327.)

PRELIMINARY PRAYERS.

In the name of the Father, etc.—*I believe in God*, etc.— One *Our Father*, and three *Hail Marys*, in the middle of which are added these words :—

—Jesus ; may He increase our faith !—*R*. Holy Mary, etc.

—Jesus ; may He strengthen our hope !—*R*. Holy Mary, etc.

—Jesus ; may He inflame our love !—*R*. Holy Mary, etc.

Glory be to the Father, etc.—*R*. As it was in the beginning, etc.

I.—THE JOYFUL MYSTERIES.

[In each of the five Mysteries say one *Our Father*, ten *Hail Marys*, and, at the end, *Glory be to the Father;* which is called *One Decade.*]

1.—Jesus, whom thou, O Virgin, didst conceive of the Holy Ghost.—*R*. Holy Mary, etc.

2.—Jesus, whom thou, O Virgin, didst bear in thy womb when visiting Elizabeth.—*R*. Holy Mary, etc.

3.—Jesus, whom thou, O Virgin, didst bring forth in a stable at Bethlehem.—*R*. Holy Mary, etc.

4.—Jesus, whom thou, O Virgin, didst present in the temple. *R*. Holy Mary, etc.

5.—Jesus, whom thou, O Virgin, didst find in the temple. *R*. Holy Mary, etc.

II.—THE SORROWFUL (DOLOROUS) MYSTERIES.

1.—Jesus, who was bathed in a bloody sweat for us.
   R. Holy Mary, etc.
2.—Jesus, who was most cruelly scourged for us.
   R. Holy Mary, etc.
3.—Jesus, who was crowned with thorns for us.
   R. Holy Mary, etc.
4.—Jesus, who carried the heavy Cross for us.
   R. Holy Mary, etc.
5.—Jesus, who died on the Cross for us. R. Holy Mary, etc.

III.—THE GLORIOUS MYSTERIES.

1.—Jesus, who rose again from the dead. R. Holy Mary, etc.
2.—Jesus, who ascended into Heaven.   R.   ,,
3.—Jesus, who sent down the Holy Ghost upon the Apostles.
   R. Holy Mary, etc.
4.—Jesus, who took thee, O Virgin, up into Heaven.
   R. Holy Mary, etc.
5.—Jesus, who crowned thee, O Virgin, in Heaven.
   R. Holy Mary, etc.

[When the whole *Rosary* or *Psalter* (15 Decades) is said at a time, the *Preliminary Prayers* are said but once.]

THE CHAPLET OF THE BLESSED SACRAMENT

Has the same Preliminary Prayers as the Rosary, and five Decades, with the following Mystery expressed in each Hail Mary:

—Jesus; may He be praised and blessed in the Most Holy Sacrament of the Altar! R. Now and for evermore! Holy Mary, etc.

THE CHAPLET FOR THE DEAD

Is said in the same manner as the preceding, with this Petition in each Hail Mary:

—Jesus; may He give eternal rest to the faithful departed!
   R. Holy Mary, etc.

CONTENTS.

	PAGE
TRANSLATOR'S PREFACE.	v.
ROSARY, as said in Germany	ix.
CHAPLET of the Blessed Sacrament	x.
CHAPLET for the Dead	ib.
EXPLANATION of Abbreviations and Marks	xv.

HISTORY OF RELIGION.

I. HISTORY BEFORE CHRIST.
    From Adam to Moses ... 3
    From Moses to Christ ... 7
II. HISTORY OF CHRIST ... 15
III. HISTORY AFTER CHRIST.
    From the Ascension of Christ to the Conversion of Constantine ... 21
    From the Conversion of Constantine to the Rise of Protestantism in the 16th Century ... 27
    From the Rise of Protestantism in the 16th Century to Pope Pius IX. ... 39
CONCLUDING REMARKS ... 54
CHRONOLOGICAL SUCCESSION OF THE POPES ... 59
ADDITIONS ... 63

CHRISTIAN DOCTRINE.

INTRODUCTION ... 65

PART I.—*On Faith.*

ACCEPTATION, OBJECT, AND RULE OF FAITH ... 69
NECESSITY OF FAITH ... 76
QUALITIES OF FAITH ... 79

XII.

On the Apostles' Creed.

	PAGE
FIRST ARTICLE	82
On God, and His Attributes or Perfections ...	ib.
On the Three Divine Persons	89
On the Creation and Government of the World	91
On the Angels	95
On our First Parents and their Fall	97
SECOND ARTICLE	103
Jesus Christ, the Promised Messias	105
Jesus Christ, True God	109
THIRD ARTICLE	113
FOURTH ARTICLE	116
FIFTH ARTICLE	120
SIXTH ARTICLE	122
SEVENTH ARTICLE	123
EIGHTH ARTICLE	127
NINTH ARTICLE	130
On the Church, and the Form of her Government	ib.
On the Marks of the Church	138
On the End of the Church, and on her Qualities resulting from this End:	142
(*a*) On the Infallibility of the Church	143
(*b*) On Salvation in the True Church of Christ alone	145
On the Communion of Saints	
TENTH ARTICLE	150
ELEVENTH ARTICLE	151
TWELFTH ARTICLE	154

PART II.—*On the Commandments.*

ON THE COMMANDMENTS IN GENERAL	159
ON THE CHIEF COMMANDMENT	160
On the Love of God	ib.
On the Love of our Neighbour	162
On Christian Self-Love	167
ON THE TEN COMMANDMENTS OF GOD	169
First Commandment of God	170
On the Veneration and Invocation of the Saints	176

	PAGE
Second Commandment of God	181
Third Commandment of God	185
Fourth Commandment of God	187
Fourth Commandment continued	193
Fifth Commandment of God	195
Sixth Commandment of God	199
Seventh Commandment of God	201
Eighth Commandment of God	205
Ninth and Tenth Commandments of God	209

ON THE SIX COMMANDMENTS OF THE CHURCH ... 211

- First Commandment of the Church ... 213
- Second Commandment of the Church ... 214
- Third Commandment of the Church ... 216
- Fourth and Fifth Commandments of the Church ... 220
- Sixth Commandment of the Church ... 221

ON THE VIOLATION OF THE COMMANDMENTS, OR ON SIN ... 22

- On Sin in General ... ib.
- On the Different Kinds of Sin ... 224
- The Different Kinds of Sin continued ... 227

ON VIRTUE AND CHRISTIAN PERFECTION ... 230

- On Virtue ... ib.
- On Christian Perfection ... 234

PART III.—*On the Means of Grace.*

ON GRACE IN GENERAL ... 240

ON THE GRACE OF ASSISTANCE ...

ON THE GRACE OF SANCTIFICATION OR JUSTIFICATION ... 243

1. *On the Sacraments* ... 247

   - Baptism ... 250
   - Confirmation ... 255
   - Holy Eucharist ... 259
     - On the Real Presence of Christ in the Blessed Sacrament ... ib.
     - On the Holy Sacrifice of the Mass ... 264
     - On Holy Communion ... 270
   - Penance ... 277

XIV.

Penance continued.

	PAGE
Examination of Conscience	280
Contrition	281
Resolution of Amendment	285
Confession	286
Satisfaction	290
Indulgences	293
Extreme Unction	297
Holy Order	300
Matrimony	303
ON SACRAMENTALS	311
2. *On Prayer*	314
On the Lord's Prayer	319
On the Angelical Salutation	323
ON RELIGIOUS PRACTICES AND CEREMONIES IN GENERAL, AND ON SOME IN PARTICULAR	327
RECAPITULATION	332

EXPLANATION
OF THE
ABBREVIATIONS AND MARKS USED IN THE SHORT HISTORY AND CATECHISM.

(d. 1584) ...	*stands for* ...	died in 1584.
B. C. ...	,,	Before Christ.
A. D. ...	,,	Anno Domini, or, in the year of our Lord.
i.e. ...	,,	id est, or, that is.
viz. ...	,,	videlicet, or, namely.
comp. ...	,,	compare.
§. 6. ...	,,	Paragraph 6th of the History.
§.§. 8. 9. 10.	,,	Paragraphs 8. 9. 10.
Concl. Rem...	,,	Concluding Remarks; see page 54.
Ex. ...	,,	Example, or, Examples.
Counc. of Tr. S. 6. ch. 11. c. 22..	,,	Council of Trent, Session 6th, Chapter 11th, Canon 22nd.
Page 107. Qu. 17. ,,	...	Page 107th. Question 17th.
Eccles. ...	,,	Ecclesiastes.
Ecclus. ...	,,	Ecclesiasticus.
Matth. 16, 18. 19. ,,	...	St. Matthew, Chapter 16th, verses 18 and 19.
Tob. 6. 8. & 11. ,,	...	Tobias, Chapters 6. 8. & 11.

See the names of the Books of the Old and New Testaments on pages 71 and 72.

* The asterisk, or little star, put before a question of the Catechism, denotes that the question and its answer may be passed over without destroying the connexion between the preceding and the following.

ERRATA.

Page 115, line 37, *for* Jesus the good shepherd,
                    read ²Jesus the good shepherd.
,, 134, ,, 31, *for* but few, heresies,
                    read but few heresies.
,, 152, ,, 26, *for* into the resurrection,
                    read unto the resurrection.
,, 176, ,, 32, *for* the Mass to God, alone,
                    read the Mass, to God alone.
,, 179, ,, 20, *for* not make to yourself,
                    read not make to yourselves.
,, 180, ,, 33, *for* Acts 19, 11. 92.
                    read Acts 19, 11. 12.
,, 188, ,, 28, *for* "God, blessed for evermore,"
                    read "God blessed for ever."
,, 189, ,, 8, *for* despise and disregard,
                    read despise or disregard.

SHORT HISTORY OF RELIGION.

HISTORY BEFORE CHRIST.

I.—*From Adam to Moses.*

1. In the beginning God created Heaven and Earth. He said, "*Let them be made,*" and they were made. In six days God created the whole world—the sun, moon, and stars; the plants, trees, and animals; and, last of all, He made man to His own image and likeness. The first man was called Adam, and the first woman, Eve. They were just and holy, and the favourites of God. They lived happy in a delicious garden, called Paradise, and they and their descendants were never to die.

2. God commanded Adam and Eve not to eat of the fruit of the tree that stood in the midst of the garden, lest they should die. But the serpent said to them: "If you eat thereof, you shall be as Gods." Adam and Eve believed the serpent, and broke the command of God. For this sin of disobedience, punishment immediately came upon them, and all

---

1. How did God create Heaven and Earth? In how many days did He create all things? When did He create man? How did He distinguish man from the other creatures? What were the names of the first man and woman? Were they also liable to sin, as we are? Where did they live? Were they, and their children, ever to die?

2. What commandment did God give to Adam and Eve? What did the serpent tell them? What did Adam and Eve do? Were they punished for it? Were they alone punished?

their descendants. They were driven from Paradise, were doomed to death and many hardships, and were to be banished from God for ever. Nevertheless, God had compassion on them, and promised them a *Saviour*, who should reconcile them again to Him, and make them partakers of eternal happiness, provided they did penance. (Gen. 3, 15.)

3. Cain and Abel, sons of our first parents, offered sacrifice to Almighty God. God was pleased with that of the virtuous Abel, but not with that of the wicked Cain. Cain, being exceedingly angry at the preference given to his brother, killed him; and, in punishment for this crime, he was cursed by God, and became a vagabond upon earth.

4. The descendants of Cain were wicked, like their father, and gradually seduced even the good; insomuch that, in process of time, all men turned away from God, and sank deeper and deeper into sin and vice. God then resolved to destroy the degenerate race of Adam by a universal deluge (B.C. about 2350). The rain fell upon the earth for forty days and forty nights, and the waters rose fifteen cubits, or twenty-seven feet and a half, above the highest mountains. All living creatures on the face of the earth perished in the flood, except the pious Noe, with his family, and the animals that were with him in the ark, which he had built by the command of God. In thanksgiving for this favour, Noe erected an altar, and offered a burnt-sacrifice to the Lord, who, in return, blessed

---

What punishment came upon them? Did God then abandon them? What did He promise them?

3. Who were Cain and Abel? How did they worship God? Was God pleased with their sacrifices? What did Cain do, and what became of him?

4. Were the descendants of Cain good or wicked? What evil did they do? What did God then resolve to do? How long did it rain? To what height did the flood rise? Did all living creatures perish? What did Noe do when he came

him and his sons, and promised him that "there should no more be waters of a flood to destroy all flesh." (Gen. 9, 15.)

5. The descendants of Noe became so numerous that they had soon to be scattered abroad into all lands. However, before separating, they determined to build a tower, the top of which should reach to Heaven. But God confounded their language, so that they were obliged to desist from building; and the tower was called the *Tower of Babel*, or *Confusion*. Noe's descendants also gave themselves up to their wicked inclinations, and degenerated so far that, instead of adoring the true God, they worshipped the sun and the moon, men and animals, and even idols of gold and silver, and of stone and wood. This shameful idolatry brought with it all kinds of sins and vices, which again prevailed in a frightful manner among mankind.

6. God, however, provided that the true faith, and the hope in a future Redeemer, should not entirely vanish from the earth. For that purpose, He chose Abraham (B.C. 1920), made a particular covenant with him, and promised him that the "*Messias*" should be born of his posterity, saying: "In thee shall all the kindred of the earth be blessed." (Gen. 12, 3.) Therefore, God also distinguished Abraham and his descendants—who were called *Hebrews*, and afterwards *Israelites* or *Jews*—from all

---

out of the ark? What new kindness did God show to Noe and his sons?

5. Did the descendants of Noe multiply much? What did they attempt to do? How was their undertaking frustrated? What was the tower called? Did the descendants of Noe remain faithful to God? What was the consequence of their idolatry?

6. Were the true religion and the hope in the Redeemer entirely to vanish? How did God prevent this? How were the descendants of Abraham called? What favour did God bestow on them?

other nations, and, in the course of time, often revealed Himself to them in a wonderful manner.

7. In order to try the faith of Abraham, God commanded him to offer his only son Isaac in sacrifice upon Mount Moria. Abraham set out without hesitation. He himself placed the wood for the burnt-offering upon his son, and ascended the mountain with him. When they had reached the summit, Isaac willingly laid himself on the wood to be offered up in sacrifice; but God saved the pious Isaac through an Angel, blessed Abraham for his obedience, and renewed His former promises to him.

> Isaac was here a figure of the future Saviour of the world, who, in obedience to His Father, took the wood of the cross upon His shoulders, and carried it to Mount Calvary, to sacrifice Himself upon it for our redemption.

8. The patriarch Jacob was the son of Isaac, and lived with his family in the land of Chanaan, the country into which God had called Abraham. He had twelve sons, who became the fathers of the twelve tribes of Israel. One of them, Joseph, was chosen by God to be, through what happened to him in his life, a figure of Jesus Christ. Having been sold by his brothers, he was carried into Egypt, where he was falsely accused, and cast into prison. After recovering his liberty, the King made him chief ruler over all Egypt; and as, by his wisdom and prudence, he saved the country during seven years from a dreadful famine, he was called "Saviour of the world." (Gen. 41, 45.)

---

7. How did God try the faith of Abraham? How did he fulfil the command of God? What did Isaac do? Did God suffer him to be killed? How did God reward Abraham? What mysterious signification does the sacrifice of Isaac contain?

8. Who was Jacob, and where did he live? How many sons had he, and what did they become afterwards? What was Joseph chosen by God to be? What happened to him?

At his invitation, Jacob also, with all his family, went to Egypt, and settled there. Before his death, he pronounced this remarkable prophecy regarding the Redeemer: "*The sceptre* (supreme power) *shall not be taken away from* (the tribe of) *Juda* (his son), *till He come, that is to be sent; and He shall be the expectation of nations.*" (Gen. 49, 10.) And, in fact, Christ, who *was sent by God*, was not born until Herod, a stranger, sat on the throne of the Kings of Juda.

II.—*From Moses to Christ.*

9. After Joseph's death, the Israelites grew into a great people, insomuch that the Egyptians, fearing they might become too powerful, reduced them to the hardest slavery. At length, the Lord appeared to Moses in a flame of fire out of the midst of a bush, and commissioned him to lead the children of Israel back to Chanaan (B. C. 1500). Pharao, King of Egypt, would not let them go; and, therefore, Almighty God sent dreadful plagues over all his dominions, and, at last, an Angel, who in one night killed all the firstborn of the Egyptians. But the destroying Angel did not hurt the Israelites, because they had sprinkled the doors of their houses with the blood of the paschal lamb, which, according to God's command, they ate that very night.

> By this was foreshown how, one day, mankind should be delivered from eternal death by the Blood of Jesus Christ, the true Divine Paschal Lamb, which we eat in the Holy Eucharist.

Did Jacob remain in Chanaan? What did he prophesy before his death, and about whom? How was it fulfilled?

9. What happened to the children of Israel in Egypt? Whom did God appoint to deliver them? How did he appear to Moses? Did Moses meet with any opposition? What did God do to the Egyptians? Did the Angel hurt also the Israelites? Why did he not hurt them? What did the blood of the paschal lamb signify?

10. Then Pharao permitted the Israelites to depart; but he soon regretted it. In all haste, he collected his troops, and pursued the unarmed Israelites to the shores of the Red Sea, who, struck with alarm and dread of being drowned or slaughtered, implored the assistance of God. Then Moses, by the command of God, stretched forth his rod over the Red Sea; and, behold, the waters were divided before them, and stood like a wall on their right hand and on their left, and they passed through on dry ground. Pharao rushed furiously after them into the midst of the sea; whereupon Moses once more stretched forth his rod over the waters, and they suddenly returned to their former place, and buried Pharao with his whole army in the deep.

11. The children of Israel had now to travel through a vast wilderness, and came, fifty days after their departure from Egypt, to Mount Sinai, where God, amidst thunder and lightning, gave them the Ten Commandments, written on two tables of stone. He also renewed with them the covenant He had made with their fathers, and regulated their religious and civil duties by most salutary laws. But the people soon forgot the Commandments and blessings of God, and continually complained and murmured; nay, they debased themselves to such a degree, that they made a golden calf, and adored it as their God.

12. In punishment of these, and many other grievous sins, the Israelites had to remain forty years in the desert, until another and better generation had grown

---

10. Did Pharao continue keeping the Israelites in bondage? What did he do soon after? What did the Israelites do on their part? How were they delivered? How did God punish Pharao?

11. Did the Israelites now go on straight to Chanaan? How long were they journeying from Egypt to Mount Sinai? What happened at Mount Sinai? Did God give them the Ten Commandments only? What return did they make for all these benefits?

12. How was their ingratitude punished?

up. Nevertheless, God continually bestowed favours upon them. He rained bread, called *manna*, from Heaven for them, and gave them water from a rock; and, at last, after Moses' death, He conducted them into Chanaan, or Palestine, the promised land, which they conquered with His powerful assistance, and divided into twelve parts, giving one of them to each of the twelve tribes.

> All this was a figure of the future salvation of mankind. (1. Cor. 10, 6.)—The deliverance from the bondage of Egypt, signifies our liberation from the slavery of Satan by Jesus Christ.—The journey through the wilderness, signifies our pilgrimage in this world, where God gives us His laws, nourishes us with the true Bread of Heaven, and strengthens us with the life-giving fountains of grace.—The land of promise, refers us to Heaven, which, by combating the world, the flesh, and the devil, we must conquer and take eternal possession of.

13. In this beautiful country, the Israelites lived happy, and were blessed by God, until, contrary to His express command, they united themselves by marriage to the Gentiles, or Pagans, and thereby fell again into vice and idolatry. As often as they turned away from God, He abandoned them to their enemies; but, when they returned to Him, He raised among them pious heroes, called *Judges*, such as, Gedeon, Jephte, and Samson, who rescued them from their foes.

14. For more than four hundred years, the people of Israel were ruled by the High-Priests and Judges,

---

Did God abandon them altogether? What favours did He still show them? When, and how, did they get possession of Chanaan? Is there not a figure in all this? What does the deliverance from Egypt signify? What does the journey through the desert signify? What does the promised land call to our mind?

13. How long did the Israelites remain happy in the promised land? What happened to them when they offended God? How did God help them when they repented?

14. Who were the first rulers of the people of Israel? How long were they governed by them?

who were invested with supreme authority over them; but now they desired to be governed, like the neighbouring nations, by a King. In compliance with their wish, God appointed Saul to be their King, and the Prophet Samuel anointed him in 1095 B.C. He was, however, rejected by God for his disobedience, and was succeeded by David in 1055. David was strong and mighty: when only a youth, he had slain the giant Goliath; and having been made King, he extended his kingdom by splendid victories. He served God with an upright heart, and composed in His honour those beautiful sacred songs, called *Psalms*, in which, by Divine inspiration, he prophesied many things concerning the Redeemer of the world, who was to be born of his family, and whose kingdom should have no end. For this reason, Christ is also called the Son of David.

15. Solomon, his son and successor, was a wise and great King. He built a magnificent temple to the Lord in Jerusalem about the year 1000 B.C. The Sanctuary, or Holy of Holies, was overlaid with plates of the purest gold; and in it was kept the Ark of the Covenant, which contained the Two Tables of Laws, written by God Himself. The High-Priest was the only person who was allowed, once a year, to enter the Sanctuary. The people of Israel had no other temple, nor was any one permitted to offer up sacrifice in any other place, except in the temple of Jerusalem.

Who was the first King of Israel? Why was he rejected by God? By whom was he succeeded? What can you tell me of David? Was he also pious? Why are his Psalms so very remarkable? Why is Christ also called the Son of David?

15. Who was Solomon? What famous building did he erect? How was the Sanctuary decorated, and what was kept in it? What did the Ark of the Covenant contain? Who was permitted to enter the Sanctuary, and how many times a year? Had the people of Israel any other temples, or altars?

Solomon, however, did not persevere in wisdom and goodness. He married Pagan wives, and had, towards the end of his life, the misfortune of being seduced by them from the service of God into the impious practices of idolatry.

16. After Solomon's death, his kingdom was divided (B.C. 980). The tribes of Juda and Benjamin remained faithful to King Roboam, his son, and formed the kingdom of *Juda*, the chief city of which was Jerusalem. The other ten tribes chose Jeroboam for their King, and made Samaria the capital of their kingdom, which from that time was called the kingdom of *Israel*. At the same time, they abandoned the religion of their fathers, built a temple for themselves at Samaria, and introduced all sorts of the most abominable idolatry. God, therefore, delivered them into the hands of the Pagan King, Salmanasar, who destroyed the kingdom of Israel for ever, and led the people to Ninive, into the Assyrian Captivity (B.C. 718). The kingdom of Juda was also repeatedly chastised by God for its many transgressions. In 606, Nabuchodonosor (Nebuchadnezzar) II. took Jerusalem, pillaged the temple, and sent the sacred vessels and a large number of Jews to Babylon; and in 588, he entirely demolished the temple and the city, and carried Sedecias, the last King of Juda, with the rest of the inhabitants, into the same Babylonian Captivity. But the kingdom of Juda was not destroyed for ever,

---

Did Solomon remain wise and good? What made him leave the service of God?

16. What happened after Solomon's death? Which tribes formed the kingdom of Juda? Who was its first King? Which was its capital? How many tribes constituted the kingdom of Israel? Whom did they choose for their King? Which was the capital of the kingdom of Israel? Did it remain faithful to God? How did God punish it? Did the kingdom of Juda also sin against the Lord? Was it also chastised, and how? Was not its punishment less severe than that of the kingdom of Israel, and why?

like the kingdom of Israel, that had forsaken the religion of its fathers.

17. These severe judgments of God did not by any means overtake them suddenly and unexpectedly. Men enlightened by God, who were called Prophets, had announced them long before, confirming their words by great miracles, in order to rouse the people to repentance. These same Prophets also promised pardon to those who should repent, and prophesied of the Redeemer who was to come. In their books, written many centuries before Christ, we read all the circumstances of His life and sufferings : His birth of a Virgin at Bethlehem, His office of teaching, His miracles, His passion, His death, His resurrection, the sending of the Holy Ghost, the destruction of Jerusalem, the conversion of the Gentiles, and the splendour of the Christian Church ; nay, Daniel foretold the very year in which the Saviour was to appear. The most remarkable amongst the Prophets are, Elias, Eliseus, Isaias, Jeremias, Ezechiel, and Daniel.

18. During the time of the Captivity, illustrious examples of rare virtues were given by Tobias at Ninive ; and at Babylon, by the chaste Susanna, by the three young men in the fiery furnace, and by Daniel in the lions' den. The Babylonian Captivity had already lasted seventy years, when Cyrus, King of Persia, took Babylon, and, by Divine inspiration, gave permission to the Jews to return to their own country (B.C. 536), and to rebuild the temple at

---

17. Did the judgments of God come upon them quite unexpectedly ? How did God forewarn the people ? Did the Prophets only announce God's judgments ? What have they foretold of the Messias ? Which Prophet foretold the time of His coming most precisely ? Which are the most remarkable among the Prophets ?

18. Who distinguished themselves by their virtues at Ninive and Babylon ? How long did the Babylonian Captivity last ? How was it brought to an end ? What did the Jews most urgently set about after their return ?

Jerusalem. In a short time, the second temple was finished; and when the old men began to complain that its magnificence was far inferior to that of the first, the Prophet Aggeus foretold them that the glory of this latter house should be greater than that of the former, because the "*Desired of all nations*," the Messias, was to enter it. (Agg. 2, 8—10.)

19. Esdras and Nehemias now re-established the Divine Service in conformity to the law, and collected the Sacred Scriptures, which thenceforth were diligently read and interpreted. All the people shed tears, and repented most sincerely. They never more returned to idolatry, which had brought upon them the grievous sufferings of their Captivity. When, some time later, Antiochus, King of Syria, tried to compel them to adore idols, they resisted most courageously under the command of the High-Priest Mathathias, and his sons; nay, many of them, animated by the glorious example of the aged Eleazar, of the seven brothers, commonly called the Machabees, and of their heroic mother, preferred to suffer the most atrocious of deaths, rather than disobey the law of God. (B.C. 170—143.)

20. Four thousand years had elapsed since the creation of the world, and the signs that were to precede the coming of the Redeemer of mankind, were now accomplished. The Jews longed for it with the greatest anxiety, and even among the Gentiles there was a current opinion that a great Ruler was to rise

---

Was the new temple as magnificent as the one that had been demolished? In what was it superior to the first one?

19. What is to be observed about Esdras and Nehemias? How did the people then behave? Did they remain faithful to their Lord and God? How did they show their fidelity? Who especially distinguished themselves at that time?

20. How many years had the world existed before the coming of the Messias? Were all the signs of His coming accomplished at that time? What was the prevalent feeling of the Jews and the Pagans?

in Judea. The corruption in which the world was sunk, was unbounded. The Jews, indeed, still acknowledged the one true God ; but impious sects, such as the Pharisees and Sadducees, had sprung up amongst them, and a great corruption of morals had gained ground. Most of them honoured God only with their lips, but their conduct was according to the sinful desires of their heart. All other nations, even the most enlightened among them, the Greeks and Romans, were devoted to the most shameful idolatry. Innumerable were the gods and goddesses to whom they built temples and altars, and offered sacrifices, even of human beings; and whom they believed they particularly honoured, when they extolled their infamous vices, and imitated them without shame or fear. Such were the Heathens, as St. Paul testifies (Rom. 1, 29—31) : " Filled with all iniquity, malice, fornication, avarice, wickedness ; full of envy, murder, contention, deceit, malignity ; whisperers, detractors, hateful to God, contumelious, proud, haughty, inventors of evil things, disobedient to parents, foolish, dissolute, without affection, without fidelity, without mercy." Who was then able to help, and save mankind ?—God alone;—and He did help, and did save them.—As He had promised to our first parents in Paradise, and foretold by the Prophets, He now showed mercy to mankind, when in their utmost degeneracy, and sent them a Redeemer and Saviour ; for, " God so loved the world, as to give His Only Begotten Son, that whosoever believeth in Him, may not perish, but may have life everlasting." (John 3, 16.)

What was the state of the world ? How did this corruption appear among the Jews ? And how, amongst the other nations ? In what did the abomination of idolatry consist ? What character does St. Paul give of the Heathens ? Was there any one then who could help mankind ? Did He help them, and how ? What did Christ Himself say on this subject ?

HISTORY OF CHRIST.

21. The world was at peace; Augustus was Emperor of Rome, and Herod, the Idumean, King of Judea (§8.), when the promise of God, and the predictions of the Prophets, were accomplished. Jesus Christ, the Son of God and Redeemer of the world, was born, in a stable at Bethlehem, of Mary, a virgin, descended from the royal family of David. His birth was announced by Angels to the shepherds at Bethlehem, and by a star to the Wise Men in the East. The cruel Herod made every effort to discover the Divine Infant, that he might put Him to death; but by the Lord's command, Joseph, the foster-father of Jesus, fled with Him and His mother to Egypt, and did not return till after the death of Herod. Jesus then led a retired life at Nazareth in Galilee, was subject to His parents, and " advanced in wisdom, and age, and grace with God and men." (Luke 2, 52.) When He was twelve years old, He went with His parents to Jerusalem to celebrate the Pasch, or Passover, and remained there three days in the temple, astonishing even the Scribes or Doctors of the Law, by His wise questions and answers. At the age of thirty, He went to the River Jordan to be baptized by John the Baptist. When He came out of the water, the Holy Ghost descended upon Him in the shape of a dove, and a voice came from Heaven, saying: " This is My Beloved Son, in whom I am well pleased." (Matt. 3, 17.)

22. Jesus then retired into the desert, and after having fasted and prayed there forty days and forty

---

21. Under what Emperor and what King was the Redeemer born? Where, and of whom, was He born? Who was first told of His birth, and by whom? What did King Herod try to discover, and why? What did St. Joseph do? Where did Jesus spend His childhood after His return from Egypt? How did He live there? What did He do when He was twelve years old? What did He do when He was thirty? What happened at His baptism?

22. What did Jesus do after His baptism?

nights, He began to preach the Gospel, that is, the good tidings of the kingdom of God on earth. He travelled about the towns and villages, and proved His Divine mission and the truth of His doctrine, by His holy life, by miracles, and prophecies. Those who heard Him, were filled with wonder and amazement. Multitudes of people followed Him, praised and extolled Him as the true Messias, and said, "Never did man speak like this man." (John 7, 46.) Jesus selected from His followers twelve men whom He called His *Apostles* or Messengers. They were to be witnesses of His doctrine and works, that after His Ascension into Heaven, they might preach what they had seen and heard of Him, to all nations. These are the names of the twelve Apostles: Simon, who is called Peter, and Andrew, his brother; James (the Elder), the son of Zebedee, and John, his brother; Philip and Bartholomew; Thomas and Matthew; James (the Less), the son of Alpheus, and Thaddeus, his brother, sometimes called Jude; Simon, the Cananean, and Judas Iscariot, who afterwards betrayed Him. Moreover, He chose seventy-two Disciples, "and He sent them two and two before His face into every city and place, whither He Himself was to come." (Luke 10, 1.) The twelve Apostles, the seventy-two Disciples, and the others who adhered to Jesus, formed the beginning of that society of all the faithful, which we call the *Church* of Christ, and against which He promised the gates of hell should never prevail. He appointed Peter to be her visible Head on earth, called him the Rock upon which He

---

What does the word *Gospel* mean? How did Jesus prove His Divine mission? What impression did He make upon the people? How many Apostles did He choose? What does the word *Apostle* signify? Why did He choose them? What are their names? How many other Disciples did He elect, and for what purpose? Who formed the beginning of the Christian Church? What did Jesus promise to His Church? Whom did He appoint to be her visible Head on earth? By what expressions did He intimate this?

said He would build His Church, and promised him the keys of the kingdom of Heaven. (Matt. 16, 18. 19.)

23. Jesus bestowed favours upon the Jews, as no one had ever witnessed before: He made the blind to see, and the lame to walk ; He restored the sick to health, and raised the dead to life; in a word, He relieved every kind of suffering and misery. Nevertheless, He had many enemies, especially among the Scribes and Pharisees, who hated Him because He reprimanded them for their sins and vices, and also, because He would not establish a temporal kingdom, and elevate them to high dignities. They watched all his words and actions; but they could not convince Him of any sin. In the third year of His public teaching, and shortly before the Pasch, or Easter, Jesus raised Lazarus to life, after he had lain four days in the grave. The people, hearing of this miracle, greatly rejoiced; and when Jesus went to Jerusalem, they came forth in crowds to meet Him, with branches of palms and olives in their hands, spread their garments in the way, and cried, saying, "Hosanna to the Son of David: Blessed is He that cometh in the name of the Lord: Hosanna in the highest." (Matt. 21, 9.) This triumphant entry of Jesus exasperated His enemies still more, and from that day they sought to put Him to death

24. Jesus knew that the time of His bitter Passion was at hand. Resigned to the will of His Heavenly Father, He prepared to pass out of this world.

What did He promise to give him ?
23. What sort of favours did Jesus confer upon the Jews ? How did the Jews behave towards Him ? Why did the Scribes and Pharisees especially hate Him ? Why did they watch all His words and actions ? Could they convince Him of any sin ? What special miracle did Jesus perform in the third year of His teaching ? What impression did this make on the people ? In what words did they express their feelings ? What effect did this reception of Jesus produce on his enemies ?
24. How did Jesus meet His approaching Passion ?

Whilst, in comformity with the Jewish law, He was eating the Paschal Lamb with His Apostles, He took bread into His holy and venerable hands, lifted up His eyes towards Heaven to God, His Almighty Father, gave thanks, blessed and broke it, and gave it to His Disciples, saying, "*Take ye and eat; this is My Body which shall be delivered for you.*" After that, He took the chalice with wine in it, again gave thanks, blessed and gave it to His Disciples, saying, "*Drink ye all of this; this is My Blood of the New Testament, which shall be shed for you and for many unto the remission of sins. As often as you do this, do it for the commemoration of Me.*" Thus Jesus instituted the Holy Eucharist, wherein, under the appearances of bread and wine, He gives Himself truly to us for the nourishment of our souls. After the Last Supper, Jesus continued speaking for some time to His Apostles in the most affectionate manner, and promised to send them, for their Comforter, the Holy Ghost, the Spirit of Truth, who should teach them all things, and abide with them for ever. After this, He went into the garden of Gethsemani, on the Mount of Olives, to pray.

25. There all His sufferings were most sensibly displayed before His soul. A violent agony came over Him, and His sweat became as drops of blood trickling down upon the ground. "My Father," said He, "if it be possible, let this chalice pass from Me. Nevertheless, not as I will, but as Thou wilt." (Matt. 26, 39.) In the meanwhile, Judas, who was about to betray Him, approached with a band of armed men;

How did He celebrate the Last Supper with His Apostles? What commandment did He give them at the end of it? What Sacrament did He institute by this? What did He promise to His Apostles after the Last Supper? Whither did He go afterwards?

25. What did Christ suffer in the garden of Gethsemani? What memorable prayer did He say there? By whom was He then betrayed?

and Jesus suffered Himself to be taken, bound, and led before the Chief Council, where He was mocked, spit upon, and buffeted. The Chief Priests then delivered Him up as guilty of death to Pontius Pilate, the Roman Governor of Judea, who, on his part, sent Him to King Herod; but neither of them could find any evil in Him. Nevertheless, He was scourged and crowned with thorns; and at last, in compliance with the clamorous and threatening demands of the Chief Priests and the Jewish rabble, who preferred the murderer Barabbas before Him, Pilate delivered Him unto them to be crucified.

26. Jesus, like one of the greatest criminals, was loaded with a heavy cross, and conducted to Mount Calvary, a place of execution, where He was crucified between two thieves. As the Prophets had foretold, so it was now accomplished: His hands and feet were pierced with nails; the soldiers divided His garments among them, and upon His vesture they cast lots. When tormented with burning thirst, they gave Him vinegar and gall to drink. Even the Chief Priests and Ancients scoffed at Him; but Jesus suffered all these cruelties with the most wonderful patience and meekness. Nay, He even prayed for His enemies, saying: " Father, forgive them, for they know not what they do." For three hours, Jesus was hanging upon the cross, suffering the most dreadful pains. The sun was darkened, and all nature mourned. At

---

And how was He apprehended? Whither did they lead Him then? How was He treated before the Chief Council? To whom did the Chief Priests, and to whom did Pilate, deliver Him up? What did Pilate and Herod think of Him? What else had Christ to suffer?

26. What did they make Jesus carry? Where, and between whom, was He crucified? How were then the prophecies fulfilled in Him? When hanging on the cross, how did He suffer, and for whom did He pray? How long did He hang on the cross? What great miracle happened during that time?

last, with a loud voice, He exclaimed, "It is consummated; Father, into Thy hands I commend My Spirit;" and bowing His head, He gave up the ghost. The moment He expired, the earth quaked, the rocks split asunder, the veil of the temple was rent in two from the top to the bottom, the graves were opened, and many bodies of the Saints that had slept, arose and appeared in Jerusalem. The Centurion or Captain, and the soldiers, who stood near the cross, were struck with awe, and said, "Indeed this was the the Son of God."—Thus Jesus became "the propitiation for our sins; and not for ours only, but also for those of the whole world." (1. John 2, 2.)

27. It was on Good Friday, about three o'clock in the afternoon, that Jesus expired. In order to assure themselves that He was dead, one of the soldiers, with a spear, opened His side, and immediately there came out blood and water. His body was taken down from the cross, and laid in a new sepulchre hewn out in a rock. The Jews sealed it, and set a guard before it. But early on the third day, before sunrise, there was a great earthquake, and Christ Crucified arose glorious from the sepulchre. During forty days afterwards, He often appeared to His Disciples, instructed them concerning the kingdom of God—that is, the Church,—gave them power to forgive sins, and installed Peter Head of the Church, with these words: "Feed My lambs; feed My sheep." (John 21, 15—17.) When He appeared for the last

---

How did our Lord expire? What miracles illustrated His death? What benefit did Jesus confer by His death on us and on the whole world?

27. On what day, and at what hour, did Jesus expire? How did they assure themselves of His death? And what resulted from this? What was done with His sacred body? What did His enemies then do? When, and how, did Christ rise to life? How long did He yet remain on earth? What did He do during that time?

time in the midst of the Eleven, He commanded them to go into the whole world, to preach the Gospel to all nations, and to baptize them " in the name of the Father, and of the Son, and of the Holy Ghost." For that purpose, He gave them the same power which He had received from His Heavenly Father, and promised to be with them all days, even to the consummation of the world. Finally, on the fortieth day after His Resurrection, He led His Disciples to the Mount of Olives, where He lifted up His hands over them, and, whilst He blessed them, ascended in their sight up to Heaven.

HISTORY AFTER CHRIST.

I.—*From the Ascension of Christ to the Conversion of Constantine.*

28. After the Ascension of our Lord, His Disciples returned to Jerusalem, where they persevered in prayer, expecting the coming of the Holy Ghost whom He had promised to send them. In the mean time, the Apostles chose Matthias, one of the Disciples, in the place of Judas. On the tenth day, the Feast of Pentecost, there came suddenly a sound from Heaven, as of a mighty wind, and it filled the whole house where they were assembled. Over the head of each one, there appeared the form of a fiery

---

What did he command His Apostles to do when He appeared the last time among them? What power, and what promise, did He give them? When, where, and how, did He ascend into Heaven?

28. How did the Disciples prepare for the coming of the Holy Ghost? Whom did the Apostles choose in the place of Judas? When, and how, did the Holy Ghost come?

tongue, and all of them being filled with the Holy Ghost, began to speak in divers languages, and to praise the Lord their God. Peter, the Head of the Apostles, stood up and declared to the innumerable multitude of the Jews who had come together, that the same Jesus whom they had crucified, and whom God had raised from the dead, was their Lord and Redeemer, and he called upon them to believe in Him. His discourse was so powerful, that no less than three thousand came at once, and asked to be baptized. Soon after, Peter and John went to the temple to pray. A lame man was lying there at the gate, and asked an alms of them. Peter said to him: "Silver and gold I have none; but what I have, I give thee: in the name of Jesus Christ of Nazareth, arise and walk;" and forthwith the lame man sprang to his feet, walked joyfully with them into the temple, thanking and praising God. All the people were filled with amazement at this miracle, and five thousand more of them asked to be baptized.

29. The Apostles preached the Resurrection of Jesus Christ with great power, and did many signs and wonders. By this, their authority increased so much, that the people brought the sick into the streets, in order that, when Peter passed by, his shadow at least might fall upon them, and deliver them from their infirmities. The Chief Priests and their adherents, seeing all this, were greatly exasperated. They caused the Apostles to be apprehended and scourged, and forbade them to preach in the name of Jesus; they stirred up the people against

---

What change did He produce in them? What did Peter, the Head of the Apostles, do? What was the result of his sermon? How was the lame man at the temple-gate healed? What effect had this miracle on the Jews?

29. By what else did the Apostles spread the doctrine of Christ? What did the people do in consequence of this? What impression did this make upon the Chief Priests and their adherents? What did they do to the Apostles?

them, insomuch that St. Stephen was stoned to death; and they perpetrated many other acts of violence. But no earthly power was able to prevent the spreading of the doctrine of Jesus. The Apostles did not cease to preach the Crucified Saviour, both in the temple and from house to house, and the number of those who presented themselves to be baptized, increased exceedingly every day. Even Saul, afterwards called Paul, the most furious enemy and persecutor of the Christians, became, through the grace of God, an Apostle of Jesus Christ, and the most zealous propagator of the Gospel.

30. The new Converts in Jerusalem and its neighbourhood formed the first Christian Community, called the *Church*. Their conduct was unblemished and irreproachable; they served God with gladness and in simplicity of heart. They all lived in the greatest harmony, and had but one heart and one soul. None of them suffered want; for the rich willingly sold, for the relief of the poor, what they could spare, such as houses and lands, and laid the proceeds at the feet of the Apostles, that they might divide them among the needy. The Apostles were the rulers of the Church, as Christ had ordained: they taught, baptized, and administered the other Sacraments; they managed all ecclesiastical affairs, and governed the Community.

31. Although many of the Jews embraced the doctrine of Christ, yet the greater part of them remained obstinate and hardened. God, therefore,

---

Who was the first Martyr? Did the Apostles, on being persecuted, cease preaching? What can you relate of St Paul?

30. Of whom was the first Christian Community composed? What was their conduct, and how did they serve God? Was there any dissension amongst them? Did any of them suffer from want? How were the poor relieved? By what authority, and how, did the Apostles govern this first Community?

31. Were the Jews all converted?

permitted the punishment they had been threatened with, to be inflicted upon them; and in the seventieth year after the birth of Christ, Jerusalem was destroyed, and the temple burnt, by the Romans. One million and a hundred thousand Jews lost their lives, and the rest were banished from their country, and dispersed all over the world, that they might be everywhere and at all times living witnesses of the Divine judgment. The stubbornness of the Jews, and still more an express command of God, had early determined the Apostles to go and preach to the Pagans or Heathens. Poor and persecuted as they were, they announced to them the good tidings of salvation under thousands of hardships and perils, even of death. Therefore, God visibly blessed their efforts, and thirty years had scarcely elapsed after the Descent of the Holy Ghost, when there were already Christian Communities in all parts of the world. Over these Churches, the Apostles placed Bishops, to whom they communicated their powers by special forms of prayer and the imposition of hands, and whom they appointed their substitutes and successors. All these Communities were most closely united together, and formed under their common Head, St. Peter, the One, Universal, that is, *Catholic* Church. St. Peter was first Bishop of Antioch, and afterwards Bishop of Rome, where he suffered martyrdom under Nero A.D.

Did those who refused to believe in Christ remain unpunished? What punishment was inflicted on them? Why were they dispersed all over the world? What determined the Apostles to go and preach to the Pagans? Under what difficulties, and with what success, did they preach to them? How did the Apostles organize the new Christian Communities? Were these Communities separated, and independent of one another? Who was their common Head? What do we call all these Communities together? What is the meaning of Catholic? Where was St. Peter Bishop, and where did he die?

65; and then, the supreme authority over the whole Church devolved on his successors, the Bishops of Rome, or the Popes.

32. The Pagans were greatly alarmed at the rapid spreading of the Christian Religion, which openly condemned their vicious lives and their monstrous idolatry, and they resolved to exterminate it. The Christians had either to abjure their faith, or to die under the most cruel torments. They were scourged and lacerated, and were cast before wild beasts; their sides were torn with iron hooks, or burnt with torches. They were thrown into caldrons of boiling oil, mutilated, sawn in pieces, and crucified; they were covered with pitch and set fire to, that they might serve to light the nocturnal games of the Pagans. Everywhere the Christians suffered tortures beyond all description. The whole earth was drenched with their blood, and hundreds of thousands of every age, sex, and condition, died under the most dreadful torments. Rome especially, the capital of Paganism, and the seat of all the abominations of idolatry, overflowed, as it were, with the blood of the Christians. The number of those who suffered martyrdom in that city surpasses all belief; and their bones, which are still to be seen in the subterraneous caverns, or Catacombs, where they were entombed by their fellow-Christians, are witnesses of it to this day.

33. These terrible persecutions lasted, with few interruptions, for three hundred years. Had Christianity been the work of man, it would certainly have

---

Upon whom did his supremacy over the whole Church devolve?
32. What impression did the spreading of Christianity make on the Pagans? How did they expect to exterminate it? What torments did they inflict upon the Christians? Were there many thus tortured and killed? Where did the persecution of the Christians chiefly rage? Have we any evidence of this now-a-days?
33. How long did these persecutions last? Was the Christian religion extirpated by them? Why not?

been extirpated by the blind fury of its enemies; but being the work of Jesus, the Son of God, it took deeper and deeper root, and spread more and more over the world. The signs and wonders which the Confessors of Christ did, but above all, the imperturbable serenity of mind and cheerfulness of heart, with which they suffered the most cruel torments and the most painful of deaths, convinced the Pagans that only the God of the Christians could be the true God. It even often happened that, whilst the Christians were suffering these most horrible tortures, many of the Pagan spectators were heard to cry out: " We also are Christians; kill us together with them!" and thus the blood of the Martyrs was the fruitful seed from which new Christians continually sprang up.

34. By permitting all this, God had sufficiently shown to the world that the establishment of the Church was His work, and that all the powers of the earth could not prevail against her. He now bestowed peace on her by calling Constantine the Great to be the protector of Christianity. This Emperor, while still a Pagan, was at war with Maxentius. Seeing that his enemy's army was far greater than his, Constantine prayed fervently to the true God for assistance, and behold, a bright cross appeared in the sky to him and to his whole army, with the following inscription upon it:—" In this sign thou shalt conquer." In imitation of his cross, Constantine ordered a banner to be made, and had it carried before his army in battle. He then bravely attacked the superior forces of Maxentius,

---

What convinced the Pagans of the Divine origin of Christianity? What occurred often-times while the Christians were tortured? With what, then, may the blood of the Martyrs justly be compared?

34. Why did God permit these persecutions? Whom did He call to put an end to them? Who was Constantine, and what can you relate concerning his victory?

and overcame them; and from that moment (A.D. 312) Constantine became the defender and protector of Christianity.

II.—*From the Conversion of Constantine to the Rise of Protestantism in the 16th Century.*

35. The cross that had hitherto been the sign of the greatest ignominy, now became a sign of honour and victory. It glittered on the imperial crown of Constantine, and was displayed in Rome, till then the principal seat of Paganism, on the pinnacle of the temple of Jupiter—the Capitol,—and it thus announced the triumph of the crucified God-Man to the whole world. Constantine granted the free practice of their religion to the Christians, built splendid churches for them, and showed marks of great honour and distinction to Priests, and especially to the Popes. His example prompted thousands of the Pagans to embrace the Divine doctrine, and their idols were soon abandoned, and their temples deserted. In a short time, Paganism was completely overthrown throughout the Roman Empire, and the Christian Religion was permanently established.

36. The Catholic Church had now to gain victories of another kind, namely, over her internal enemies, the Heretics. Several Heretical and Schismatical doctrines had already been broached at different times and in different places; they had, however, soon disappeared. But now, by God's permission, some new

---

In what year did Constantine gain the battle and become the protector of Christianity?

35. What had the cross been before this, and what did it become now? Where was it particularly seen, and what did it announce to the world? What did Constantine do for the Christian Religion? What effect had his example upon the Pagans? What became of Paganism, and what was established in its place?

36. Were the contests of the Church now at an end? Who were her new enemies? Had there not been Heresies before?

Heretics arose, and gained many followers by cunning and fraud. They impudently left the Church, and formed separate and vast Communions, or Sects, which were mostly named after their founders; as, the Arians, Nestorians, Eutychians, Pelagians, etc. These Heretics often succeeded in gaining the favour of Princes and Emperors, under whose protection they most cruelly oppressed and persecuted the faithful. In the same way, as the Apostles had formerly assembled in order to settle, by the inspiration of the Holy Ghost and under the presidency of St. Peter, such differences as had arisen in matters of religion (Acts 15); so now also their successors, the Bishops of the Catholic Church, assembled under the presidency of the Pope, or of his Legates, consulted about the Heretical doctrines, and then condemned them. Such an assembly of Bishops is called a *General Council*; and the decisions of such a Council in matters of faith, when confirmed by the Pope, are infallible, because they proceed from the Church, which the Holy Ghost invisibly governs and preserves from all error. One of the most famous Councils is that of Nice, in Bithynia, which was held in 325. Three hundred and eighteen Bishops were assembled there, and amongst them were many holy men who, during the persecutions, had suffered for Christ's sake, and had lost their hands, or eyes. They unanimously condemned the impious doctrine of Arius, who obstinately maintained that Jesus Christ was not God from all eternity, and

---

And what was the difference between them, and these new ones? Whence did the Sects take their names? How did they behave towards the faithful? How did the Church oppose these Heresies? What is the name of a general assembly of the Bishops of the Catholic Church? When, and why are the decisions of a General Council infallible? When was the Council of Nice held? How many, and what Bishops were assembled there? What sentence did they pass? What error did Arius maintain?

they cut him off from the Communion of the faithful. Although this Sect, called Arians, was at that time very powerful, the Church, by her solemn decision had set the seal of reprobation on it, and consequently it was gradually to vanish from the face of the earth. The same sentence of condemnation was passed on all the other Heresies that sprang up in subsequent ages, and however hard the conflicts were in which the Church had to engage, she has always come off victorious.

37. During this period, God illustrated His Church also by many holy and learned men, who gloriously defended the true doctrine. They are called *Doctors of the Church*, or *Fathers of the Church*. Such were St. Athanasius, Patriarch of Alexandria, who had to endure from the Arians a long and severe persecution for the true faith (d. 373); St. Basil the Great, Archbishop of Cæsarea (d. 379); St. Gregory Nazianzen (d. 389), and St. John, surnamed Chrysostom, that is, *Golden Mouth* (d. 407), both Patriarchs of Constantinople; St. Cyril, Archbishop of Jerusalem (d. 386), and St. Cyril, Patriarch of Alexandria (d. 444); St. Ambrose, Archbishop of Milan (d. 397); St. Jerome, celebrated for his Latin translation of the Holy Scriptures, called the *Vulgate* (d. 420); St. Augustine, Bishop of Hippo in Africa, one of the brightest luminaries of the Church (d. 430); and the Holy Popes St. Leo the Great (d. 461), and St. Gregory the Great (d. 604). Whilst the Holy Fathers of the Church especially distinguished themselves as defenders of the true faith, the *Hermits*, or *Solitaries*, and Monks shone as models of the most austere

---

What became of these Sectarians after their condemnation? How did it fare with all subsequent Heresies? And what became of the Catholic Church?

37. By whom did God especially illustrate His Church at this time? How are those holy and learned men called? Can you name any of them? Did any other men distinguish themselves in the Church about this time?

penance. The *Hermits* were pious Christians who fled from the seductive pleasures of the world, to prepare themselves in solitude by prayer and self-denial for a happy death. A cavern in a rock, or a hut made of branches, was their abode; the bare ground, or a few leaves, their bed; roots and herbs were their food, and water was their drink. They renounced all the comforts of life, that they might entirely die to the world, and live only for God. The first Hermit was St. Paul, who died about 340. St. Antony, to satisfy the importunities of others, built the first Monastery, and is called the *Patriarch of Monks* (d. 356). Thus the *Solitary Life* gave rise to the *Monastic Life*, which was so opportunely and successfully propagated in the West by the great St. Benedict, so noted for the wonders he has done. For, not to speak of his miracles, we may safely say that Europe is especially indebted to the Religious Order he established, for the cultivation of its soil, and the conversion of its inhabitants. He died in 543. St. Augustine, the Apostle of England, was a Benedictine Monk, and introduced this Order into England in 596.

38. In the fifth and sixth centuries, the Church was exposed to new dangers, when rapacious Pagan nations left their own wild homes, and overran the Christian countries in countless swarms, laying waste all before them with fire and sword. This is called the *Migration of Nations*. Some of them were named

---

Who were the Hermits? What was their abode? What was their food and drink? Why did they renounce all comforts? Who were the first and most famous Hermits? What did the Solitary Life give rise to afterwards? Who built the first Monastery? Who particularly advanced the Monastic Life in Europe? For what is Europe especially indebted to the Benedictine Order? When, and by whom, was it introduced into England?

38. What was the cause of the dangers to which the Church was exposed during the fifth and sixth centuries? What is this called in History?

Huns, Alans, Heruli, Goths, Suevi, Lombards, Burgundians, Vandals, Franks, Angles, Saxons; but the most merciless and savage of all these barbarian tribes were the Huns, under their King Attila, who called himself the *Scourge of God*. The most celebrated towns were utterly destroyed, and whole countries laid waste and almost depopulated. The Roman Empire, more than one thousand years old, and once so powerful, could no longer resist these savage tribes, and was at last completely overthrown. Odoacer, King of the Heruli, took Rome, and was proclaimed King of Italy in 476. It is impossible to describe the extent of misery which these barbarous hordes inflicted on all Europe, until, finally, God subdued and civilized them by means of that very Church which they had threatened with destruction. Holy men were sent by the Popes to announce the good tidings of salvation to them. They took the Cross and the Gospel in their hands, and although they were exposed to the greatest dangers, they preached with no less courage and confidence in God, the doctrine of the Saviour of the world. In the fifth, sixth, seventh, and eighth centuries, Germany was also converted and civilized. St. Severinus is called the *Apostle of Austria*, because he converted that country to the Christian faith. He died in 482. St. Columban and St. Gall, both natives of Ireland, preached near the Lake of Constance, and in Switzerland; St. Kilian, a holy Irish Monk, and St. Willibald, an English West-Saxon, in Franconia; St.

Can you name any of these rapacious tribes? Which of them was the most savage and cruel? Who was their King, and what did he call himself? Did these savage tribes do much harm? What became of the Roman Empire? Who was made King of Italy? In what year? By what means did God subdue the barbarians? How was this done? In what centuries was Germany converted and civilized? Who is the Apostle of Austria? Can you name any more of the Missionaries to whom Germany owes its conversion?

Rupert and St. Corbinian, both French Missionaries, in Bavaria and the surrounding countries; St. Ludger, a native of Friesland, in Westphalia; St. Anscharius, a French Benedictine Monk, in Scandinavia and Lower Germany (d. 865). But the most indefatigable and successful preacher of the Gospel in Germany was St. Winfrid or Boniface, who is therefore justly called the *Apostle of the Germans.* He was born at Crediton, in Devonshire, about the year 680, and was a Benedictine Monk at Exeter. On account of his great merits, he was created Archbishop of Mentz, in 732, by Pope Gregory III., and, whilst he was engaged in preaching the Gospel to the infidel inhabitants of the northern parts of Friesland, he was martyred in 755. As soon as the Missionaries had got a footing in a country, they made it their first business to erect one or several Monasteries. These sanctuaries of religion then sent forth holy men to spread the seeds of Christianity over the country, established schools for the education of young Priests, and taught the barbarians to leave off their savage manners, and to follow peaceful and useful occupations. Thus the wild Germans were taught agriculture, the duties of domestic life, trades, and mechanical arts. By the industry and labour of the Monks, deserts were changed into rich fields, and dark forests into pleasant abodes—in all respects, they were the greatest benefactors of mankind. The Emperor Charlemagne, who had especially the propa-

---

Who is called the Apostle of the Germans? Where was he born? To what Order did he belong? Of what town was he made Archbishop? How, and in what year, did he die? What did the Missionaries usually do when they had settled in a country? What did, then, the Monasteries do for the spreading and strengthening of the faith? For what else is Germany indebted to the Monks? What Emperor in those days interested himself particularly for the prosperity of the Christian Church, and what did he do?

gation and prosperity of the Christian Church at heart, founded more than twenty-four Monasteries, and raised several Episcopal Sees, which he most liberally endowed with lands and estates. His example was followed by the pious King Stephen, to whom Hungary is indebted for her conversion to Christianity.

39. Whilst the Christian faith was propagated in the West with gratifying success, most fatal and deplorable disturbances arose in the East. The Greek Emperors at Constantinople, instead of humbly submitting themselves to the Church, wanted to rule her and obtrude upon her their opinions as articles of faith. The people were heedless, the Clergy frequently forgot their duties, and pride and dissension supplied at last what was still wanting to bring about that lamentable Schism by which the greater portion of the Greek or Eastern Church seceded from the Pope, the common Head of the Church of Christ (A.D. 1054). But God did not delay to inflict upon them the punishment they had so well deserved. As in former times He had chastised the Israelites for the neglect of His laws, so He now punished the degenerate Christians also. In the beginning of the seventh century (A.D. 622), there had appeared in Arabia an arrogant impostor, called *Mahomet*, who pretended to be a messenger of God, and patched up a new religion out of Pagan, Jewish, and Christian observances and doctrines. At the head of a band of robbers, he first plundered caravans, soon after took cities and countries, and, sword in hand, forced the

---

To whom does Hungary owe her conversion?

39. What happened in the East, whilst the Christian faith was successfully spread in the West? Who was the chief cause of those disturbances? To what were the people and the clergy inclined? What was the unfortunate result of all this? Did God suffer all this to remain unpunished? Who was Mahomet? What did he pretend to be? Of what did he form his new religion? How did he spread it?

inhabitants to embrace his religion. His successors, who were called Caliphs, continued, by the force of arms, to subdue one country after another in Asia and Africa, and to spread the doctrine of their false prophet, and, at the same time, barbarism, profligacy, and the most oppressive slavery. Christianity, it is true, was not entirely rooted out in those countries; but being separated from the true Church, it fell into a state of torpidity and debasement, under which it is still languishing at the present time.

40. In the year 637, Jerusalem, the Capital of the Holy Land or Palestine, had fallen under the power of the Mahometans or Saracens (*i.e.* Arabians; so called from *sara*, a desert), and had groaned under their yoke four hundred and forty-two years, when, in 1079, it was conquered, together with the fairest portions of Western Asia, by the *Seljukian Turks*, a Tartar tribe, who came in 1048 from the Caspian Sea, and had in the eighth century embraced Mahometanism. The latter were the most relentless foes of Christianity. The enormities which they committed in the Holy Land, and the cruel treatment which they inflicted upon the Christian pilgrims who resorted thither from the West, gave rise, about the close of the eleventh century, to the *Crusades*. Peter of Amiens, a pious Hermit, who had made a pilgrimage to Jerusalem, reported to Pope Urban II. how the Holy Places, where our Saviour had lived and suffered, were profaned by the Infidels, and to what

---

What did his successors do ? Was the Christian religion totally destroyed under them ? What became of it, and what was the reason ?

40. In what year did Jerusalem fall under the power of the Mahometans ? What do you understand by Mahometans, and what by Saracens ? When was Jerusalem conquered by the Turks ? What do you call those Turks, and whence did they come ? What was their religion ? Were they friends of the Christians ? What was the cause of the Crusades ? Who was Peter of Amiens, and what did he report to Urban II. ?

outrages the Christians were there exposed. The Pope was so sensibly affected that he resolved to put an end to the insolence and insatiable rapacity of the Mahometans. He summoned the Christian Princes and Knights to a Council at Clermont in Auvergne (A.D. 1095), called upon them to engage in a military expedition against the Infidels, and excited their enthusiasm to such a pitch, that the whole Assembly spontaneously exclaimed, "*God wills it! God wills it!*" This cry re-echoed through the whole West, and shortly after, there stood ready a tremendous host of men armed at all points. They wore, as a badge of their engagement, a red *cross* on their right shoulder, whence originated the name of *Crusaders* and *Crusade*, Full of joy and courage, they marched to Palestine. After having endured inexpressible hardships, and fought many a hot battle, they at last took Jerusalem, and the brave hero, Godfrey of Bouillon, Duke of Lorraine, was proclaimed King A.D. 1099. Being presented with a golden crown, he refused to wear it, saying, that he would never consent to wear a crown of gold, where the Redeemer of the world had worn a crown of thorns; and he never gave himself any other title but that of Duke Godfrey. The new Kingdom, however, lasted only eighty-eight years. Owing to the treachery of the Greeks, and to the want of discipline and harmony among the Crusaders, it was unable to resist the superior forces of the Turks, although it repeatedly obtained auxiliaries from the West; and thus Jerusalem was taken by Saladin, Sultan of Egypt, in 1187.

What did the Pope do? What did he effect at the Council of Clermont? In what year was the Council of Clermont held? What ensued in the West? What is the origin of the name of Crusade? What can you relate of the first Crusade? In what year was Jerusalem taken? What can you relate of Godfrey of Bouillon? How long did the Christian Kingdom of Jerusalem last? What caused its fall? When, and by whom was it conquered?

About the year 1300, fresh hordes of Turks, called the *Ottomans*, poured down from Tartary, subdued the Seljukians, and extended their conquests over Western Asia, Rumelia, Moldavia, Servia, Bulgaria, Greece, and the Morea; until at last, under that monster of brutality and voluptuousness, called Mahomet (II.) the Great, they rendered themselves masters of Constantinople, the Capital of the Greek Empire (A.D. 1453); which calamity God, no doubt, permitted in punishment for the grievous offences it had committed against Him. The further progress of the Turks, however, was checked by the ardent zeal and heroic valour of the Christian Princes Hunniades and Scanderbeg, of the Knights Hospitallers of St. John of Jerusalem (who from 1310 were called Knights of Rhodes, and from 1530, Knights of Malta), and of other Christian Orders of Chivalry, till they were at last completely overthrown by the united forces of the Pope, of Spain, and Venice, and by the evident help of the Glorious Mother of God, in the famous battle of *Lepanto* (A.D. 1571). The result of this victory was not only a check to the progress of the Ottomans, but also the beginning of the decline of their power; and thus Catholic Europe, and especially Germany, was saved from the imminent danger of being likewise overrun and subjugated by those ferocious Infidels.

41. In the Western countries of Europe, the Crusades everywhere roused the people to a more vigorous exertion of their mental powers and to a new spiritual life. During the destructive Migration of

---

About what year, and by what Turks were the Seljukians subdued, and how far did they extend their conquests? In what year, and by whom was Constantinople taken? Who checked the further progress of the Turks? By whom were they at last completely overthrown? In what battle, and in what year? What was the result of this victory?

41. What influence had the Crusades on Western Europe?

Nations (§ 38), the sciences had found an asylum in the Monasteries; but now they spread among the people, and were ardently cherished by them. Celebrated Schools and Universities were established, and men of wonderful erudition, as, St. Anselm (d. 1109), Albertus Magnus (d. 1280), St. Thomas of Aquino (d. 1274), and others, occupied the professorial chairs. Those times, generally called "*The Middle Ages*," are still more renowned for the lustre of Christian virtues, for the firmness of faith, for childlike simplicity, and for an ardent love of God and man. Even at the present time, we behold with surprise and wonder those ancient gigantic Cathedrals which were erected by the piety of our ancestors; and we are enraptured at the most tender devotion, expressed in the paintings and statues with which they adorned the buildings consecrated to God. Such great and charming works could only be produced by the Religion which filled their hearts and governed all their actions. This same Religion also poured out the greatest blessings over the earth through the holy Founders of Religious Orders, St. Romuald (d. 1027), St. Bruno (d. 1101), St. Norbert (d. 1134), St. Bernard (d. 1153), St. Dominic (d. 1221), St. Francis of Assisium, surnamed the Seraphic (d. 1226), and many other men of God. The numerous Monasteries which they built, not only produced many great Saints and enlightened Prelates, but they also cherished piety and religious zeal among the lower classes of the people. They relieved the wants of the poor, sheltered and nursed the sick, and

---

Where had the sciences found an asylum during the invasions by the barbarians, and among whom were they now spread? What learned men of those times can you name? What do we call those times, and what are they particularly remarkable for? What monuments give, even at the present time, evidence of the piety of our ancestors? What enabled them to produce such stupendous works? Through whom in particular did the Catholic Religion pour out its blessings at that time? What fruits did the numerous Monasteries bring forth?

redeemed those who had been made prisoners and slaves; they sent Missionaries into all parts of the world, and obtained, by their devout prayers, abundant graces from Heaven on countries and nations.

42. In the mean time, there appeared also an exuberant growth of cockle among the wheat in the field of God (Matt. 13). There were pernicious feuds and wars, various acts of injustice and violence, and many scandals. In several places, and particularly in Germany, the custom had been introduced by temporal Princes, of putting the newly elected Bishops and Abbots in possession of their benefices, by giving them the *Ring* and the *Crosier*, the symbols of Pastoral authority; which ceremony was called *Investiture*, and seemed to imply the conferring of spiritual jurisdiction. -Not content with this, the Emperor Henry IV. used to bestow Bishoprics and Abbeys upon the most unworthy candidates, and even on such as offered him the largest sums of money. Pope Gregory VII. courageously inveighed against those crying abuses, and hence ensued, about 1076, a long and tedious contest, called *The Contest of Investiture*, out of which the Church indeed came forth victorious, but not till after many hard trials. After that, there arose Heretics, who kindled the fire of revolt first against the Ecclesiastical, and then against the Secular authorities; as, in France the Albigenses, in Upper Italy the Waldenses, in England the Wickliffites or Lollards, in Bohemia the Hussites. Peace, it is true, was restored

---

42. Was there in those times no cockle in the field of God? What kind of cockle was it? What custom had been introduced in some places by the temporal Princes? What is symbolized by the Ring and Crosier? What was this ceremony called, and what did it seem to imply? What did the Emperor Henry IV. use to do? Who opposed him? What is this contest called, and when did it take place? How did the Church get out of it? What evil came afterwards on the West of Europe? Which were the most notorious Heretics of that time?

to the Church, and men, mighty in words and deeds, as, St. Vincent Ferrer (d. 1419), and St. John Capistran (d. 1456), went through the countries of Europe, preaching penance to Princes and people. Nevertheless, an unholy fire lay hidden under the ashes: feelings of disrespect and hostility to the Church, and a fondness for innovations, had gained ground, and were increased by many other attendant evils. Nothing was wanted for the fatal eruption of this volcano of wickedness and rebellion, but an opportunity; and this presented itself in the beginning of the sixteenth century in Germany. Like a contagious disease, this lamentable evil spread abroad: thousands and thousands abandoned the Catholic Church; bloody wars, revolts, and corruption of morals, ensued; the most splendid establishments, founded by the piety of former ages, were destroyed, and unspeakable misery was prepared both for time and eternity.

III.—*From the Rise of Protestantism to Pope Pius IX.*

43. Martin Luther, an Augustinian Monk and a Professor in the University of Wittenberg, a man of an irritable and turbulent disposition, began in 1517 by exclaiming against the abuses, which are said to have been practised in the publication of the Indulgences granted by Pope Leo X. to those who should contribute to the rebuilding of St. Peter's Church in Rome. But soon after he arbitrarily set himself up as a reformer of the Church, inveighed against the Ecclesiastical authorities, especially against the Pope, whose supreme power he denounced as usurpation and tyranny, and which he said he would bring to a mise-

---

Whom did God send to preach penance to them? Was the evil then entirely suppressed? How, and when did the slumbering fire break out into a flame? What was the consequence of this?

43. Who was the author of Protestantism? What sort of a man was he? When, and how did he begin his conflict with the Church? Did he stop there? How did he behave towards the Pope?

rable end. In pursuance of his wrong views, he rejected many articles of faith which the Church had received from Christ and His Apostles. He discarded the Holy Sacrifice of the Mass, Fasting, Confession, Prayers for the Dead, and many other pious practices; he declared good works to be useless, and taught that man is justified and saved by faith alone. Moreover, he threw open the Monasteries and Convents, and gave leave to the Monks and Nuns to marry; and he presumed to award to Princes and Sovereigns the right of confiscating the property of Churches and Convents, and of assigning it to any use they pleased. Finally, he broke the vow of chastity which he had solemnly made as a Monk and as a Priest, and committed the double sacrilege of taking a Nun for his wife. Luther boasted that he took his doctrine from the Bible only; but being misled by the false rule of private judgment in its interpretation, he soon fell into the most palpable contradictions and errors. Thus he asserted that " man has no free will, and consequently can neither keep the commandants, nor avoid evil;"* " that sin does not condemn man, provided he firmly believe;"† &c. Nevertheless, he soon obtained many followers; for the thoughtless multitude were very much pleased with such easy doctrine which allowed them to lead a dissolute life, and covetous Princes found nothing more conformable to their wishes than the suppression of Churches and Monasteries. Besides, Luther eagerly

---

What innovations did he introduce? What did he do with regard to Monasteries, Monks, and Nuns? What pretended right did he give to Princes and Sovereigns? Was his conduct edifying? Whence did he pretend to take his doctrine? How did he interpret the Bible? Did he teach the pure Word of God? Can you name any of his errors? How was his doctrine received by the people, and how by some Princes?

---

* De Servo Arbitrio.
† Epist. ad Melancht. an. 1521.—De Captivit. Babyl., Tom. 2. fol. 284.

embraced any opportunity of increasing his party, and for this purpose, he permitted the Landgrave of Hesse to contract a second marriage whilst his first wife was still living. The way of innovation and revolt being once opened by Luther, several others soon followed him, and they went even farther than he did. Zwinglius, in Switzerland, denied the real presence of Jesus Christ in the Holy Eucharist. Calvin, at Geneva, taught that " God has predestined a part of mankind, without any fault of theirs, to eternal damnation, and that therefore He blinds and hardens the heart of sinners."† The Anabaptists proclaimed a kingdom of Christ on earth, in which there was to be no private property, no law, no magistrates. Zwinglius, Calvin, and other Sectarians, totally demolished in the Churches what had been spared by Luther. The images of the Crucified Redeemer and of the Saints, pictures as well as statues, and masterpieces of art, were hewn in pieces; the organs and altars were shattered; nay, even the graves were ransacked, and the bones of the Saints trampled upon and burnt to ashes. Although these pretended Reformers combated and anathematized one another, nevertheless their several doctrines spread most rapidly. Only united in their hatred against the Catholics, they contrived all imaginable measures to gain the superiority over them. By thousands and thousands of pamphlets they disseminated their erroneous principles, and, at the same time, they most virulently attacked and calumniated the Pope and the

---

What did he do to gain the favour of the Landgrave of Hesse? Did any imitate Luther's example? Where, and what did Zwinglius teach? Where, and what did Calvin teach? What did the Anabaptists proclaim? What havoc did the Zwinglians and the Calvinists make? Did the different Sects agree among themselves? Did their disagreement prevent the spread of their doctrines? In what were they united? What measures did they contrive to propagate their principles?

---

* Instit. Relig. Christ.

Catholic Clergy. Moreover, in many places, crying acts of violence were committed, and people were forced by all sorts of oppression and persecution to renounce the Holy Catholic Faith.

44. The Catholics, on their part, made several attempts to restore peace to the Church, by entering into amicable discussions with their opponents ; but the hatred which Luther bore to the Pope, the Head of the Church, continued implacable. To check the progress of heresy and wickedness, the Emperor Charles V. assembled in 1529 a second Diet at Spire, where a decree was issued, that, until the decision of a General Council, Lutheranism should be tolerated wherever it had already been established, but should not be spread any further ; that no one should be hindered from saying or hearing Mass, and that all invectives against any Religion should be prohibited. The Lutherans *protested* against this decree, and from this circumstance is derived their name of *Protestants;* which appellation has since been given also to the other Sects into which they have divided. At length, the Holy Father convoked a General Council at Trent, in the Tyrol, in the year 1545. The doctrine of the Innovators was examined and unanimously condemned ; at the same time, many excellent decrees concerning Ecclesiastical institutions and the reformation of abuses, were issued ; in a word, the eminent transactions of this Council gave fresh beauty and new vigour to the Catholic Church. The Protestants

---

What means did they use in many places to make the Catholics renounce their faith ?

44. What did the Catholics do for the restoration of peace, and what was the result ? In what year, and by whom, was the Diet of Spire assembled ? What famous decree was issued there ? How did the name of *Protestants* originate ? Are only the Lutherans now called Protestants ? What measures did the Holy Father at last take ? In what year was the Council of Trent convoked, and what was done by it ? What did the Church gain by this Council ?

had been repeatedly invited to the Council, as they had in the beginning expressly wished for it in order to adjust their differences; but they refused to appear at Trent. Consequently, the unfortunate Schism continued, and brought unspeakable misery and endless calamities upon the greater part of Europe.—Luther had preached liberty and reviled the Emperor, the Princes and Bishops; the peasants lost no time in freeing themselves from their Masters. They traversed the country in lawless bands, burnt down the castles and monasteries, and committed the most horrible cruelties against the Nobility and Clergy. More than one hundred thousand persons were slain during this frightful insurrection (A.D. 1525). Other religious wars ensued, and Germany, which once had been so flourishing, became at last the scene of the most frightful desolation and of the most horrible atrocities during the Thirty Years' War (1618—1648). The other countries which had embraced the new doctrine were likewise devastated by religious and civil wars. In Switzerland, Zwinglius fell in a bloody battle which he fought against his own countrymen. In France, the Calvinists, called Huguenots, kept, with a devastating army, the field for many years against the Crown and the Church. In their blind fury, they massacred numbers of Priests, Monks, and Nuns; they ravaged villages and towns, and burnt or pulled down many thousands of churches, some of which were magnificent monuments of Christian art. England also suffered severely for her apostasy, begun by King Henry VIII., who abandoned the Catholic Church

---

Did the Protestants come to it? What was the effect of Luther's preaching liberty? What took place during the war of the peasantry? Were there any other wars in Germany, and how long did the great religious war last in that country? What was the consequence of this war? Were any other countries involved in war, and which? Where, and how did Zwinglius end his life? What are the French Protestants called, and what atrocities did they commit? Who introduced Protestantism into England, and for what reason?

because the Pope would not allow him to repudiate his lawful wife Catharine, and marry Anne Boleyn. From that time, the country was drenched in human blood; even King Charles I., a successor of the tyrannical Henry, was beheaded by rebels who boasted of professing and practising the *purest* of all Christian Doctrines.

45. The loss which the Church had suffered from the apostasy in Europe, was to be amply compensated by the conversion of innumerable Heathens in other parts of the globe. Missionaries went forth in every direction, and announced the salutary doctrines of the Gospel with wonderful success. It is truly astonishing what St. Francis Xavier, the Apostle of the Indies, who was so eminently favoured by Heaven, alone accomplished. Glowing with zeal for the salvation of the Pagans, he crossed the vast ocean, and landing at Goa in the year 1542, he began his mission by walking through the streets with a bell in his hand, and calling the children to come and be instructed. They joyfully attended and listened to the holy man, who spoke to them so affectionately of their dear Redeemer. When they had returned home, they repeated what they had heard, and so induced the adult persons to come likewise and hear the holy preacher. God rewarded his zeal, and granted him, as He had done to the first Apostles, the power of healing the sick, of raising the dead to life, of commanding the storms; in short, the power of working the most stupendous miracles. With untiring energy he went from country to country, from island to island, through all India and Japan, and converted, in the short period of ten

---

Did England gain anything by the change? What do you know of Charles I.?

45. How was the Church compensated for her loss in Europe? How was this effected? What is the name of the Apostle of the Indies? Where did he land, and in what year? How did he begin his mission? What did the children do? How did God reward and assist his zeal? In what countries did he work, and

years, many tribes and kingdoms. He himself testifies in one of his letters, that in one month he administered Holy Baptism to ten thousand Heathens. After his death, other Missionaries continued the pious work, and introduced the Religion of Jesus into China also, that immense, unknown, and till then inaccessible Empire. That these Heathens had been truly converted, was proved in the most convincing manner when the persecution of the Christians broke out in Japan. About one million and a hundred thousand* died for their faith, and the greatest part of them were most horribly tortured. Even tender children, weak old men, and women of rank, hastened with joy to martyrdom, dressed in their holiday attire, as if they were going to a wedding-feast. A fanatical hatred of Christianity is still prevalent in Japan at the present time.—In America also, that newly discovered world, the light of the Gospel spread, and overthrew the most abominable idolatry with all its horrors and vices. No people on earth offered up more human sacrifices than the Americans. The Mexicans sacrificed about twenty thousand human victims every year, and when they had no captives for this purpose, they did not spare even their own children. It is impossible to describe what the heroic Missionaries suffered, and what dangers they incurred among those bloodthirsty cannibals. They had to struggle not only against the cruelties and vices of the natives, but also against the insatiable avarice of the European settlers. Yet their labours were

---

how long? What was the result of his labours? How many Heathens did he christen or baptize in one month? Was Christianity also introduced into China? How was the sincerity of the new Christians, especially in Japan, proved? How many were martyred in Japan? Does the hatred against the Christians still continue there? What can you relate of America in general, and of Mexico in particular? Was the work of the Missionaries easy there? What particular obstacles did

---

* Some authors reckon 1,200,000.

crowned with success, and the Christian faith was firmly and permanently established on that Continent. The mission of Paraguay, in South America, especially flourished. The brutish natives, who lived among the wild beasts in the forests, who thought of nothing but plundering, murdering, and revenge, who delighted only in eating human flesh, in voluptuousness and drunkenness,—were transformed, by the indefatigable Missionary Priests, into devout Christians, who became models of modesty and charity, of innocence and piety, and by their untiring industry and labour, changed their wild country into a delicious paradise.

46. The holy men who, with such indefatigable zeal, and often even to the shedding of their blood, devoted themselves to the conversion of the Pagans, belonged for the most part to Religious Orders. Francis Xavier, and those others who planted the faith in China and Paraguay, were Jesuits, that is, Members of the Society of Jesus. This Order was founded in 1540 by St. Ignatius of Loyola, a man filled with the most ardent zeal for the honour of God. These Religious exerted themselves especially in propagating the Catholic Faith, and defending it against the new-fangled doctrines; and consequently they drew upon themselves implacable hatred and grievous persecutions from the enemies of Religion. God raised also other Orders, that they might, in concert with the Secular Clergy, heal the wounds which Luther and other Heretics had inflicted on the Church. The pious

---

they encounter ? Did they succeed the less for all that ? How did the Savages of Paraguay live ? What did they become after their conversion to Christianity ?

46. To what class of men did most of the Missionaries belong ? Of what Order were the Apostle of the Indies, and the first planters of Christianity in China and Paraguay ? When, and by whom was this Order established ? In what did these Religious especially exert themselves ? How were they requited for their labour by the enemies of Religion ? Did God raise any other Orders at that time, and for what purpose ? When,

Capuchins, who sprang in 1528 from the Order of St. Francis of Assysium, laboured especially for the salvation of souls, and distinguished themselves by their affectionate zeal and austere life. The Oratorians, or Fathers of the Oratory, which was founded in 1574 by St. Philip Neri, devoted themselves to prayer and the instruction of the people, to visiting the hospitals, to attending the poor and the sick, and to literary pursuits. The Fathers of the Pious Schools occupied themselves with the instruction of youth, and other Religious again, with the nursing of the sick. There arose also Communities of Religious women for the training up of young girls to a pious and godly life; as, the Orders of the Visitation, of the Ursulines, and of the Good Shepherd, and the Institute of English Ladies.* Above all, this period was exceedingly rich in heroes of faith and virtue. St. Charles Borromeo, Cardinal Archbishop of Milan (d. 1584), set a bright example of true Christian charity during the plague, by visiting the sick in the most dangerous places, in lazarets and hospitals, and by giving up all his property, even his bed, for the relief of the sufferers. St. Francis of Sales, Prince-Bishop of Geneva (d. 1622), converted, by the irresistible power of his meekness and humility, seventy-two thousand Savoyards from

---

and how did the Order of Capuchins originate, and by what were they particularly conspicuous ? When, and by whom was the Oratory founded, and to what does it devote itself ? What was the object of the Fathers of the Pious Schools, and of other Orders ? What Communities of Religious women arose at that time ? What do they devote themselves to ? What is the origin of the Institute of the English Ladies ? In what was this epoch especially rich ? Can you tell me anything remarkable of St. Charles Borromeo ? What do you know of St.

---

* This Institute was established in the Netherlands for English Ladies who were persecuted under Queen Elizabeth for their attachment to the Catholic Faith, and soon spread over Germany, where it is still flourishing under the above name, though its members have long ceased to be English.

the errors of Calvin to the true Faith. St. Vincent ot Paul (d. 1660) devoted his whole life to the poor and distressed; no misery, of whatever kind or form, escaped the ardour and abundance of his love. He founded orphanages and foundling-hospitals; he established a Congregation of Missionary Priests (called Lazarists from St. Lazarus' College in Paris) for the instruction of ignorant country people; an Association for the reforming of convicts, and also the admirable Institute of the Sisters of Charity for nursing the sick. In Germany, especially in Austria and Bavaria, and in Switzerland, the Venerable Peter Canisius opposed himself as a mighty barrier against Heresy; he combated it by his writings and incessant preaching, and founded Schools and Pious Institutions for preserving and enlivening the true faith established by Christ and His Apostles. The sixteenth and seventeenth centuries were also illustrated by St. John of God, St. John of the Cross, St. Thomas of Villanova, St. Cajetan, St. Peter of Alcantara, St. Camillus of Lellis, St. Joseph Calasanctius, St. Joseph of Cupertino, St. Francis Borgia, St. Pius V., St. Fidelis of Sigmaringen, St. Aloysius Gonzaga, St. Stanislas Kostka, and by many other men eminent for the sanctity of their lives; and among the female sex were especially distinguished St. Teresa, St. Rose of Lima, St. Angela of Brescia, St. Mary Magdalen of Pazzi, St. Jane Frances de Chantal, St. Catharine of Ricci, &c. In the eighteenth century there shone among others, as one of the brightest ornaments of the Catholic Church, St. Alphonsus Maria Liguori, Bishop

---

Francis of Sales? What did St. Vincent of Paul in general do for the temporal and eternal welfare of his fellow-men? What Charitable Institutions did he found in particular? Who especially laboured in the 16th century in Germany and Switzerland for the preservation of the true faith? Were there any other principal Saints who shone in the 16th and 17th centuries, and who were they? By what Saints was the female sex distinguished at that time? What Saint did particularly illustrate the 18th century?

of St. Agatha, near Naples (d. 1787), who established the Congregation of the Redemptorists for the instruction of the people. All these Saints did great deeds, and wrought innumerable miracles by their mighty intercession with God; and thus they irrefragably proved that the true spirit of Christianity, the spirit of charity, of humility and self-denial, had not departed from the Church, as the blind adversaries of our faith unfortunately often assert.

47. Awful events, which make nature shudder, remain as yet to be related. We would fain pass them over in silence, if they were not most instructive for us. As with all human productions, so it fared with the doctrine of Luther; it became antiquated, it altered and entirely changed. Sects upon Sects arose: Baptists, Presbyterians, Episcopalians, Quakers, Methodists, Moravians, &c. Each one of these Sects presumed, after the example of Luther, to reform the faith. At last, impious free-thinkers, first in England and afterwards in France, carried their presumption to the highest pitch, and contrived the infernal scheme totally to abolish Religion, and to exterminate for ever the Belief in Christ. Under the pretence of enlightening mankind, they deluged the world with writings in which they scoffed at all holy things, grossly calumniated the Pope and the Clergy, and openly advocated the most shameful licentiousness. Their books, written in most attractive language, and sparkling with witticism and satire, found their way too readily among all classes of people, and at the same time the spirit of profligacy and impiety spread with surprising rapidity. The enemies of God now felt themselves

---

What Religious Order did he found? What did all these Saints especially do, and what did they prove by their works and miracles?

47. What became, in process of time, of the doctrine of Luther? What was the final result of its alterations and changes? What did the Sectarianism lead to? What did the free-thinkers contrive to do? What principal means did they make use of? Why were their books well received by the peo-

powerful enough to execute their horrible plan. They first attacked the Priesthood, that they might the more easily scatter the sheep, after they had smitten the shepherd. The Ecclesiastical property was confiscated and sold in France about the close of the eighteenth century; the Monks and Nuns were turned out of their peaceable abodes by force, and the Religious Houses were plundered and pulled down. Soon after, a sanguinary edict was issued against all Priests who should continue faithful to the discharge of their duties. Was any one discovered refractory, he was cast into prison, or immediately hanged up to the nearest lamp-post. The Christian Era was annulled, the celebration of the Sundays and Festivals was abolished, the churches were profaned and devastated. Every thing that reminded them of Christianity was destroyed. Finally, the madness of these men arrived at such a pitch, that they proclaimed *Reason* to be the Supreme Being, and conducted a vile woman, as an emblem of the Deity, on a triumphal car into the Cathedral of Paris, where they placed her on the high altar, in the place of the figure of our Crucified Redeemer, and sang hymns in her honour. Order, prosperity, and public safety disappeared together with Religion; even the throne was overturned and shattered to pieces. Louis XVI., a pious and benevolent, but rather too good-natured King, was beheaded in 1793, and soon after him, his wife and his sister suffered the same death. France was for two years the scene of such horrible atrocities as are unequalled in the annals of history. Human blood flowed in

---

ple? Whom did the Infidels first attack, and why? What became of the Ecclesiastical property, the Monks and Nuns, and the Religious Houses? What edict was issued against the Priests? What did the Infidels do to destroy the very name of Christianity? With what particular infamy did they brand themselves in their madness? Why did prosperity and public safety disappear? What happened to Louis XVI. and his family? What became then of France? Were children at

torrents. Neither age nor sex was safe from the fury of those monsters. In the Vendée, five hundred children, the oldest of whom was fourteen, were shot, because their fathers remained faithful to God and their King. The total number of the people slaughtered in this Reign of Terror was, according to some, two millions. And all this was done under the pretence of promoting the happiness of mankind. *Enlightenment* was their word when they abolished Religion; *Liberty* and *Equality*, when they murdered their fellow-men. At last, the sanguinary despots began to tremble for their own lives, and in order to stop the complete anarchy that prevailed, they solemnly proclaimed that the nation should once more believe in God and the immortality of the soul. In the year 1799, Napoleon, in quality of First Consul, seized upon the sovereign power; but he did not venture to govern a people without Religion. He, therefore, restored the Catholic Religion in France, and made a solemn Concordat with the Pope (A.D. 1801). However, the Church did not long enjoy this peace. Napoleon, blinded by fortune, attempted to extort from the Supreme Head of the Church certain concessions which he could not grant. The French troops invaded Rome, and carried away Pius VII. prisoner in 1809. But as God had visibly protected His Church ten years before, when Pope Pius VI. had died a captive at Valence in France, so now He did not abandon her to her enemies. Napoleon was vanquished by the Confederate Powers of Europe, and dispos-

---

least spared? How many people are said to have been slaughtered during the Reign of Terror? Under what pretence were all these horrible crimes committed? What did the impious wretches finally do in the utmost necessity? By whom, when and why was the Catholic Religion restored in France? Did Napoleon remain a faithful son of the Church? How did he treat Pius VII.? Did God ever withdraw His hand from the Church? What became of Napoleon, and what of the Pope?

sessed of his crown, and the Pope re-entered triumphant into Rome (A.D. 1814). Pius VII. was succeeded in the Holy See by Leo XII., Pius VIII., and Gregory XVI.; and from the 16th of June, 1846, to the present time, the Papal throne has been occupied by Pius IX., who, in an uninterrupted succession of Popes from St. Peter, is the two hundred and fifty-fifth. (See p. 59—63.)

48. By this terrible French Revolution, Divine Providence intended to show to the world, what misery awaits those who fall off from God and the Religion of Jesus Christ. Unfortunately, this warning was not generally heeded, and the pretended Enlightening System of the French Freethinkers was also adopted in other countries. Many ancient and venerable Institutions were abrogated, Monasteries and Convents were suppressed, the authority and influence of the Church diminished, her rights derogated, her benefits and blessings disowned, and shameless infidelity, with its pernicious principles, was publicly taught in the Universities. However, Almighty God has not ceased to protect His Church, and even to glorify her by many incontestable miracles. But the greatest miracle perhaps is the continual spreading of the Church in all parts of the world, notwithstanding the great and numerous obstacles which are everywhere thrown in her way. This is peculiarly striking in North America, where, in the United States alone, forty-eight Dioceses, with Seminaries, Monasteries, Convents, Colleges, and other pious Institutions, have been founded within less than sixty years. Among

---

In what year did Pius VII. return to Rome ? Who were his Successors ? Who is the present Pope ? How many Popes have there been from the time of St. Peter ?

48. What does the French Revolution teach us ? Was this warning properly heeded ? What influence had this Revolution on other countries ? Did God cease to protect His Church ? Which is the greatest miracle of that time ? How does this in North America, especially in the United States ? How

some nations of Asia, the blood of Martyrs has become the seed of new Christians. In England, the Catholic Churches, Monasteries, Convents, and Schools are visibly multiplying, owing to the continual increase of the number of those who re-enter into the pale of the true Church. In Germany also, a great change for the better has been effected. Monasteries, Convents, and Charitable Institutions have been re-established for nursing the sick, for instructing youth, for educating poor children, for opening asylums to penitents of both sexes, and for promoting the propagation of Faith. Literary pursuits have become more Christian, a new zeal has been revived, and it is being more and more understood that unity, peace, and eternal salvation, are only to be found in the Catholic Church. If, on the other hand, many Christians, enslaved to the love of earthly things, have become indifferent towards God and His Holy Religion, if the Church is still continually oppressed and persecuted, this ought not to shake our faith, but rather confirm us in it; for even in this we see the accomplishment of the Prophecies recorded in the Gospel, and of the prediction, that one day a great revolt shall take place from God and Christ, the Saviour of the world. (2 Thess. 2, 3, 4. Luke 18, 8.) Every one, therefore, must take heed that he be not led astray, but remain faithful until death, that he receive the crown of life. (Apoc. 2, 10.)

---

in Asia? How in England? What change has taken place in Germany? Where can one be sure to find unity, peace, and eternal salvation? What should we think of the indifferentism of some Christians, and of the continual persecution of the Church? What, therefore, should every one of us do?

CONCLUDING REMARKS

ON THE HISTORICAL EVIDENCES OF THE TRUTH OF OUR DIVINE RELIGION.

We have now, in a small compass, surveyed the History of our Holy Religion, and considered the blessings it has conferred upon mankind from Adam, our first parent, to our Lord and Saviour Jesus Christ, and from Him, the Divine Head and Founder of our Church, to His present Vicegerent, Pius IX. How sublime and beautiful is the Religion we profess! Every thing connected with it, calls out to us: No one but God could give such a Religion to mankind.

1. No, man has not invented it; God Himself has taught it to us, and commanded us to observe it. He revealed it by holy men in the Old Testament (§.§. 6.11.7.); and in the New, precisely as the Prophecies of the Old Testament had foretold, His Only-Begotten, Eternal Son appeared on earth, and most convincingly confirmed His Divine Doctrine by numerous miracles, especially by His Resurrection from the dead (§.§. 21. 22. 23. 26. 27.). God has spoken, and no one has a right to be indifferent to His word; to despise or reject it, would be to condemn oneself to everlasting hell fire.

2. The Religion to which we belong, did not take rise only a few centuries ago; properly speaking, it dates from the beginning of the world. For its first seeds were laid in Paradise, when God promised a Redeemer to our First Parents after their fall; and the whole of the Old Law, with its sacrifices and won-

---

What have we now surveyed? What have we chiefly considered in the History of our Religion?

1. Whence does our Religion come? By whom has God revealed it to us? How did Jesus Christ confirm His Divine Doctrine? Is it indifferent which religion we profess?

2. How old is our Religion? How do you explain and prove its great age?

derful events, was but a figure of the New Law, which contains the fulfilment and accomplishment of the Old. (§§ 2. 7. 9. 12. and others.) The Old Law believed in the Redeemer who was to come, and the New believes in Him who has come. But it is the same belief in the same Redeemer, and therefore it is essentially the same Religion.

3. Although our Holy Religion has a beginning coeval with the beginning of mankind, and its history embraces about six thousand years, yet it is not lost in obscure fables of ancient times; on the contrary, its truth is evident and obvious to all. For it exhibits, from the remotest antiquity down to the present time, an uninterrupted series, as it were, of public and universally known facts and events, which perfectly agree with one another, and with all the monuments of past ages, also with the annals of the various nations of the world, and with the discoveries made by natural philosophers; and which have been so manifoldly and irrefragably attested, that he who would not believe them, might just as well deny any other historical truth. We count, and can even name, the generations exactly as they succeeded one another from Adam to Christ (Luke 3. Matt. 1.), and all the Supreme Pastors or Popes, from St. Peter to our Holy Father, Pius IX., who is now gloriously governing the Church established by the Son of God. (§47. at the end; and p. 59—63.) What a wonderful concatenation, and what an unparalleled succession!

4. Even the Jews, the most obstinate adversaries of our faith, bear witness to its truth. For they carefully keep upon record, in their Holy Books, the whole history and all the Prophecies of the Old Testament, to which we appeal in order to prove the Divine Origin

---

3. Is the history of our Religion perhaps uncertain, because it dates from the origin of the world, and embraces so long a period? Why not?

4. What evidence do even the Jews give to the truth of our Religion? What does this prove?

of Christianity; insomuch that no one can for a moment suppose that the Christians had perverted or invented such passages in the Old Testament, as refer to our Saviour (§. 17.).

5. Nor can it be denied that it was entirely through the mighty help of God that the Christian Religion has spread over the whole earth. The Apostles who first preached it were from the lowest class of the people, poor, unknown, even without eloquence or learning. Their doctrine of the Cross, which contains the inscrutable mysteries of penance, humility, and mortification, was not likely to please the proud and licentious Pagans, who found in their abominable mythology (*i.e.*, fabulous history of their Gods), not only an excuse, but even a justification for all their vices. The rich and the great looked with disdain upon the poor fishermen; the witty and the learned derided them; and the mighty Rulers of the earth, as even Pagan writers testify, took all possible pains to destroy them with fire and sword. During three centuries, persecution and martyrdom were the common lot of the Christians. Nevertheless, the doctrine of the poor fishermen, as we have seen, triumphed over all its enemies, and thus proved to be the Doctrine of God (§29—35). It spread so rapidly that, soon after the death of the Apostles, St. Justin ventured to affirm before the whole world: "There is no people, neither among the Barbarians, nor among the Greeks, nor in any other known nation, among whom prayers and thanksgivings are not offered up to the Father and Creator of the Universe in the name of Christ Crucified." Who else but the Almighty could have performed such an inexplicable wonder? St. Augustine, the celebrated Father of the Church, makes a striking

---

5. How do you prove that the Christian Religion was spread through the help of God? About what time did St. Justin live? What does he testify of the propagation of Christianity? What observation does St. Augustine make?

observation upon this: "If the miracles," he says, "wrought by the Apostles, could be denied, this would be the greatest miracle, that the world believed without miracles."

6. But the Christian Church is not only founded on miracles; her duration itself is a continual and perpetual miracle. Kingdoms and Empires, in spite of their power, perish in the course of time; the Kingdom of Christ alone outlasts them all, and is constantly increasing. If it decreases in one part of the world, it spreads so much the more in another (§ 45). From the time of its foundation, it has been assailed by innumerable enemies from within and from without, their power is terrible, their hatred implacable; the Church of Christ, on her part, has no army to repulse their assaults, no sword to oppose their rude violence. Had not the arm of God protected her, she would long since have been overcome by the force and fraud of her enemies. (§§ 32, 36, 38, 39, 42, 43, 47, 48).

7. The Christian Church appears still more glorious, if we consider the benefits and blessings which she has at all times conferred on mankind. It was she that subdued the brutality of the barbarians, that abolished slavery and human sacrifices, and promoted public and domestic happiness. It was she that founded Charitable Institutions and innumerable Hospitals for the reception of the sick and distressed; it was she that amended the existing laws or made new ones; it was she that taught concord and charity, and diffused learning and true enlightenment (§§ 30, 38, 41, 45, 46). She can truly be called the Tree of Life which God has planted, that all men should peacefully rest under its shade, and refresh themselves with its fruit. Never has a nation abandoned this Tree of Life without plunging itself into indescribable misery. We

---

6. How do you prove that the duration or permanent continuance of the Christian Church is a miracle?

7. What fruits did the Christian Faith produce for mankind?

know very well what has become of the nations in Asia and Africa who were formerly so happy, and what fruit the Anti-Christian Freethinkers have produced in Europe (§§ 39, 47, 48). If "the tree is to be known by its fruits" (Matt. 7, 16), every one must see that the Christian Faith, which diffuses nothing but happiness and blessings, is the most valuable gift of God; that, on the contrary, Infidelity, which produces but misery and vexation, can only proceed from the spirit of evil.

8. Now, this Church which Almighty God has founded on miracles, nay, which is herself a continual miracle; this Church, which incessantly pours out the greatest benefits over the universe, can be no other but the Roman Catholic Church. History clearly proves that it is she, and no other, that forms that Community of the faithful, which Christ has established for the salvation of the world, in which the Bishops, as the Successors of the Apostles, under the supreme authority of the Pope, the Successor of Saint Peter, exercise their Teaching and Pastoral Offices in an uninterrupted succession (§§ 22, 30, 31). It is impossible that any Sect, whatever may be its name, should be the Church founded by Christ; for it is well known that every one of them began to exist long after Christ, and that even then they owed their origin to their defection and separation from the Church of Christ (§§ 36, 42, 43). We see, therefore, that in all these Sects the words of Jesus are sooner or later fulfilled: "Every plant which My Heavenly Father hath not planted, shall be rooted up." (Matt. 15, 13.) Their existence is not lasting; they spring up, make some noise, and disap-

---

What, on the contrary, were the fruits which Heresy and Infidelity brought forth? What conclusion must we draw from these different fruits?

8. How do you prove from History that the Church established by God, can be no other than the Roman Catholic? What has Christ foretold of all Sects? What promise has He given to the Catholic Church?

pear again. (§ 36 at the end; § 47 at the beginning.) It is not so with the Catholic Church. Thousands of years pass away; neither does she vanish, nor does she grow old; for to her was made the promise of our Lord: "Upon this rock I will build My Church, and the gates of hell shall not prevail against her." (Matt. 16, 18.)

CHRONOLOGICAL SUCCESSION
OF
THE POPES.

	FROM		FROM
St. Peter at Rome*	42	St. Soter	168
St. Linus	67	St. Eleutherius	177
St. Cletus (Anacletus)		St. Victor I.	192
St. Clement	92	St. Zephyrinus	202
St. Evaristus	100	St. Callistus (Calixtus) I.	219
St. Alexander I.	109		
St. Sixtus (Xystus) I.	119	St. Urban I.	223
St. Telesphorus	127	St. Pontian	230
St. Hyginus	139	St. Antherus	235
St. Pius I.	142	St. Fabian	236
St. Anicetus	157	St. Cornelius	251

* The dates of the accession of the first Popes cannot be accurately given.

	FROM		FROM
St. Lucius	252	Pelagius I.	555
St. Stephen I.	253	John III.	560
St. Sixtus II.	257	Benedict I.	574
St. Dionysius	259	Pelagius II.	578
St. Felix I.	269	St. Gregory I.	590
St. Eutychian	274	Sabinianus	604
St. Caius	283	Boniface III.	606
St. Marcellinus	296	St. Boniface IV.	607
St. Marcellus I.	308	St. Deusdedit	615
St. Eusebius	310	Boniface V.	619
St. Melchiades	311	Honorius I.	625
St. Sylvester	314	Severinus	638
St. Marcus	336	John IV.	640
St. Julius I.	337	Theodorus I.	642
St. Liberius	352	St. Martin I.	649
St. Damasus I.	366	St. Eugenius I.	654
St. Siricius	385	St. Vitalian	657
St. Anastasius	398	Adeodatus	672
St. Innocent I.	402	Donus or Domnus I.	676
St. Zosimus	417	St. Agatho	679
St. Boniface I.	418	St. Leo II.	682
St. Celestine	423	St. Benedict II.	683
St. Sixtus III.	432	John V.	685
St. Leo I.	440	Conon	687
St. Hilary	461	St. Sergius I.	687
St. Simplicius	468	John VI.	701
St. Felix II.	483	John VII.	705
St. Gelasius I.	492	Sisinnius	708
St. Anastasius II.	496	Constantine	708
St. Symmachus	498	St. Gregory II.	715
St. Hormisdas	514	St. Gregory III.	731
St. John I.	523	St. Zachary	741
St. Felix III.	526	Stephen II.	752
Boniface II.	530	Stephen III.	752
John II.	533	St. Paul I.	757
St. Agapetus I.	535	Stephen IV.	767
St. Silverius	536	Adrian I.	772
Vigilius	540	St. Leo III.	795

	FROM		FROM
Stephen V.	816	Benedict VII.	975
St. Paschalis	817	John XIV.	983
Eugenius II.	824	John XV.	985
Valentinus	827	Gregory V.	996
Gregory IV.	827	Sylvester II.	999
Sergius II.	844	John XVII.	1003
St. Leo IV.	847	John XVIII.	1003
Benedict III.	855	Sergius VI.	1009
St. Nicolas I.	858	Benedict VIII.	1012
Adrian II.	867	John XIX.	1024
John VIII.	872	Benedict IX.	1033
Marinus	882	Gregory VI.	1044
Adrian III.	884	Clement II.	1046
Stephen VI.	885	Damasus II.	1048
Formosus	891	St. Leo IX.	1049
Boniface VI.	896	Victor II.	1055
Stephen VII.	896	Stephen X.	1057
Romanus	897	Nicolas II.	1058
Theodorus II.	898	Alexander II.	1061
John IX.	898	St. Gregory VII.	1073
Benedict IV.	900	Victor III.	1086
Leo V.	903	Urban II.	1088
Christopher	903	Paschalis II.	1099
Sergius III.	904	Gelasius II.	1118
Anastasius III.	911	Callistus (Calix-	
Lando	913	tus) II.	1119
John X.	914	Honorious II.	1124
Leo VI.	928	Innocent II.	1130
Stephen VIII.	929	Celestine II.	1143
John XI.	931	Lucius II.	1144
Leo VII.	936	Eugenius III.	1145
Stephen IX.	939	Anastasius IV.	1153
Martin II.	943	Adrian IV.	1154
Agapetus II.	946	Alexander III.	1159
John XII.	956	Lucius III.	1181
John XIII.	965	Urban III.	1185
Benedict VI.	972	Gregory VIII.	1187
Donus or Domnus II.	974	Clement III.	1187

	FROM		FROM
Celestine III.	1191	Pius II.	1458
Innocent III.	1198	Paulus II.	1464
Honorius III.	1216	Sixtus IV.	1471
Gregory IX.	1227	Innocent VIII.	1484
Celestine IV.	1241	Alexander VI.	1492
Innocent IV.	1243	Pius III.	1503
Alexander IV.	1254	Julius II.	1503
Urban IV.	1261	Leo X.	1513
Clement IV.	1264	Adrian VI.	1522
Gregory X.	1271	Clement VII.	1523
Innocent V.	1276	Paulus III.	1534
Adrian V.	1276	Julius III.	1550
John XXI.	1276	Marcellus II.	1555
Nicolas III.	1277	Paulus IV.	1555
Martin IV.	1281	Pius IV.	1559
Honorious IV.	1285	St. Pius V.	1566
Nicolas IV.	1288	Gregory XIII.	1572
St. Celestine V.	1294	Sixtus V.	1585
Boniface VIII.	1294	Urban VII.	1590
Benedict XI.	1303	Gregory XIV.	1590
Clement V.	1305	Innocent IX.	1591
John XXII.	1316	Clement VIII.	1592
Benedict XII.	1334	Leo XI.	1605
Clement VI.	1342	Paulus V.	1605
Innocent VI.	1352	Gregory XV.	1621
Urban V.	1362	Urban VIII.	1623
Gregory XI.	1370	Innocent X.	1644
Urban VI.	1378	Alexander VII.	1655
Boniface IX.	1389	Clement IX.	1667
Innocent VII.	1404	Clement X.	1670
Gregory XII.	1406	Innocent XI.	1676
Alexander V.	1409	Alexander VIII.	1689
John XXIII.	1410	Innocent XII.	1691
Martin V.	1417	Clement XI.	1700
Eugenius IV.	1431	Innocent XIII.	1721
Nicolas V.	1447	Benedict XIII.	1724
Callistus (Calixtus III).	1455	Clement XII.	1730
		Benedict XIV.	1740

	FROM		FROM
Clement XIII.	1758	Leo XII.	1823
Clement XIV.	1769	Pius VIII.	1829
Pius VI.	1775	Gregory XVI.	1831
Pius VII.	1800	Pius IX.	1846

ADDITIONS.

See Preface.

Page 11. and in 588, he entirely——Babylonian Captivity.
,, 16. These are the names——betrayed Him.
,, 21. In the meantime, the Apostles——in the place of Judas.
,, 30. The first Hermit was St. Paul——Patriarch of Monks (d. 356.).
,, ,, For, not to speak of his miracles——into England in 596.
,, ,, Some of them were named Huns——Angles, Saxons.
,, 31. Odoacer, King of the Heruli——of Italy in 476.
,, 34. In the year 637, Jerusalem——foes of Christianity.
,, 35. They wore, as a badge of their——Crusaders and Crusade.
,, ,, And thus Jerusalem was taken——those ferocious Infidels.
,, 38. In several places——spiritual jurisdiction.
,, 42. To check the progress——into which they have divided.
,, 47. The Oratorians——literary pursuits.
,, ,, Note. This Institute——ceased to be English.
,, 59. The Chronological Succession of the Popes from St. Peter to Pius IX.

A FULL CATECHISM

OF

THE CATHOLIC RELIGION.

INTRODUCTION.

On the End of Man.

1. For what end are we in this world?

We are in this world, that we may know God, love Him, and serve Him, and thereby attain Heaven.

2. What is Heaven?

Heaven is a place of eternal and perfect happiness.

3. Are not then the things of this world intended to make us happy?

No, the things of this world cannot possibly make us happy.

4. Why cannot the things of this world make us happy?

Because all earthly things are vain and perishable; and 2. Because man is made for God and an everlasting happiness.

1. "I heaped together for myself silver and gold and the wealth of kings, and provinces. And whatsoever my eyes desired, I refused them not, and I withheld not my heart from enjoying every pleasure. But I saw in all things vanity, and vexation of mind, and that nothing was lasting under the sun." Thus spoke Solomon, the happiest of kings. (Eccles. 2,8—11.) What is your life? It is a vapour which appeareth

for a little while, and afterwards shall vanish away." (James 4, 15.) 2. "For Thyself, O God, Thou hast made us; therefore, our heart will be restless until it rests in Thee." (St. Augustine.)

5. For what end then were the things of this world principally given to us?

That we may use them for the purpose of knowing and serving God.

"All men are vain, in whom there is not the knowledge of God, and who by these good things that are seen, could not understand Him that is, neither by attending to the works have acknowledged who was the Workman." (Wisd. 13, 1.) "Whether you eat or drink, or whatsoever else you do, do all to the glory of God." (1. Cor. 10, 31.)

6. Why does God require us to know Him, love Him, and serve Him?

God requires us, 1. To know Him, because He is the eternal Truth; 2. To love Him, because He is the most bountiful and most amiable Good; and 3. To serve Him, because He is the Sovereign Lord.

7. What will become of those who will not know, love, and serve Him?

God will cast them from Him for ever.

"The unprofitable servant cast ye out into the exterior darkness. There shall be weeping and gnashing of teeth." (Matt. 25, 30.)

8. What is then most necessary in this life?

In this life the most necessary thing is, that we should know, love, and serve God, and thereby obtain eternal happiness.

"Seek ye first the kingdom of God and His justice." (Matt. 6, 33.) "For what doth it profit a man, if he gain the whole world, and suffer the loss of his own soul?" Matt. 16, 26.)

9. What must we do, if we would know and serve God, and be eternally happy?

1. We must believe all that God has revealed; 2. We must keep all the Commandments which God has ordered to be kept; and 3. We must use the means of grace which God has ordained for our salvation.

Or in other words: We must have Religion; for *Religion* (from *religare*) is the lively *union* of man with God, which springs from faith, charity, and grace, and is confirmed by the faithful observance of the Divine Commandments.

10. Why must we, in order to be saved, believe, keep the Commandments, and make use of the means of grace?

We must, in order to be saved, 1. Believe, because it is only by faith, that we get a right knowledge of God; 2. We must keep the Commandments, because by keeping the Commandments, we serve God; and 3. We must also use the means of grace, because by them we obtain the help necessary to salvation.

11. Where do we get a right knowledge of the truths of Divine faith, of the Commandments, and of the means of grace?

In the Christian Doctrine.

12. What do you call the book which briefly contains the Christian Doctrine in question and answer?

The *Catechism*.

13. What then does the Catechism treat of?

1. Of *Faith*;
2. Of the *Commandments*; and
3. Of the *Means of Grace*, namely, the Sacraments and Prayer.

Application.—Never neglect going to the instructions on Christian Doctrine; and, when there, be always attentive, that you may learn to know and love God properly, and thus attain your last end, which is eternal happiness in Heaven.—"Blessed is the man that findeth wisdom (i.e., the knowledge and love of God)! She is more precious than all riches; and all the things that are desired, are not to be compared with her. She is a tree of life to them that lay hold on her; and he that shall retain her, is blessed." (Prov. 3, 13—18.)

PART I.

ON FAITH.

§. 1. *Acceptation, Object, and Rule of Faith.*

1. What is the Faith of a Catholic Christian?

Faith is a virtue infused by God into our souls, by which we believe, without doubting, all those things which God has revealed, and proposes by His Church to our belief.

"*To believe*" means, in general, to hold to be true what another says, and for this reason, because he says it. *To believe God* means, therefore, to hold firmly and without doubting what God has revealed, and because He has revealed it, although we can neither see nor comprehend it; for faith is founded, not on our seeing or comprehending, but on the word of God. "Faith is the evidence of things that appear not." (Hebr. 11, 1.)

2. Why do we say that faith was infused by God into our souls?

Because it is a gift of God, and an effect of His grace, which enlightens our understanding, and moves our will, to believe, without doubting, all those things which God has revealed.

"For by grace you are saved through faith, and that not of yourselves, for it is the gift of God." (Eph. 2, 8.)

3. Why must grace not only enlighten our understanding, but also move our will?

Because a *good will* also belongs to faith; for no one can believe but he who is willing to believe.

Therefore faith is also rewarded by God, and infidelity punished. "He that believeth and is baptized shall be saved; but he that believeth not shall be condemned." (Mark 16, 16.)

4. Why must we believe all that God has revealed ?
Because God is the eternal and infallible truth.

5. What means, "*all that God has revealed ?*"
It means all that God has made known for our salvation by the Patriarchs and Prophets, and at last, by His Son, Jesus Christ, and the Apostles.

" God, who, at sundry times and in divers manners, spoke in times past to the fathers by the Prophets, last of all, in these days hath spoken to us by His Son." (Hebr. 1, 1. 2.)

6.* Was it necessary that God should have revealed to us the truths of salvation, in order that we might know them ?
Yes, because without Divine Revelation, we should have known many of them but with great difficulty, and very imperfectly; and most of them would have remained entirely unknown to us.

" And hardly do we guess aright at things that are upon earth : and with labour do we find the things that are before us. But the things that are in Heaven, who shall search out ? And who shall know Thy thought, except Thou give wisdom, and send Thy Holy Spirit from above ?" (Wisd. 9, 16. 17.)

7. How did Divine Revelation come down to us ?
Divine Revelation came down to us, partly by *writing*, that is, by the Holy Scripture, or the Bible; partly by *word of mouth*, that is, by Tradition.

8. What is the Holy Scripture ?
The *Holy Scripture* is a collection of books which were written by the inspiration of the Holy Ghost, and acknowledged by the Church as the Word of God.

" Prophecy came not by the will of man at any time but the holy men of God spoke, inspired by the Holy Ghost." (2 Pet. 1, 21.)

9. How is the Holy Scripture divided ?
The Holy Scripture is divided into the books of

the Old and New Testament, or of the Old and New Law.

10. What Revelations does the Old Testament contain?

The Old Testament contains the Divine Revelations which were made to man before the coming of Christ.

11. Of what books does the Old Testament consist?

The Old Testament consists, 1. Of *Twenty-one Historical Books*, which relate the Creation of the world, the lives of the Patriarchs, and the History of the Jewish nation; 2. Of *Seven Moral Books*, which are collections of Psalms, of holy maxims, and of rules of life; and 3. Of *Seventeen Prophetical Books*, which mostly contain prophecies.

The *Historical Books* are: The Pentateuch, or five Books of Moses (Genesis, Exodus, Leviticus, Numbers, Deuteronomy); the Book of Josue; the Book of Judges; the Book of Ruth; the four Books of Kings; the two Books of Chronicles or of Paralipomenon; the Book of Esdras; the Book of Nehemias, which is also called the Second of Esdras; the Book of Tobias; the Book of Judith; the Book of Esther; and the two Books of the Machabees.

The *Moral Books* are: The Book of Job; the Psalms; the Proverbs; Ecclesiastes, or the Preacher; the Canticle of Canticles; the Book of Wisdom; and Ecclesiasticus, or Jesus the Son of Sirach.

The *Prophetical Books*: Isaias; Jeremias; Baruch; Ezechiel; Daniel; Osee; Joel; Amos; Abdias; Jonas; Micheas; Nahum; Habacuc; Sophonias; Aggeus; Zacharias; and Malachias.

12. What Revelations does the New Testament contain?

The New Testament contains the Revelations which we have received through Jesus Christ and the Apostles.

13. Of what books does the New Testament consist?

The New Testament consists, 1. Of the *four*

Gospels according to St. Matthew, St. Mark, St. Luke, and St. John, which relate the history of Jesus; 2. Of the *Acts of the Apostles*, by St. Luke; 3. Of *fourteen Epistles* of St. Paul, and *seven* by other Apostles, which contain dogmatical and moral instructions; and 4. Of the *Apocalypse*, or the Revelation of St. John, which foretells the combats and victories of the Church.

The Epistles of St. Paul are: One to the Romans; two to the Corinthians; one to the Galatians; one to the Ephesians; one to the Philippians; one to the Colossians; two to the Thessalonians; two to Timothy; one to Titus; one to Philemon; and one to the Hebrews.

The other Epistles are: One of St. James; two of St. Peter; three of St. John; and one of St. Jude, surnamed Thaddeus.

14. Is it enough to believe that only which is contained in the Holy Scripture?

No; we must also believe *Tradition*, i.e., those revealed truths which the Apostles preached, but did not commit to writing.

St. Paul, therefore, exhorts the first Christians by saying: "Therefore, brethren, stand fast; and *hold the traditions* which you have learned, whether *by word*, or by our Epistle." (2 Thess. 2, 14.)

15. Have not then the Apostles written all that Jesus Christ has taught?

No; the Apostles have not even written all that Jesus has done, far less, all that He has taught; for Christ did not commission them to *write*, but to *preach* His doctrine. (Mark 16, 15. Matt. 28, 19.)

"Many other signs also did Jesus in the sight of His disciples, which are not written in this book." (John 20, 30.)

The Bible, therefore, does not contain the entire Revelation of God. The Bible nowhere tells us, how many Divine books there are, and which they are; if we did not know this for certain from Tradition, we should not even have a Bible.—The Bible does not, in doubtful passages, decide upon the true meaning of its words;

therefore, all Sects always appealed to the Bible, in order to prove their contradictory doctrines, and each one of them pretended to have hit on its true meaning.—If we would consult the Bible *only* without Tradition, we ought, for instance, still to keep holy the Saturday with the Jews, instead of the Sunday, and refrain ourselves from things strangled, and from blood (Acts 15, 20.) moreover, we ought, with the Anabaptists, to let little children, who are incapable of being instructed, die without Baptism; since Christ has commanded, first to teach, and then to baptize. (Matt. 28, 19.)

16. Why is the unwritten doctrine of the Apostles called "*Tradition?*"

It is called Tradition, because, since the times of the Apostles, it has, without interruption, been *transmitted* or handed down in the Catholic Church from generation to generation.

" And the things which thou hast heard of me by many witnesses, the same commend to faithful men, who shall be fit to teach others also." (2 Tim. 2, 2.)

17. How has Tradition been handed down to us?

It has been handed down to us partly by word of mouth, and partly by the decrees and rites of the Church, and the writings of the Holy Fathers.

18.* What is to be thought of the writings or of the doctrine of the Holy Fathers?

The uniform doctrine of the Holy Fathers is the doctrine of Jesus Christ, which they have received from the Apostles or their Successors; therefore, we are never to deviate from it.

19. But why must we believe Tradition, as well as what is contained in the Holy Scripture?

Because Catholic Tradition was revealed by God, as well as that which is contained in the Holy Scripture.

20. What then must the Catholic Christian in general believe?

He must believe all that God has revealed, and the

Catholic Church proposes to his belief, whether it be contained in the Holy Scripture or not.

The Church is considered to *propose* a truth to our belief, when recognizing it to be revealed by God, she commands us to believe it.

21 Why is it necessary that the Catholic Church should propose the revealed truths to our belief?

Because it is only from the Catholic Church that we can infallibly know what God has revealed.

22. Why can we from the Catholic Church alone infallibly know what God has revealed?

1. Because it is only from the Catholic Church that we have the Scripture and Tradition, which contain the Divine Revelations; and 2. Because it is through her alone that we infallibly know the true meaning of the Scripture and of Tradition.

23. Why do we say that it is only from the Catholic Church that we have the Holy Scripture and Tradition?

1. Because the Catholic Church alone has received the Scripture and Tradition from the Apostles, and has always, with the special assistance of the Holy Ghost, preserved them uncorrupted; and 2. Because it is she alone who gives us incontestable security for their Divine origin.

It is from his Church alone that the Catholic receives with full confidence the Books of the Holy Scripture. He is not only sure, 1. Of their *Authenticity* and *Credibility*, because this has been so frequently and undeniably proved, that it is impossible to question it without rejecting all historical truth (see Short History of Religion: Concluding Remarks §§. 3 and 4); and 2. Of their *Integrity* or *Incorruptness;* because the Holy Scripture has always been revered by the Church as the Word of God, and, consequently, most scrupulously preserved from any corruption whatever; but he is also sure, 3. Of their *Divine Origin;* because this is founded on the testimony of the Catholic Church, which was established by Christ to teach us the truth, and has also been manifestly proved and confirmed through all ages as a Divine and infallible institution.—(Short History of Religion: Concluding Remarks §§. 5, 6, 7, and 8.)

24. And why do we say that through the Catholic Church alone we infallibly know the true meaning of the Scripture and of Tradition?

Because the Catholic Church alone is *"the pillar and ground of the truth"* (1 Tim. 3, 15), and, therefore, cannot err in the interpretation of the Word of God.

25. May no one, then, presume to explain the Scripture and Tradition contrary to the interpretation of the Catholic Church?

No; for this would be as if he understood the Scripture and Tradition better than the Holy Ghost, who inspires the Church with the true meaning of it.

26. But is the meaning of the Holy Scripture not clear in itself, and easy to be understood by every one?

No; for the Holy Scripture is a Divine and mysterious book, "*in which,*" as St. Peter says, speaking of the Epistles of St. Paul, "*are certain things hard to be understood, which the unlearned and unstable wrest to their own destruction.*" (2 Petr. 3, 16.)

"What else gives rise to so many heresies, but because the Scripture, which is good in itself, is ill understood?"—St. Augustine.

27. Is it not then true that the Bible alone is the only Rule of Faith? Or, in other words: Is not then every private individual to search the Bible, and nothing but the Bible, until he finds out what he has to believe?

No; for not the Bible alone, but the Bible and Tradition, *both* infallibly interpreted by the Church, are the right Rule of Faith.

1. If it was the will of our Saviour that we should arrive at the knowledge of the truths of salvation simply by reading and searching the Scripture, why then is it

written: "Faith cometh by *hearing*, and hearing by the (preaching of the) *Word* of Christ?"—(Rom. 10, 17.) And why then did not Christ Himself write? Why did He not commission His Apostles to write? Why did they not write but after the lapse of a long space of time, and only upon some special occasion? Why did they not all write? Why did He Himself "*give some Apostles, and some Prophets, and other some Evangelists, and other some Pastors and Doctors?*"—(1 Cor. 12. Eph. 4.) Why did He not command that every one, or, at least, every Christian should learn to read? Why then was printing invented so late? etc.

2. The Christian Religion had been spread, and flourished, before the Books of the New Testament were written; and even after they had been written, there were many Christian nations, as St. Irenæus testifies, who did not so much as possess the Holy Scriptures.

28.* What has the Church decreed with regard to the reading of the Bible in the vulgar tongue?

1. That we should have the learning and piety requisite for it; and 2. That the translation should be accompanied with explanations, and that both should be approved of by the Church.

By this wise provision, the Church by no means intends to withhold the Word of God from the faithful, since she desires nothing more than that all should know it, and meditate upon it; she merely wishes to guard them against corrupted Bibles, which are often designedly offered to ignorant people, and against erroneous interpretations, sects, and schisms.

Application.—In matters of faith, never trust your own judgment, but always humbly submit to the decisions of Holy Church; for when you believe what the Church teaches, you believe the Word of God.

§. 2. *Necessity of Faith.*

29. Is faith necessary to salvation?

Faith is absolutely necessary to salvation; for "*without faith it is impossible to please God.*" (Hebr. 11, 6.)

"He that doth not believe, is already judged." (John 3, 18.) "He that believeth not, shall be condemned." (Mark 16, 16.)

30. Will any faith save us?
No; only the true faith, which Christ our Lord has taught, will save us.

"He that believeth in the Son, hath life everlasting; but he that believeth not the Son, shall not see life; but the wrath of God abideth on him." (John 3, 36.)

31. Why will that faith only, which Christ has taught, save us?
Because by this faith alone, and by no other, we are made partakers of Christ, and without Christ there is no salvation.

"For there is no other name under Heaven given to men, whereby we must be saved." (Acts 4, 12.)

32. Is it then a sin to say, that it does not matter what faith we profess?
Yes, it is a grievous sin to say so, or even only to think so; for we despise God by it, who has given us the one true faith, and, therefore, has sent His Only Begotten Son into the world. (Short Hist. of Rel.; Concl. Rem. §. 1.)

If it did not matter what we believe, it would not have been necessary for God to reveal a religion, and our ancestors might all have remained Heathens or Jews. But "*this is the judgment,*" says Jesus Christ, "*because the light is come into the world, and men love darkness rather than the light;*" (John 3, 19.) i.e., because many were obstinate in their unbelief, although they saw the truth, or could have seen it, provided they had been sincere.

33.* But is it not written: "*He that feareth God, and worketh justice, is acceptable to Him?*" (Acts 10, 35.)
Yes; but he who fears God, does also believe all that He has revealed, as Cornelius did. (Acts 10.) He, on the contrary, who does not believe all that God has revealed, does not fear Him either, but rejects His Word, and denies His Veracity.

"He that believeth not the Son, maketh Him a liar."
(1 John, 5, 10.)

34. Which Church has the true faith, taught by Christ?

It is only the Catholic Church that has the true faith taught by Christ.

35. Why is it only the Catholic Church that has the true faith taught by Christ?

Because the Catholic Church alone has received from Christ Himself, through His Apostles, this faith as a Heavenly gift committed to her trust, and has always preserved it uncorrupted. (1 Tim. 6, 20.)

36. Have not the Protestant Sects also received their doctrine from Christ Himself, and preserved it uncorrupted?

No; for 1. It is impossible that they should have received it from Christ Himself, since they did not begin to exist till long after Christ; and

2. It is equally impossible that they should always have preserved uncorrupted whatsoever of the doctrine of Christ and His Apostles has devolved to them, because they teach at different times different principles, whereas Christ and the Apostles always taught the same.

"Our preaching which was to you, was not, *It is*, and *It is not;* for the Son of God, *Jesus Christ*, who was preached among you by us, was not, *It is*, and *It is not*, but, *It is*, was in Him." (2 Cor. 1, 18. 19.)

37. If then the true faith is essentially necessary to salvation, and the Catholic faith is the only true one; is it not a great grace to be a Catholic Christian?

To be a Catholic Christian is an invaluable grace, for which we cannot thank God enough, and which we ought most earnestly to turn to our advantage.

Application.—Rejoice, and often thank God that you are a child of the Catholic Church; for "*there is*," as St. Augustine says, "*no greater wealth, no greater treasure than the Catholic Faith*," provided we live as our faith teaches us. This truth is especially confirmed at the hour of death.

§. 3. *Qualities of Faith.*

38. What must be the qualities of our faith?
Our faith must be 1. *Universal*; 2. *Firm*; 3. *Lively*; and 4. *Constant*.

39. When is our faith *universal?*
Our faith is universal, when we believe not only *some*, but *all* the truths which the Catholic Church proposes to our belief.

40. Is then no one at liberty to admit and believe only some points of the Christian faith?
No; for 1. Christ says without exception: "Preach the *Gospel* to every creature; he that believeth not shall be condemned;" (Mark 16, 15. 16.) and again: "Teach them to observe *all* things whatsoever I have commanded you." (Matt. 28, 20.) And St. John says: "Whosoever *revolteth*, and continueth not in the doctrine of Christ, hath not God." (2 John 1, 9.) And 2. He who believes of the doctrine of Christ only what he pleases, has no faith at all; for such a one does not believe God, but his own judgment.

41. When is our faith *firm?*
Our faith is firm, when we believe without the least doubt.

EXAMPLES: Abraham, rewarded for his firm faith: "In the promise of God he staggered not by distrust; but was strengthened in faith; and, therefore, it was reputed to him unto justice." (Rom. 4, 20. 22.) Moses and Aaron, punished on account of a doubt. (Numb. 20, 12.)

42. When is our faith *lively?*
Our faith is lively, when we live up to it; that is, when we avoid evil and do good according as our faith prescribes.

"As the body without the spirit is dead; so also faith without works is dead." (James 2. 26.)

43. Will a dead faith also save us?

No; our faith must prove active by charity, or else it is not sufficient for obtaining eternal salvation.

"In Christ Jesus neither circumcision availeth any thing, nor uncircumcision; but faith that worketh by charity." (Gal. 5, 6.) "And if I should have all faith, so that I could remove mountains, and have not charity, I am nothing." (1 Cor. 13, 2.)

44. When is our faith *constant*?
Our faith is constant, when we are ready to lose all, even our life, rather than fall away from it.

"Take heed, brethren, lest perhaps there be in any of you an evil heart of unbelief, to depart from the living God." (Hebr. 3, 12.) Example of the holy Martyrs.

45. What leads people to fall away from their faith?
1. Pride and subtile reasoning on the mysteries of our religion; 2. Neglect of prayer and of the other religious duties; 3. Worldliness and a wicked life; and 4. Reading irreligious books; intercourse with scoffers at religion; and such matrimonial or other connections as endanger the true faith.

1. "I confess to Thee, O Father, Lord of heaven and earth, because Thou hast hid these things from the wise and prudent, and hast revealed them to little ones." (Matt. 11, 25.) 2. "The kingdom of God shall be taken from you, and shall be given to a nation yielding the fruits thereof." (Matt. 21, 43.) 3. "Having faith and a good conscience, which some rejecting have made shipwreck concerning the faith." (1 Tim. 1, 19.) 4. "Beware of false prophets, who come to you in the clothing of sheep, but inwardly they are ravening wolves." (Matt. 7, 15.) "A little leaven corrupteth the whole lump." (Gal. 5, 9.)

46. How do we especially show that our faith is firm and constant?
By never denying it, not even in appearance, but by candidly professing it on every occasion by word and deed.

"Every one that shall confess Me before men, I will also confess him before My Father who is in heaven. But he that shall deny Me before men, I will also deny him before My Father who is in heaven." (Matt. 10, 32. 33.) "With the heart, we believe unto justice; but, with the mouth, confession is made unto salvation." (Rom. 10, 10.) Example of Eleazar.

47. Is there also a particular sign by which Catholics profess their faith?

Yes, the *Sign of the Cross.*

48. Why do we use the sign of the cross in order to profess our faith?

Because it expresses the two principal mysteries of our religion; namely, the mystery of the Most Blessed Trinity, and the mystery of our Redemption by Christ on the cross.

49. Whence comes the custom of making the sign of the cross?

This custom is very old, and descends from the apostolic times.

50. When should we make the sign of the cross?

It is good and wholesome to make it frequently, as the first Christians did; especially, when we rise and go to bed, before and after prayers, before every important occupation, and in all temptations and dangers.

51. Why is it wholesome frequently to make the sign of the cross?

Because by devoutly making the sign of the cross, we arm ourselves against the snares of the devil, and draw the blessing of Heaven upon us.

52. Why do we usually make the sign of the cross on our forehead, mouth, and heart, at the reading of the Gospel?

That God, through the merits of Christ Crucified, may give us grace to comprehend the Gospel with our mind, to profess it with our mouth, and to love it with our heart.

Application.—Never be ashamed of the Catholic

faith, or of the sign of the cross; let this be your motto: "But God forbid that I should glory, save in the cross of our Lord Jesus Christ." (Gal. 6, 14.)—Shun most carefully all intercourse with irreligious and wicked persons, and especially beware of such books as might stagger you in the true faith, or lead you astray from the path of virtue.

ON THE APOSTLES' CREED.

1. Where are the chief things, which we must above all know and believe, briefly contained?
In the twelve Articles of the Apostles' Creed.

2. Why is it called the *"Apostles' Creed?"*
Because it descends from the Apostles.

THE FIRST ARTICLE.

"I believe in God the Father Almighty, Creator of Heaven and Earth."

§. 1. *On God.*
"I believe in God."

3. What is God?
God is an infinitely perfect Spirit, the Lord of Heaven and Earth, and the Author of all good.

4. Why do we call God a *"Spirit?"*
We call God a Spirit, because He has understanding and free will, but no body. (John 4, 24.)

5. And why do we say that *"God is infinitely perfect?"*
Because God is not, like created beings, good only in some measure, but because He unites in Himself all good perfections without measure, or bounds, or number.

6. Which are the principal Attributes or Perfections of God?

These: God is eternal and unchangeable, omnipresent, omniscient or all-knowing, all-wise, all-powerful; He is infinitely holy and just; infinitely good, merciful and long-suffering; infinitely true and faithful.

7. What means, "*God is eternal?*"

God is eternal means, that He is always, without beginning and without end.

"Before the mountains were made, or the earth and the world was formed; from eternity and to eternity Thou art God." (Ps. 89, 2.)

8. What means, "*God is unchangeable?*"

God is unchangeable means, that He remains eternally the same, without any change either in Himself, or in His decrees.

"With whom (God) there is no change, nor shadow of alteration." (James 1, 17.) "My counsel shall stand, and all My will shall be done." (Isai. 46, 10.)

9. What ought we to do, since God is eternal and unchangeable?

We ought to serve and love Him for ever and ever.

"Thou art the God of my heart, and the God that is my portion for ever." (Ps. 72, 26.)

10. What means, "*God is omnipresent?*"

God is omnipresent means, that He is everywhere: in Heaven, on Earth, and in all places.

"Do not I fill Heaven and Earth? saith the Lord." (Jer. 23, 24.) "God is not far from every one of us; for in Him we live, and move, and are." (Acts 17, 27. 28.) Although God fills all space, nevertheless He is everywhere entire and perfect, and encompassed by no space; for He is *immense*.

11. What means, "*God is omniscient?*"

God is omniscient means, that He knows all things perfectly and from all eternity: He knows all things past, present, and to come, even our most secret thoughts.

"The eyes of the Lord are far brighter than the sun,

beholding round about all the ways of men, and the bottom of the deep, and looking into the hearts of men, into the most hidden parts; for all things were known to the Lord God, before they were created: so also after they were perfected he beholdeth all things." (Ecclus. 23, 28. 29.) See the whole Psalm 138. Examples; Predictions of Christ and of the Prophets.

12. What benefit do we derive from the frequent remembrance of God's omnipresence and omniscience?

1. It keeps us everywhere, even in secret, from evil, and incites us to good; and 2. It gives us courage and consolation in all difficulties and troubles.

1. "It is better for me to fall into your hands without doing it, than to sin in the sight of the Lord." (Dan. 13, 23.) —"That thy alms may be in secret, and thy Father who seeth in secret will repay thee." (Matt. 6, 4.)—2. "Though I should walk in the midst of the shadow of death, I will fear no evils, for Thou art with me." (Ps. 22, 4.)—"Behold my witness is in heaven, and He that knoweth my conscience is on high." (Job. 16, 20.)

13. What means, "*God is all-wise* ?"

God is all-wise means, that He knows how to dispose all things in the best manner, in order to attain His end.

"How great are Thy works, O Lord! Thou hast made all things in wisdom." (Ps. 103, 24.)—Examples: The child Moses saved; Joseph exalted; Aman disgraced.

14. What means, "*God is all-powerful or almighty* ?"

God is all-powerful means, that He can do any thing, and has only to will, and the thing is done.

"Whatsoever the Lord pleased he hath done, in heaven, in earth, in the sea, and in all the deeps." (Ps. 134, 6.)—"Because no word shall be impossible with God." (Luke 1, 37.)— Examples: The Creation; the wonders in Egypt and in the desert.

15. To what should our belief in God's infinite power and infinite wisdom incite us?

It should incite us, 1. To place all our confidence

in God; and 2. To be always resigned to His dispensations.

1. "Put not your trust in the children of men, in whom there is no salvation. Blessed is he whose hope is in the Lord his God." (Ps. 145, 3. 5.)—Ex.: Gedeon.—2. "Commit thy way to the Lord, and trust in Him, and He will do it." (Ps. 36, 5.)—Ex.: Job.

16. What means, "*God is holy?*"
God is holy means, that He loves and wills only what is good, i.e., what agrees with His perfections, and abhors all that is evil.

"Thou hast loved justice, and hatedst iniquity." (Ps. 44, 8.) Ex.: The giving of the Law on Mount Sinai.

17. What means, "*God is just?*"
God is just means, that He rewards and punishes men according to their deserts.

"He will render to every one according to his works; . . . . for there is no respect of persons with God." (Rom. 2, 6. 11.)—Examples: The world punished by the deluge, and Sodom and Gomorrha destroyed by fire from heaven; but Noe and Lot preserved.

18. When will perfect retribution be made?
Perfect retribution will not be made till in the other world;† there is, however, even in this life, no true happiness for the wicked,‡ and no true unhappiness for the just.§

† Parable of the cockle and the wheat (Matt. 13, 30.)—of the rich man and Lazarus. (Luke 16.)—‡ "We wearied ourselves in the way of iniquity and destruction, and have walked through hard ways." (Wisd. 5, 7.)—Examples: Cain, Absalon, Achab, Antiochus.—§ "The souls of the just are in the hand of God." (Wisd. 3, 1.)—Examples: Joseph, Tobias, Susanna, Daniel, St. Paul. (2 Cor. 7, 4.)

19. To what should the remembrance of God's holiness and justice animate us?
It should animate us, 1. Carefully to avoid all evil, and to become more and more holy; and 2. Not to pride ourselves in our pretended righteousness.

1. "Fear ye not them that kill the body, and are not able to kill the soul; but rather fear Him that can destroy both soul and body into hell." (Matt. 10, 28.)—"I am the Lord your God; be holy because I am holy." (Levit. 11, 44.) —2. "I am not conscious to myself of anything, yet I am not hereby justified; but He that judgeth me, is the Lord." (1. Cor. 4, 4.)

20. What means, "*God is good?*"

God is good means, that out of love He will do good to all creatures, and that He really bestows innumerable blessings upon us.

"Thou lovest all things that are, and hatest none of the things which Thou hast made." (Wisd. 11, 25.) "Thus saith the Lord: Can a woman forget her infant, so as not to have pity on the son of her womb? And if she should forget, yet will not I forget thee." (Isai. 49, 15.)

21. Which is the greatest proof of God's love and goodness?

That He delivered His Own Son up to death for the salvation of us sinners.

"God is charity. By this hath the charity of God appeared towards us, because God hath sent His Only-begotten Son into the world, that we may live by Him." (1 John 4, 8. 9.)

22. What means, "*God is merciful?*"

God is merciful means, that He is disposed to avert all evil from His creatures, and, therefore, willingly pardons all truly penitent sinners.

"The mercy of God is upon all flesh." (Ecclus. 18, 12. Comp. Jon. 4, 11.) "As I live, saith the Lord God, I desire not the death of the wicked, but that the wicked turn from his way, and live." (Ez. 33, 11.) Ex.: The Ninivites. Parable of the prodigal son. (Luke 15.)

23. What means, "*God is long-suffering?*"

God is long-suffering means, that He often waits a long time before He punishes the sinner, in order to give him time for repentance.

"Thou overlookest the sins of men for the sake of repentance." (Wisd. 11, 24.) Ex.: Manasses (2 Paral. 33.); Jerusalem (Matt. 23, 37.); Parable of the barren fig-tree Luke 13)

24. What should we do, since God is so good, so merciful, and so long-suffering?

We should 1. Be thankful to God, and love Him with all our heart; 2. When we have sinned, we should with confidence beg pardon of Him; and 3. We should be good and merciful to our neighbours.

1. "Give glory to the Lord, for He is good: for His mercy endureth for ever." (Ps. 106, 1.) Ex.: Ingratitude of the Israelites in the desert punished. 2. "I will arise and will go to my father." (Luke 15, 18.) 3. "Be ye therefore merciful, as your Father also is merciful." (Luke 6, 36.) Parable of the unmerciful servant. (Matt. 18.)

25. What means, "*God is true?*"

God is true means, that He reveals nothing but truth, because He can neither err nor lie.

"It is impossible for God to lie." (Hebr. 6, 18.)

26. What means "*God is faithful?*"

God is faithful means, that He surely keeps what He promises, and executes what He threatens.

"And thou shalt know that the Lord thy God, He is a strong and faithful God, keeping His covenant and mercy to them that love Him, and repaying forthwith them that hate Him, so as to destroy them." (Deut. 7, 9. 10.)

27. What does the truth and faithfulness of God oblige us to do?

1. To believe most firmly in the word of God, and steadfastly to trust in His promise; and 2. Always to speak the truth, and to keep the promise we have made.

1. "Blessed are they that have not seen, and have believed." (John 20, 29.) Ex.: Abraham. 2. Punishment of Ananias and Saphira. (Acts 5.)

28. Can we also see God?

No, we cannot see God with corporeal eyes, because He is a Spirit.

29. How then have we come to the knowledge of God and His perfections, since we cannot see Him?

God has made Himself known to man in a natural, and especially in a supernatural manner.

30. How has God made Himself known to man in a natural manner?

1. By the *visible world*, which he has created, and continually governs; for nobody can reasonably think that the world has made itself, or that the regular and perfect order in it originated and subsists by itself. Only "The fool hath said in his heart: There is no God." (Ps. 13, 1.)

Therefore St. Paul says of the Gentiles, that they are inexcusable, if they do not believe in God; "For the invisible things of Him, from the creation of the world, are clearly seen, being understood by the things that are made; His eternal power also, and Divinity." (Rom. 1, 20.) "Nevertheless He left not Himself without testimony, doing good from Heaven, giving rains and fruitful seasons, filling our hearts with food and gladness." (Acts 14, 16. Comp. Wisd. 13.)

2. By the *voice of conscience*, which admonishes us to dread an invisible avenger of sin, and to hope in a rewarder of virtue. (Rom. 2, 15.)

Conscience does not come from ourselves; for it punishes us. It comes, therefore, from that Holy and Just Being, who created us, and formed our heart.

31. How has God made Himself known to man in a supernatural manner?

By the *Revelation*, which He has given us by the Prophets, and at last, by His Son. (See p. 70. Q. 5.)

"No man hath seen God at any time: the Only-begotten Son who is in the bosom of the Father, He hath declared Him." (John 1, 18.)

32. Is there more than one God?

No, there is but one God.

"I am God, and there is no God beside, neither is there the like to Me." (Isai. 46, 9.)

33. Why do we say, "*I believe in God*," and not only, "*I believe God?*"

Because we must not only believe that there is a God, and that all that He has said is true; but we must likewise give ourselves up to God with love and confidence.

Application.—"My son, give Me thy heart." (Prov. 23, 26.) Oh! give it to Him, the Eternal, the infinitely Beautiful, Rich, Good, and Faithful God—without delay—for ever and ever! God alone has a right to possess it, and He alone has the power to render it happy through all eternity.

§. 2. *On the Three Divine Persons.*

"I believe in God the Father."

34. Why do we say, "I believe in God the *Father?*"

1. Because God is our invisible Father in Heaven; and 2. Because in God there is more than one Person, the first of whom is called Father.

35. How many Persons are then in God?

There are three Persons in God: the Father, the Son, and the Holy Ghost.

"Going therefore, teach ye all nations; baptizing them in the name of the Father, and of the Son, and of the Holy Ghost." (Matt. 28, 19.) "There are three who give testimony in Heaven, the Father, the Word, and the Holy Ghost, and these three are One." (1 John 5, 7.)

36. Is each one of the three Persons God?

Yes, the Father is true God, the Son is true God, and the Holy Ghost is true God.

37. Are they not, then, three Gods?

No, the three Persons are but one God.

38. Why are the three Persons but one God?

Because all three Persons have one and the same indivisible nature and substance.

39. Is any one of these Persons older, or more powerful, than the others?

No; all three Persons are from eternity; all three

are equally powerful, good, and perfect; because all three are but one God.

40. Is there, then, no distinction at all between the Father, the Son, and the Holy Ghost?

As to the Persons, they are distinct; but as to the substance, they are one.

41. How are the three Divine Persons distinct from one another?

By this, that the Father is begotten of no one, nor proceeds from any one; the Son is begotten of the Father; and the Holy Ghost proceeds from the Father and the Son.

42. But if the Son is begotten of the Father, and the Holy Ghost proceeds from both, why, then, is none of the Divine Persons older than the others?

Because the Son is begotten from all eternity, and the Holy Ghost also proceeds from all eternity.

43. And if none of the Divine Persons is older or greater than the others, why then is the Father called the *first*, the Son the *second*, and the Holy Ghost the *third* Person?

They are so called, not to show any superiority, but the order in which the one proceeds from the other from all eternity.

44. What works are principally attributed to each of the three Divine Persons?

1. To the Father are attributed the works of Omnipotence, and particularly the Creation; 2. To the Son, the works of wisdom, and particularly the Redemption; and 3. To the Holy Ghost, the works of love, and particularly the Sanctification; although these works are common to all three Persons.

The works of *Omnipotence* and Creation are particularly attributed to the Father, because He is the principle to which the two other Persons owe their eternal origin. The works of *Wisdom*, to the Son, because the Father begets the Son by the knowledge of Himself, wherefore the Son is also called the essential "*Image*," the eternal "*Word*" of the Father.

The works of *Love* are attributed to the Holy Ghost, because He proceeds from the mutual love of the Father and of the Son.

45. What do we call the mystery of one God in three Persons?

We call it the mystery of the *Most Blessed Trinity*.

46. Can we comprehend this mystery?

No; it is impossible that our weak intellect, which understands even created things but imperfectly, should comprehend a mystery which is infinitely above all created things.

"Great art Thou in counsel, and incomprehensible in thought." (Jer. 32, 19.)—" For we know in part. We see now through a glass in a dark manner." (1 Cor. 13, 9. 12.) —However incomprehensible this mystery may be, yet it does not contradict any of the truths acknowledged by reason; for we do not say that God has one nature and three natures, but that, though He has but one nature, yet there are three Persons in Him. The Unity refers to the nature, and the Trinity to the Persons. (Comparison with the soul.)

47.* Is the doctrine of the Most Holy Trinity also important to us?

Yes, it is most important; for it is the principal and fundamental doctrine of Christianity, in so much that to reject it would be to deny the Christian Faith.

Application.—That the grace of this saving Faith may not be withdrawn from you, never forget what thanks you owe to the Most Blessed Trinity for the inestimable benefits of your creation, redemption, and sanctification, and what you have solemnly promised to the same Trinity in the holy Sacrament of Baptism.—(Feast of the Blessed Trinity.)

§. 3. *On the Creation and Government of the World.*
" Creator of Heaven and Earth."

48. Why is God called " *Creator of Heaven and Earth?*"

Because God created, i.e., made out of nothing, the whole world, the Heavens and the Earth, and all that is in them.

49. By what has God created the whole world?
By His almighty will.

"Thou hast created all things; and for Thy will they were, and have been created." (Apoc. 4, 11.)

50. Did God create the world, because He needed it?
No; God is infinitely rich and happy in Himself, and needs nothing besides Himself.

"Thou art my God, for Thou hast no need of my goods." (Ps. 15, 2.)

51. If God needs nothing besides Himself, why then did He create other beings?
He created them, because He is infinitely good, and desired to impart His goodness also to other beings.

"We are, because God is good." (St. Augustine.)—"God was not impelled to create by any other cause than a desire to communicate to creatures the riches of His bounty." (Cat. of the Counc. of Tr.)

52. Did then God create the world for His creatures?
No; God created the world for Himself, that is, for His glory; but nevertheless, for the good of His creatures.

"The Lord hath made all things for Himself." (Prov. 76, 4.)—"And every one that calleth upon My name, I have created him for My glory, I have formed him, and made him." (Isai. 43, 7.)

53. What does God still do, that the world which He has created may not return into its original nothing?
He preserves and governs it.

54. How does God preserve the world?
By the same power of His will, with which He created the world, He causes it also to continue, in the manner He pleases, and as long as He pleases.

"How could any thing endure, if Thou wouldst not?" (Wisd. 11, 26.)

55. How does God govern the world?

He takes care of all things,† orders all things, and, in His wisdom and goodness, directs all things to the end for which He has created the world.‡

† "God made the little and the great, and He hath equally care of all." (Wisd. 6, 8.)—"But the very hairs of your head are all numbered." (Matt. 10, 30.) ‡ "She (the wisdom of God) reacheth therefore from end to end mightily, and ordereth all things sweetly." (Wisd. 8, 1.)—Ex.: Deliverance of the Jews through Esther.

56. What do we call this supreme care of God in preserving and governing the world?

Divine Providence.

57. But if God orders and directs all things in the world, why then is there so much evil done? Does He will it?

No, God wills not the evil; but He permits it; 1. Because He has created man free; and 2. Because He knows also how to turn evil into good, i.e., how to avail Himself of the evil in order to execute His eternal decrees.

Examples: The history of Joseph in Egypt: "You thought evil against me; but God turned it into good." (Gen. 50, 20.)—Thus God, the Almighty, caused the murder of our Saviour by the Jews to turn to the salvation of the world, and the impenitence of the same Jews, to the conversion of the Heathens. And thus He still avails Himself every day of the designs of the wicked in order to glorify His Church; "for there is no wisdom, there is no prudence, there is no counsel against the Lord." (Prov. 21, 30.)

58. And if God takes care of all things, why then are we subject to so many sufferings?

1. That the sinner may acknowledge the chastisement of God, and mend his ways, and not perish for ever; and 2. That the just man may be more and more purified, and more abound in merits, and thus obtain a greater reward in Heaven.

1. Ex.: The Brothers of Joseph: "We deserve to suffer these things, because we have sinned against our brother." (Gen. 42, 21.) Manasses (2 Paral. 33.) Jonas (Jonas 2.) 2. "Gold and silver are tried in the fire, but acceptable men in the furnace of humiliation." (Ecclus. 2, 5.) "Blessed are ye when they shall revile you, and persecute you, and speak all that is evil against you, untruly, for My sake. Be glad and rejoice, for your reward is very great in heaven." (Matt. 5, 11. 12.)

59.* But why does God often permit the wicked to prosper, whilst evil befalls the good?

1. Because He will not only deter the sinner from his evil ways by punishment, but will also win him by benefits; 2. Because He reserves to himself to punish the wicked, and to reward the good, especially in eternity; and 3. Because He will not even leave the little good, which the wicked may do, entirely unrewarded, and, therefore, as He cannot reward it in the next world on account of their impenitence, He will reward it here below.

1. "What is there that I ought to do more to My vineyard that I have not done to it? Was it that I looked that it should bring forth grapes, and it hath brought forth wild grapes?" (Isai. 5, 4.) 2. "The Lord patiently expecteth, that when the day of judgment shall come, He may punish them in the fulness of their sins." (2 Mach. 6, 14.) 3. "Woe to you that are rich; for you have your consolation," that is, your reward here in this world. (Luke 6, 24.) Ex.: Achab: "Because Achab hath humbled himself for My sake, I will not bring the evil in his days." (3 Kings 21, 29.)

60. How, then, ought we to receive the sufferings that come upon us?

We ought to receive them as graces of God; for "Whom the Lord loveth, He chastiseth" † (Hebr. 12, 6.), and "Before he be glorified, it (his heart) is humbled." (Prov. 18, 12.)

† "For it is a token of *great* goodness when sinners are not suffered to go on in their ways for a long time, but are presently punished." (2 Mach. 6, 13.)

Application.—"Cast all your care upon the Lord,

for He hath care of you." (1 Pet. 5, 7.)—" Behold the birds of the air, for they neither sow, nor do they reap, nor gather into barns, and your Heavenly Father feedeth them. Consider the lilies of the field," etc. (Matt. 6, 26—33.) Take willingly every thing that is disagreeable to you, as coming from the hand of God: ("As it hath pleased the Lord, so is it done; blessed be the name of the Lord." Job 1, 21.) and never be so rash as to complain of the dispensations of God. Whatever may come, "To them that love God, all things work together unto good." (Rom. 8, 28.)

§. 4. *On the Angels.*

61. Has God created nothing else but the visible world?

God has also created an invisible world; namely, innumerable Spirits, called Angels. (Dan. 7, 10.)

The Angels are divided into nine different Orders or Choirs, namely, Angels, Archangels, Virtues, Powers, Principalities, Dominations, Thrones, Cherubim, and Seraphim. (Col. 1, 16. Eph. 1, 21. Ezech. 10. Isai. 6, 2.)

62. In what state were the Angels, when God had created them.

They were all good and happy, and endowed with excellent gifts.

63. Did the Angels all remain good and happy?

No; many rebelled against God; therefore they were cast away from Him for ever, and hurled into Hell.

"God spared not the Angels that sinned, but delivered them, drawn down by infernal ropes to the lower hell, unto torments." (2 Pet. 2, 4. Comp. Jude 6.)

64. How has God rewarded the Angels that remained faithful?

He has rewarded them with eternal happiness, which consists in seeing and possessing Him everlastingly.

"Their Angels in Heaven always see the face of My Father who is in Heaven." (Matt. 18, 10.)

65. How are the good Angels affected towards us?
The good Angels love us; therefore, they protect us in soul and body, pray for us, and exhort us to do good.

"He hath given His Angels charge over thee, to keep thee in all thy ways." (Ps. 90, 11.) Ex.: Agar, Lot, Tobias, Judas Machabeus (2 Mach. 10, 29. 30.), Peter in prison, Cornelius, the Centurion.

66. How do we call those Angels who are particularly given to man for his protection?
Guardian Angels.

67. What is our duty towards our Guardian Angels?
We must venerate them with great devotion, be thankful to them, and readily follow their admonitions.

"Behold I will send My Angel, who shall go before thee. Take notice of him, and hear his voice, and do not think him one to be contemned." (Exod. 23, 20. 21.).

68. How are the fallen or wicked Angels affected towards us?
The wicked Angels, through hatred and envy, lay snares for us, in order to injure us in soul and body, and by enticing us to sin, to plunge us into eternal perdition.

"Your adversary the devil, as a roaring lion, goeth about seeking whom he may devour." (1 Pet. 5, 8.) Examples: Eve, Job, Sara, the Demoniacs, Judas. See also Luke 8, 12. and Apoc. 12.

69. Why does God permit the wicked Angels to lay snares for us?
He permits it, because He knows how to make their snares redound to His own honour and to the salvation of men.

"And they talked among themselves, saying: What word is this, for with authority and power He (Jesus) commandeth the unclean spirits, and they go out? And the fame of Him was published into every place of the country." (Luke 4, 36. 37.) "And the people with one accord were attentive to those things which were said by Philip, hearing and seeing the miracles which He did. For many of them had unclean spirits who, crying with a loud voice, went out." (Acts 8, 6. 7.)

70. What must we do on our part, in order that the snares of the wicked Angels may redound to our salvation?

We must fight against them full of faith and confidence, making use at the same time of the arms of prayer, and of the blessings sanctioned by the Church, and firmly resisting all temptations to evil.

"For our wrestling is not (only) against flesh and blood; but against the spirits of wickedness in the high places (i.e. in the air)." (Eph. 6, 12.) "In all things taking the shield of faith, wherewith you may be able to extinguish all the fiery darts of the most wicked one." (Eph. 6, 16.) "Resist the devil, and he will fly from you." (James 4, 7.) Ex.: Tobias and Sara. (Tob. 6, 16—19. and 8, 4—10.)

Application.—Beware of being like the evil spirits by sinning, or of being even their accomplice in seducing others to sin. Imitate the good Angels; be innocent, docile, pious, devout, and always ready to promote the welfare of your neighbour. Daily venerate your Guardian Angel, and recommend yourself to Him in all dangers of soul and body. (Feast of the Holy Guardian Angels.)

§. 5. *On our First Parents and their Fall.*

(See Short Hist. of Religion 1. 2.)

71. How did God make the first man, Adam?

God formed a body of the slime of the earth, and breathed an immortal soul into it; and the first man was made. (Gen. 2, 7.)

72. Of what did God form Eve?

God formed Eve of a rib of Adam, whilst he was sleeping. (Gen. 2, 21.)

73.* Why did God make the woman of a bone of the man?

Because man and woman, as husband and wife,

are to love one another, as if they were one body and one soul.

74. How did God distinguish man at his creation from all other creatures?
By creating him to His own image. (Gen. 1, 27.)

75. How was the first man the image of God?
By this, that he was endowed with natural and supernatural gifts, which made him resemble God.

76. In what do the *natural* gifts consist?
Especially in this, that the human soul is an immortal spirit, endowed with understanding and free will.

77. In what do the *supernatural* gifts consist?
Especially in this, 1. That the first man possessed sanctifying grace, and together with it the sonship of God, and the right of inheriting the kingdom of Heaven; 2. That in him the senses never rebelled against reason; and 3. That he was never to be subjected to hardships and sufferings, nor to death.

78. Why are the latter called supernatural gifts?
They are called supernatural gifts, because they are not, like the natural ones, essential attributes of our nature, but because they were an extraordinary free gift of God.

79. Did our first parents receive this Divine free gift for themselves alone?
They received it also for all their descendants; and therefore, according to God's dispensation, not only their natural, but also their supernatural gifts were to devolve upon the whole human race.

80. Upon what condition did they receive these supernatural gifts for themselves, and for their descendants?
Upon condition that they should keep the commandment of God not to eat of the fruit of a certain tree. (Gen. 2, 17.)

81. Why did God give them this commandment?
He gave it them, that, by their obedience to it, they

might merit that supernatural happiness, for which they had received sanctifying grace.

82. Did Adam and Eve keep this commandment which was so easy to be observed?
No; they broke the commandment of God, and ate of the forbidden fruit. (Gen. 3, 6.)

83. Was this transgression a grievous sin?
Yes; it was a very grievous sin; for though they were filled with the knowledge of God, yet they believed the serpent (which is the devil, Apoc. 20, 2.) more than God, rebelled against Him, and wanted to be like God. (Gen. 3.)

84. What punishment came upon Adam and Eve?
1. They forfeited all their supernatural gifts, and at the same time were also weakened in the faculties of their souls; 2. They were expelled from Paradise, in which God had placed them; and 3. They became liable to eternal damnation.

85. Did our first parents lose these supernatural gifts for themselves only?
No; as by their obedience they would have preserved them not only for themselves, but for all their descendants; so by their disobedience they lost them not only for themselves, but also for us all, and have thereby plunged the whole human race into the greatest misery.

86. In what does the misery consist into which our first parents have plunged the whole human race?
In this, that sin, with its fatal consequences, has passed from Adam to all mankind, insomuch that we now all come into this world infected with sin.

"By one man, sin entered into this world, and by sin death; and so death passed upon all men, in whom all have sinned." (Rom. 5, 12.) "Behold I was conceived in iniquities; and in sins did my mother conceive me." (Ps. 50, 7.) The Blessed Virgin Mary alone was, by a particular grace and privilege, perfectly preserved, through

H

the merits of Jesus Christ, not only from all actual sin, but also from every stain of original sin.

87. What do we call this sin in which we are all born?

We call it *Original Sin*, because we have not actually committed it, but have, as it were, inherited it from our first parents, who were the *origin* or source of all mankind.

88. Is original sin, though not actually committed, nevertheless truly sin?

Yes, it is the death of the soul—it is truly and properly sin. (Counc. of Tr. Sess. V.)

Owing to the sin of Adam, the entire human race lost its original sanctity and righteousness, i.e., sanctifying grace, and all the supernatural gifts which were intended for it. Man was thereby impaired in soul and body, by nature spiritually dead, fallen off and separated from God, and no more capable of attaining his higher, supernatural end. God saw then His generous and gracious design defeated, and could no longer look down with satisfaction upon degraded man. "*We all were by nature children of wrath*," because "*we were dead in sin.*" (Eph. 2, 3.)

89. What fatal consequences have, with original sin, passed to all men?

1. Their disgrace with God, and at the same time their loss of the sonship of God, and of the right of inheriting the kingdom of Heaven; 2. Ignorance, concupiscence, and proneness to evil; and 3. All sorts of hardships, pains, calamities, and at last, death.

1. See Eph. 2, 3.—"Unless a man be born again of water and the Holy Ghost, he cannot enter into the kingdom of God." (John 3, 5.) 2. "I see another law in my members, fighting against the law of my mind." (Rom. 7, 23.) "The imagination and thought of man's heart are prone to evil from his youth." (Gen. 8, 21.) 3. "Great labour is created for all men, and a heavy yoke is upon the children of Adam, from the day of their birth, until the day of their burial." (Ecclus. 40, 1.) God created man incorruptible; but by the envy of the devil, death came

into the world." (Wisd. 2, 23. 24.) This doctrine of Divine revelation is confirmed by experience, and by the sad history of mankind. (Comp. Rom. 7, 18—24.)

90. Did the fatal consequences of sin fall upon man only?

The punishment of God was also inflicted upon the earth, which had been created for man.

"Cursed is the earth in thy work," said God to Adam; "with labour and toil shalt thou eat thereof all the days of thy life. Thorns and thistles shall it bring forth to thee." (Gen. 3, 17. 18.)

91. What would have become of man, if God had not shown him mercy?

No one could have any more received grace, and been saved.

92. Why could no one have any more received grace?

Because the Divine justice demanded a satisfaction adequate to the sin, and no creature, but least of all man, who had fallen so deeply, was able to give such satisfaction.

93. How did God show mercy to man?

He promised him a Saviour, who, by a full satisfaction, should take sin away from him, and regain for him grace, and the right of inheriting the kingdom of Heaven. (Gen. 3, 15.)

"Therefore, as by the offence of one (Adam), (judgment came) unto all men to condemnation; so also by the justice of one (Christ), (grace came) unto all men to justification of life; . . . . that as sin hath reigned to death, so also grace might reign by justice unto life everlasting." (Rom. 5, 18. 21.)

94. If without the grace of the Redeemer no one can be saved, how then could those who lived before the coming of Christ, go to Heaven?

Those who lived before the coming of the Redeemer of the world, could not indeed go to Heaven before Him; but with the grace which God gave them on account of the Redeemer to come, they could merit the kingdom of Heaven, and then enter into it with Him.

The whole of the Old Testament bears witness of the many eminent graces which God gave to the Israelites, and of the just who lived among them. (Short Hist. of Rel. §. 6—19.)

95.* Did God give grace also to the Pagans for the salvation of their souls?

Yes; He manifested Himself also to the Pagans, and in many ways exhorted them to repentance and amendment:

1. By the voice of conscience and interior impulse; 2. By natural benefits; 3. By His judgments; 4. By extraordinary men whom He raised among them, or sent to them; 5. By the Israelites whom, with their holy books, He dispersed among them; and 6. Sometimes also by Angels, dreams, wonderful apparitions or events.

1. "Who (the Gentiles) shew the work of the law written in their hearts, their conscience bearing witness to them." (Rom. 2, 15.) 2. "He left not Himself without testimony, doing good from heaven, giving rains and fruitful seasons," etc. (Acts 14, 16.) 3. Deluge; punishment of Sodom, of Egypt, of Chanaan, and of other places. (Compare Wisd. 12. and 16—18.) 4. Job, Balaam, Jonas, Daniel, etc. 5. "He hath therefore scattered you (Israelites) among the Gentiles, who know not Him, that you may declare His wonderful works, and make them known that there is no other Almighty God besides Him." (Tob. 13, 4.) 6. Cornelius, the centurion, was advised by an Angel (Acts 10, 3); Nabuchodonosor, by dreams (Dan. 2. 4); Baltassar, by a mysterious hand (Dan. 5); Balaam, by an ass. (Num. 22, 28—30.)

96. Why did the Redeemer not come immediately after the fall of our first parents?

Because mankind had first to learn by experience into what great misery sin had plunged them, and that no one but God could save them.

Application.—My child, be a beautiful image of God, and hate sin, which has brought all evils into the world. "Sin maketh nations miserable." (Prov. 14, 34.)

The Second Article.

"And in Jesus Christ, His Only Son, our Lord."

1. What does this Second Article of the Creed teach us?
It teaches us that the Redeemer whom God promised and sent to us, is the Only Son of God, Jesus Christ, our Lord.

2. What does the name *Jesus* signify?
The name *Jesus* signifies *Saviour* or *Redeemer*.

"Thou shalt call His name *Jesus*; for He shall save His people from their sins." (Matt. 1, 21.)

3. What does the word *Christ* signify?
The word *Christ*, in Hebrew *Messias*, signifies *Anointed*.

4. Why is Jesus called the Anointed?
Because in the Old Law the Prophets, High-priests, and Kings were anointed with oil, and Jesus is our greatest Prophet (Acts 3, 22), Priest (Hebr. 4, 14), and King (John 18, 37).

"Jesus of Nazareth: how God anointed Him with the Holy Ghost, and with power." (Acts 10, 38.) The anointing of Jesus is the plenitude of the Divinity that dwells in Him.

5. Why is Jesus called our Prophet, Priest, and King?
Jesus is called, and is, 1. Our *Prophet*, because He revealed the mysteries of God to us, and taught us all that we are to believe, to hope, and to do, in order to be saved; 2. Our *Priest*, because He offered Himself for us on the cross, and offers Himself daily on the altar, and is also our mediator and intercessor for ever in Heaven; and 3. Our *King*, because he established a spiritual kingdom (the Church), the Head of which He is, and will be through all eternity.

6. Why is Jesus Christ called the "*Only Son of God*?"
Because Jesus Christ, as the Second Person of the

Most Blessed Trinity, is the only true and real Son of God, i.e., Son of God from eternity, of one nature and substance with God the Father.

"To which of the angels hath He said at any time: Thou art My Son, to-day (i.e., at present, from eternity) have I begotten Thee?" (Hebr. 1, 5.) The Catholic Church has, in the Œcumenical Council of Nice, expressed this fundamental doctrine of the Christian Religion, "*respecting the one nature and substance of Jesus Christ with God the Father,*" in the following terms: "I believe in one Lord Jesus Christ, the only-begotten Son of God, and born of the Father before all ages; God of God, Light of Light, true God of true God; begotten, not made; *consubstantial* to the Father, by whom all things were made."

7. Are we not then also children of God?

Yes, we are children of God, but not by nature and from all eternity; we are only children adopted by grace.

"As many as received Him, He gave them power to be made the sons of God." (John 1, 12.)

8. Why is Jesus Christ called "*Our Lord?*"

Jesus Christ is called, and is, our Lord, 1. As *God*, because being consubstantial with the Father, He is like Him Lord and Creator of Heaven and Earth; and 2. As *Man*, because, in the human nature, He has redeemed us, and therefore bought us, with His Blood, as His property; † and because, in the same nature, He will be one day our Judge,‡ and our Head and King through all eternity.§

† "For you are bought with a great price." (1 Cor. 6, 20.) ‡ "It is He who was appointed by God, to be judge of the living and of the dead." (Acts 10, 42.) § "And He (God) hath subjected all things under His feet, and hath made Him Head over all the Church." (Eph. 1, 22.)

Application.—Constantly cherish the most ardent love and devotion to Jesus, "in whose name every knee should bow, of those that are in heaven, on earth, and under the earth." (Philip. 2, 10.) Often invoke, with the greatest veneration and confidence, this Holy

Name, especially in times of temptation. Take a delight in using this beautiful form of salutation: "**Praised be Jesus Christ—For evermore, Amen.**"† (Feast of the Holy Name of Jesus.)

† This mode of saluting one another is quite common in Germany and Switzerland. An indulgence of one hundred days has been granted by Sixtus V., in 1587, and by Benedict XIII., in 1728, to those who salute each other, the one saying, " Praised be Jesus Christ," and the other answering, "Amen," or " For evermore, Amen." To those who have generally used this form of salutation during their life, a Plenary Indulgence is granted at the hour of death. The same indulgences are imparted to those who teach others this holy practice. (The Transl.)

§. 1. *Jesus Christ, the Promised Messias.*

9. How do we know that Jesus Christ is the *Messias* or *Redeemer*, promised by God?

We know it, because in Him has been fulfilled all that the Prophets have foretold of the Redeemer, as may be seen in the life and sufferings of Christ. (On the Prophets see Short Hist. of Rel. §. 17.)

10. What have the Prophets foretold of the Messias?

1. The time of His coming, the circumstances of His birth, of his life, passion, and death; 2. His Resurrection and Ascension, and the sending down of the Holy Ghost; 3. The destruction of Jerusalem, which happened after His death; the rejection of the Jews, and the conversion of the Gentiles; and 4. The founding, spreading, and duration of His Church.

11. How did they indicate the time of His coming?

The Prophet Daniel (9, 24.etc.) foretold that not quite *seventy* weeks of years, *i.e.* 490 years, should elapse from the time when it was commanded that Jerusalem should be rebuilt, until the death of Christ; 2. Jacob prophesied that at the time of the coming of the Messias, the sceptre should have been taken away from Juda. Others again foretold, that then the temple of Jerusalem should still exist, and the world be in great expectation. And all this was exactly fulfilled in Jesus. (Short Hist. of Rel. §§. 8 and 18.)

12. What did they prophesy of His birth?
That He should be born at Bethlehem of a Virgin, of the tribe of Juda and family of David, and should be adored by kings from distant countries. (Isai. 7, 14; 11, 1; and 60, 6. Mich. 5, 2. Ps. 71, 10.)

13.* What account do they give us of His life?
They give us an account of His public teaching, of His miraculous cures, of His forbearing charity and meekness, of His entering into Jerusalem upon an ass, etc. (Isai. 61. and 35, 3. etc. Zach. 9, 9.)

14.* What do they relate of His passion and death?
They relate almost all, even the least circumstances; for example, that they would sell Him for thirty pieces of silver, strike Him, pull out His hair, spit in His face, give Him gall and vinegar to drink, pierce His hands and feet, and cast lots for His garment; that those who see Him would mock Him, and wag their heads, saying, "He hoped in the Lord, let Him deliver Him." (Zach. 11, 12. 13. Isai. 50, 6. Ps. 21, 7. etc., and 68, 22.)

The Prophets did indeed promise a great King, but not a King of this world, as the Jews are still expecting; otherwise they would not have described Him as "a man of sorrows," (Isai. 53, 3. 4.) nor called Him, the "reproach of men, and the outcast of the people" (Ps. 21, 7); but a King of a spiritual and supernatural Kingdom of God (the Church), which was indeed to begin and spread on earth, but is to be consummated only in Heaven, and to last for ever.

15.* What do they say of His Resurrection and Ascension, and of His sending down the Holy Ghost?
They say, that His sepulchre shall be glorious, and that He shall not see corruption, but shall mount above the Heaven of heavens, and pour out His Spirit upon all flesh. (Ps. 15, 10; and 67, 19. 34. Isai. 11, 10. Joel 2, 28. 29.)

16.* What did the Prophets foretell of the destruction of Jerusalem, and of the rejecting of the Jews?

1. After the Messias shall have been slain, a people with their leader shall come, and destroy Jerusalem and the temple, and the desolation shall continue even to the consummation, and to the end; 2. The Jews, blinded, rejected, dispersed among all nations, shall have no longer a sacrifice, nor a temple; however, they shall not be extirpated by God, but the remnant may be saved at the end of the world. (Dan. 9, 26. 27; Ps. 68, 24—26. and 108; Isai. 10, 21. and 59, 20.)

How this was accomplished, see Short Hist. of Rel. §. 31.)

17.* What did they prophesy of the conversion of the Gentiles, and of the foundation, spreading and duration of the Church?

All that we see already accomplished, or being accomplished. They prophesied, 1. That the Messias shall be the light of the Gentiles, and that all nations of the earth shall be blessed in Him; (Gen. 22, 18; Ps. 71; Isai. 42, 6. etc.) and 2. That He shall establish a new sacrifice, and a new priesthood, and found a kingdom of God, that shall reach from sea to sea to the end of the earth, and shall never be destroyed, but stand for ever. (Mal. 1, 11; Isai. 66, 21; Jer. 3, 15; Zach. 9, 10; Dan. 2, 44; and 7, 14. etc.)

18. Did the Prophets prophesy long before the coming of Christ?

Malachias, the last of the Prophets, prophesied four hundred and fifty years before Christ.

19. Were their prophecies also known long before Christ?

Yes; they had already been written many centuries before Christ, and were preserved and read by the Jews as Divine writings; they were also translated into other languages, and spread among the Pagan nations.

20. Did not also Christ and the Apostles appeal to the testimony of the Prophets?

Yes; Christ and the Apostles proved to the Jews from the writings of the Prophets, that the Messias was come, and that He Himself—Jesus of Nazareth—was the Messias.

"Search the Scriptures," said *Jesus* to the Jews, "and the same are they that give testimony of Me." (John 5, 39.) He convinced also the unbelieving Disciples from the Prophets. (Luke 24, 25—27; and 44, 47.) *St. Peter* convinced by the prophecies, the three thousand, and the five thousand who were baptized." (Acts 2 and 3.) *St. Paul* protested before King Agrippa, saying: "Being aided by the help of God, I stand unto this day, witnessing both to small and great, saying no other thing than those which the Prophets and Moses did say should come to pass." (Acts 26, 22.) The *Evangelists*, in their narrative, always refer to the Prophets. It is also said of *Apollo:* "With much vigour he convinced the Jews openly, shewing by the Scriptures, that Jesus is the Christ," *i.e.*, the Promised Messias. (Acts 18, 28.)

21. Do we see nothing else fulfilled in Christ, but the Prophecies?

We see also in Him the fulfilment of all the Figures, by which the deeds and sufferings of the Messias were indicated many centuries before.

22. Which are the most remarkable Figures of the Messias?

1. His Passion and Death were prefigured by Abel, Isaac, Joseph, David, the Paschal Lamb, the Propitiatory Sacrifice, and the Brazen Serpent; 2. His Priesthood, chiefly by Melchisedech; 3. His Office of Prophet and Mediator, by Moses; 4. His Resurrection, by Jonas in the whale's belly; and 5. His Church and the Holy Sacraments, by the Ark, the Red Sea, the Manna, and the Temple with its various appurtenances and sacrifices. (Hebr. 9.)

Application.—How happy you are, to know and possess the promised Saviour of the world, for whom the holy Patriarchs sighed so long and so ardently!

May He always find in your heart a dwelling agreeable to Him! Endeavour, therefore, at all times, and especially during the holy season of Advent, to prepare it well for Him.

§. 2. *Jesus Christ, True God.*

23. Whence do we know that Jesus Christ is the Son of God, and true God?

We know it, 1. From the Prophecies; 2. From the testimony of His Heavenly Father; 3. From His own testimony; 4. From the teaching of the Apostles; and 5. From the doctrine of the Catholic Church.

24. What do the Prophets say?

They call the promised Redeemer: "God, God with us, the Saint of Saints, the Wonderful, the Father of the world to come." (Isai. 7, 14. and 9, 6. Dan. 9, 24.) Isaias (35, 4.) says of Him: "God Himself will come and will save you;" and Jeremias (23, 6.) says: "This is the name that they shall call Him: The Lord, Jehova, Our Just One."

25. What is the testimony of His Heavenly Father?

At the Baptism of Christ in the Jordan, and at His Transfiguration on Mount Tabor, a voice from Heaven was heard, saying: "This is My Beloved Son, in whom I am well pleased." (Matt. 3, 17. and 17, 5.)

26. What is the testimony of Christ?

Christ, 1. Testified that He is the Son of God, and true God, like His Father; 2. He confirmed His testimony by the holiness of His life, as well as by miracles and prophecies; and 3. He sealed it with His death.

"I and the Father are one. Believe that the Father is in Me, and I in the Father." (John 10, 30. 38.) "He that seeth Me, seeth the Father also." (John 14, 9.) "All things whatsoever the Father hath, are Mine." (John 16,

15.) "What things He (the Father) doth, these the Son also doth in like manner. For as the Father raiseth up the dead, and giveth life, so the Son also giveth life to whom He will; that all men may honour the Son, as they honour the Father." (John 5, 19. 21. 23.) "Amen, amen, I say to you, before Abraham was made, I am." (John 8, 58. etc.) When Peter said to Jesus: "Thou art Christ, the Son of the living God;" (Matt. 16, 16.) and Thomas said to Him: "My Lord, and My God" (John 20, 28); our Saviour confirmed the faith, and the declaration of both the Apostles.

27. What are miracles?

Miracles are such extraordinary works as cannot be done by natural powers, but only by the Omnipotence of God.

28. Which are the principal miracles, wrought by Christ?

He changed water into wine; with five loaves He filled several thousands; with one word He calmed the winds and the waves, cured diseases of all sorts, cast out devils, and raised the dead to life. When He died, all nature mourned; three days after His death, He rose again from the grave, and forty days later, He ascended into Heaven in the sight of His Disciples.

The miracles of Jesus were such, that all Judea must have known whether they had been really wrought, or not. Yet, no one has denied or questioned them, not even His most bitter enemies. On the contrary, thousands, nay, millions of people have given up all they possessed, even their lives, in testimony of their belief in these miracles.

29. How do these miracles prove the Divinity of Christ?

They prove, 1. That when Christ said that He is the Son of God, He spoke the truth, since God cannot possibly confirm a lie by miracles; and 2. That Christ possessed Divine power, since of Himself He wrought miracles.

1. "If you will not believe Me (My words), believe My

works, that you may know and believe that the Father is in Me, and I in the Father." (John 10, 38.) 2. "What things soever the Father doth, these the Son also doth in like manner. .... For as the Father raiseth up the dead, and giveth life, so the Son also giveth life to whom He will." (John 5, 19. 21.)

30. How did Jesus confirm the doctrine of His Divinity by Prophecies?

By this, that He foretold many things which God alone could know; for instance: His betrayal by Judas, and His denial by Peter; the manner of His death; His resurrection; His ascension, &c.

31. Which Prophecies of Christ do we still see being accomplished?

These, for instance, 1. That the Gospel shall be preached in the whole world (Matt. 24, 14); 2. That the gates of hell shall not prevail against the Church (Matt. 16, 18); and 3. That of the temple of Jerusalem there shall not be left a stone upon a stone. (Mark 13, 2.)

With a view to frustrate the prediction of our Lord and of the Prophets, the apostate Emperor Julian resolved, in 363, to rebuild the Temple of Jerusalem. Full of joy, the Jews came in great haste from all countries, set to work, and cleared away the rubbish of the old temple, insomuch that not one stone was left upon another. But when they were going to commence the building, terrible flames flashed out of the ground, which partly killed the workmen, and partly put them to flight. This occurred at each fresh attempt that was made, until they gave up their undertaking. This miracle is attested by contemporary Pagan, as well as Christian, writers.

32. How did Jesus seal the doctrine of His Divinity with His death?

Being adjured by the living God before the tribunal of the High-priest, He solemnly confessed that He was "The Christ, the Son of God, and that they shall see Him sitting on the right hand of the power of God, and coming in the clouds of Heaven;" and, on account of this confession, He suffered death. (Matt. 26, 63. 64. John 19, 7.)

As it would be the most grievous sin, falsely to pretend to be God; so it is the greatest dishonour to Jesus Christ, not to give credit to His protestation that He is God.

33. What do the Apostles teach of Jesus Christ?

The Apostles explicitly teach, 1. That Jesus Christ is true God; 2. That He possesses all the fulness of the Godhead, and the infinite Perfections of God; and 3. That all creatures should adore Him.

1, "We know that the Son of God is come. This is the true God and life eternal." (1 John 5, 20.) "Christ, who is over all things, God blessed for ever. Amen." (Rom. 9, 5.)

2. "In Him (Christ) dwelleth all the fulness of the Godhead corporally;" i.e., substantially. (Col. 2, 9.) Of Christ, the Son of God, St. John says: "In the beginning was the Word, and the Word was with God, and the Word was God. The same was in the beginning with God. All things were made by Him, and without Him was made nothing that was made." (John 1, 1—3.) "In Him (Christ) were all things created in heaven and on earth, visible and invisible, whether thrones, or dominations, or principalities, or powers: all things were created by Him and in Him; and He is before all, and by Him all things consist." (Col. 1, 16. 17.) "By His Son God made the world, who, being the brightness of His glory, and the figure of His substance, upholds all things by the word of His power." (Hebr. 1, 2. 3.)

3. "In the name of Jesus every knee should bow, of those that are in heaven, on earth, and under the earth; and every tongue should confess that the Lord Jesus Christ is in the glory of God the Father." (Phili. 2, 10. 11.) "Let all the angels of God adore Him." (Hebr. 1, 6.)

The Apostles also confirmed their doctrine of the Divinity of Jesus by innumerable miracles which they wrought in the name of Jesus, and by the most stupendous of all miracles, the conversion of the world. (Short Hist. of Rel. §§. 28, 29, etc.)

34. What does the Catholic Church teach of Jesus Christ?

The Catholic Church has ever believed and taught, that Jesus Christ is true God, and of one substance with God the Father; and, in defence of this fundamental Christian doctrine, she composed, at the Council of Nice, a peculiar Creed, and excommunicated those who taught the contrary. (See Short Hist. of Rel. §. 36. and Catech. Page 103. Quest. 6.)

The holy Martyrs also professed this belief, and suffered with joy indescribable torments, nay, death itself, for it; and it often pleased God to confirm their profession by undeniable miracles. One of these is particularly remarkable; it took place in Africa in 484, and is attested by many unobjectionable eye-witnesses. For when Hunnerich, King of the Arian Vandals, who most cruelly persecuted those who professed the Divinity of Christ, had had the tongues of the orthodox Christians of the city of Tipasa torn out, they spoke without tongues as fluently and distinctly as before, and proclaimed everywhere that Jesus Christ is true God, and of one substance with the Father. About sixty of them fled to Constantinople, where all the town saw them, and heard them speak daily, and that for many years.

Application.—Wickedness dims the understanding. Be always pious and virtuous, and you will never have any doubts respecting the truth of your faith. If any man will do the will of Him that sent Me, he shall know of the doctrine, whether it be of God. (John 7, 16. 17.)

THE THIRD ARTICLE.

"Who was conceived by the Holy Ghost, born of the Virgin Mary."

(See Short Hist. of Rel. §§. 21, 22, 23.†)

1. What does the Third Article of the Creed principally teach us?

It teaches us that the Son of God, through the operation of the Holy Ghost, became Man, i.e., that He took to Himself a body and a soul like ours.

The Word (the Only-begotten of the Father) was made flesh, and dwelt among us. (John 1, 14.)

---

† The History of the Birth, Life, and Passion of Christ is to be learned from the Short History of Religion.

2. What do we call this Mystery?

The *Incarnation* of the Son of God.

3. What is then our belief concerning Jesus Christ, when we believe the Mystery of the Incarnation?

We believe that Jesus Christ is both true God and true Man, or that He is a God-Man: He is God from eternity, and became Man in time.

When Christ says: "I and the Father are one," He speaks of Himself as God; and when He says: "The Father is greater than I," He speaks of Himself as Man.

4. How many natures then are there in Jesus Christ?

There are two natures in Jesus Christ, the Divine and the human.

5. Are there also in Jesus Christ two wills distinct from one another?

Yes, in Jesus Christ there is a Divine will, and a human will, which, however, is always in perfect subjection to the Divine will.

"Father, not My will, but Thine be done." (Luke 22, 42.)

6. Are there also two Persons in Jesus Christ?

No; Jesus Christ is only one Divine Person; for the two natures are inseparably united in the one Person of the Son of God.

7. Why is the Incarnation of the Son of God attributed to the operation of the Holy Ghost?

Because it is especially an effect of the Divine love and mercy towards man. (Comp. Page 90. Quest. 44.)

"God so *loved* the world, as to give His Only-begotten Son." (John 3, 16.)

8. From whom did the Son of God take His human nature?

From Mary, the purest of Virgins; therefore, she is also called "Mother of God." (Feast of the Annunciation of B. V. Mary.)

9. Why is Mary called "the purest of Virgins?"

Because she always remained a Virgin incomparably pure, and entirely undefiled, not only before, but also at and after the birth of the Divine Child.

"Behold, a Virgin shall conceive, and bear a son, and His name shall be called *Emmanuel*," that is, *God with us*. (Isai. 7, 14.) In the Holy Scriptures near relations are often called brethren; as Lot and Abraham; in like manner the cousins of Jesus are called His brethren. (Matt. 12, 46.)

10. Why is Mary called "Mother of God," since Christ took only His *human* nature from her?

She is justly so called, because Christ who was born of her according to the flesh, is true God.

"The Holy which shall be born of thee, shall be called the Son of God." (Luke 1, 35.) The doctrine of Nestorius, that Mary is not to be called Mother of God, was condemned as heretical by the General Council of Ephesus in 431.

11. Had Jesus Christ also a Father?

As Man, Jesus Christ had no father; for Joseph, the virgin-spouse of Mary, was only His foster-father.

"Jesus being (as it was supposed) the Son of Joseph." (Luke 3, 23.)

12. Why did the Son of God become Man?

1. That He might be able to suffer, and die for us; for as God He could neither suffer nor die; and 2. That by the example of His life, as well as by His word, He might teach us virtue and holiness.

13. What virtues does Jesus teach us by His example?

All virtues in the highest degree, especially, zeal for the honour of God,[1] and for the salvation of men;[2] meekness,[3] humility,[4] patience,[5] kindness and mercy towards every one,[6] even our greatest enemies;[7] and obedience to His Heavenly Father unto death.[8]

[1] Chastisement of the profaners of the temple. Jesus the good shepherd. [3] Reprimand of the Apostles who were going to call fire from Heaven. [4] Washing of the feet of

the Apostles. ⁵ His passion. ⁶ Jesus, the merciful Samaritan; Jesus at the well of Jacob; in the house of Zacheus; etc. ⁷ "Friend, whereto art thou come?" "Father, forgive them." ⁸ " Father, not My will, but Thine be done."

14. What example does Jesus give in particular to young people?

He teaches them by His example, readily to obey, to take delight in prayer and instruction, to love to stay in the house of God, and to advance in wisdom and grace, as they do in age.

The Child Jesus in the temple, and at Nazareth.

15. Why did Jesus Christ make choice of a poor and humble life?

1. That He might suffer for us from the very beginning of His life; and 2. To teach us, that we ought not to love and seek the vain goods of this world.

Application.—Give thanks to God with your whole heart for having taken the form of a servant, and become a poor Child for the love of you; especially when you hear the Angelus-bell ring in the morning, at noon, and at night. Resolve also to perform all your actions in the manner you know Jesus did His. If you do this, you will be sure to please God, whether you be rich or poor. (Feast of the Nativity of our Lord, or Christmas-day.)

THE FOURTH ARTICLE.

" Suffered under Pontius Pilate, was crucified, dead, and buried."

(See Short Hist. of Rel. §§. 25, 26.

1. What does the Fourth Article of the Creed teach us?

It teaches us that Jesus Christ suffered for us, died on the cross, and was laid in the grave.

2. Did Christ really die?

Yes, His soul was truly separated from His body.

3. Was His Divinity also separated from it?

No; the Divine Person always remained inseparably united with His body and with His soul.

4. Why did Christ wish to be buried?

In order that His Death might be the more undeniable, and His Resurrection the more glorious and credible.

5. Did Christ suffer as God, or as Man?

Christ suffered as Man, that is, according to His human nature.

6. Was Christ compelled to suffer death?

No; Christ suffered death of His own free will; "He was offered, because it was His own will." (Isai. 53, 7.)

"I live in the faith of the Son of God, who loved me, and delivered Himself for me." (Gal. 2, 20. Comp. John 10, 17. 18. and 18, 4—9.)

7. Why was it the will of Christ to suffer and die?

In order to satisfy the Divine Justice for our sins, and thereby to redeem and save us. (P. 101. Q. 91—93.)

By His voluntary obedience unto the death of the cross, Christ has given full, nay, superabundant satisfaction to the Divine Majesty for the manifold offences given to Him by our disobedience, and thus He has redeemed us from the eternal punishment, which he had deserved. Therefore, St. Paul says (Rom. 5, 19.): "As by the disobedience of one man (Adam), many were made sinners; so also by the obedience of One (Jesus Christ), many shall be made just." And St. Peter (1 Pet. 2, 22. 24.): "Who did no sin, who His Ownself bore our sins in His body upon the tree, that we, being dead to sins, should live to justice; by whose stripes you were healed." And Isaias (53, 4. 5.): "Surely He hath borne our infirmities, and carried our sorrows. But He was wounded for our iniquities, He was bruised for our sins."

8. For what sins has Christ given satisfaction?

"For the sins of the whole world" (1 John 2, 2), namely, for original sin, and all the other sins of mankind.

9. Why could no one but Christ make full reparation for our sins?

Because the offence given to the infinite Majesty of God demanded a satisfaction of infinite value, which Christ alone was able to give.

"No brother can redeem, nor shall man redeem; he shall not give to God his ransom. Nor the price of the redemption of his soul: and shall labour for ever, and shall still live unto the end." (Ps. 48, 8. 9.)

10. Why is the satisfaction of Christ of infinite value?

It is of infinite value, because a Divine Person made it; for the greater the dignity of the person who satisfies, the greater also is the value and merit of the satisfaction.

11.* Was it necessary for a perfect satisfaction that Christ should suffer such indescribable torments?

No; for even the least suffering of a God-Man would in itself have been satisfactory, because each of His works is of infinite value.

12.* Why then would He suffer so much?

In order that we might be the more sensible of the greatness of His love, and of the punishment which sin deserves; and also, that we might bear our cross the more patiently.

13. From what has Christ redeemed us by His sufferings and death?

He has redeemed us, 1. From sin; 2. From the slavery of the devil who had subdued us by sin; and 3. From eternal damnation which we have deserved by sin.

1. "He hath loved us, and washed us from our sins in His own blood." (Apoc. 1, 5.) 2. "He Himself hath been partaker of flesh and blood, that, through death, He might destroy him who had the empire of death, that is to say, the devil." (Hebr. 2, 14.) 3. "God hath not appointed us unto wrath (damnation), but unto the purchasing of salvation by our Lord, Jesus Christ, who died for us." (1 Thess. 5, 9. 10.)

14. What more has Christ gained for us through His sufferings and death?

He has 1. Reconciled us with God; 2. Re-opened Heaven to us; and 3. Merited abundant graces for us, in order to enable us to lead a holy life, and to obtain eternal happiness.

1. "When we were enemies, we were reconciled to God by the death of His Son." (Rom. 5, 10.) 2. "Having therefore, brethren, a confidence in the entering into the Holies (Heaven) by the blood of Christ; a new and living way which He hath dedicated for us through the veil, that is to say, His flesh." (Hebr. 10, 19. 20.) 3. "God hath blessed us with all spiritual blessings in heavenly places (things) in Christ, . . . according to the riches of His grace, which hath superabounded in us." (Eph. 1, 3. 7. 8. Comp. Rom. 5, 15—21.)

15. Has Christ merited grace and eternal salvation for those only, who are really saved?

No, He has merited it for all men without exception, as He died also for all without exception. (2 Cor. 5, 14. 15.)

"Christ Jesus, who gave Himself a redemption for all." (1 Tim. 2, 6.)

16. If Christ has merited eternal salvation for all men, why then are not all saved?

Because not all do, on their part, what is necessary for obtaining salvation; that is, because they do not all believe, keep the Commandments, and use the Means of Grace.

"He (Christ) became to all that *obey* Him, the cause of eternal salvation." (Hebr. 5, 9.) Example of St. Paul: Col. 1, 24. "He who made you without your concurrence, will not save you without it." (St. Augustine.)

Application.—Oh, that you would never forget how much Jesus has loved you, and what He has suffered for you! For out of mercy, and "*for His exceeding charity wherewith He loved us, even when we were dead in sins.*" (Eph. 2, 4. 5.) He has redeemed us through His most bitter passion and death, and placed us in the kingdom of His grace. Let this charity of Christ urge you to live unto Him who died for you, and rose again. (2 Cr. 5, 14. 15.)—(Devotion to the Sufferings of Christ; the Way of the Cross, or Stations; Visiting the Holy Sepulchre in Holy Week; Abstinence on Fridays; etc.)

THE FIFTH ARTICLE.

"He descended into hell, the third day He rose again from the dead."
(See Short Hist. of Rel. §. 27.)

1. What means, "He descended into hell?"

That the soul of Jesus Christ, after His death, descended into "Limbo," i.e., to the place where the souls of the just who died before Christ, were detained, and were waiting for the time of their redemption.

"He was put to death indeed in the flesh, but enlivened in the spirit; in which also coming He preached to those spirits that were in prison," that is, announced them their redemption. (1 Pet. 3, 18. 19.)

2. Why were the souls of the just detained in Limbo?

Because Heaven was closed through sin, and was first to be opened by Christ. (Hebr. 9, 6—8.)

3. Why did Christ descend into Limbo?

1. To comfort and set free the souls of the just; and 2. To show forth His power and majesty even there in the lower regions. (Phili. 2, 10.)

4. What means, "The third day He rose again from the dead?"

That, on the third day after His death, Christ reunited, by His own power, His soul to His body, as He had foretold, and rose again from the grave. (Easter day.)

"Destroy this temple, and in three days I will raise it up. But He spoke of the temple of His body." (John 2, 19. 21. Comp. John 10, 18.)

5. How did Christ rise again?

He came forth glorious and immortal from the grave, secured as it was by a heavy stone, and guarded by soldiers.

6. Did Christ no longer retain in His glorified body any mark of His sufferings ?

He still retained in His hands, feet, and side, the marks of His wounds; therefore, He said to Thomas: "*Put in thy finger hither* (into the place of the nails), *and see My hands; and bring hither thy hand, and put it into My side.*" (John 20, 27.)

7. Why has He still retained these marks?

1. In testimony of His victory over hell; 2. As a proof, that He rose again in the very same body in which He had suffered; and 3. To show them on the day of judgment for the consolation of the just, and for the confusion of the wicked.

8. Whence do we know that Christ rose from the dead ?

From the testimony of His Apostles, and His Disciples, who often saw Him after His resurrection, touched Him, ate, spoke, and conversed with Him; and who everywhere loudly proclaimed His resurrection, even before the Chief Council who had condemned Him to death, although, by this conduct, they drew upon themselves nothing but mortal hatred and persecution.

It is true that the soldiers who guarded the grave, being bribed with a large sum of money, spread the report that, while they were asleep, the Disciples of Jesus came and stole His body. But, 1. If they were asleep, how could they see then that His Disciples stole the body? 2. Whence did the timid Disciples, who expected now nothing more from their deceased Master, get on a sudden that undaunted courage? 3. How did it happen, that not even one of the sleeping guards awoke at the rolling away of the heavy stone? 4. Why were the guards not punished for the neglect of their duty? (Comp. Acts 12, 19.)

If the evidence of the Apostles and the Disciples had not been so certain and quite unexceptionable, they would never have convinced the world, in opposition to the most powerful and crafty enemies of Jesus, that He who, like a malefactor, had been publicly executed and buried, had on the third day risen again glorious from the dead. They have nevertheless so firmly convinced the world of this truth, that numberless persons have endured the most painful martyrdom for their firm belief in it.

9. What effect ought the doctrine of the resurrection of Christ to produce in us?

It ought, 1. To strengthen our belief in His Divinity, and our hope of our own future resurrection; and 2. To incite us to rise from the death of sin to a new and holy life.

1. "God raised Him up from the dead, and hath given Him glory, that your faith and hope might be in God." (1 Pet. 1, 21.)

2. "We are buried together with Him by baptism into death; that as Christ is risen from the dead by the glory of the Father, so we also may walk in newness of life." (Rom. 6, 4.)

Application.—He who is still deeply buried in the grave of sin, i.e., in evil habits, or sinful desires, is not risen yet to a new life. All our thoughts, all our exertions should tend towards Heaven. "If you be risen with Christ, seek the things that are above; where Christ is sitting at the right hand of God. Mind the things that are above, not the things that are upon the earth." (Col. 3, 1. 2.)

THE SIXTH ARTICLE.
"He ascended into Heaven, sitteth at the right hand of God the Father Almighty."

(See Short Hist. of Religion §. 27.)

1. What is meant by "He ascended into Heaven?"

That Jesus Christ, by His own power, with soul and body went up into Heaven. (Feast of the Ascension of our Lord.)

2. Did Christ ascend alone into Heaven?

No; He took also with Him into Heaven the souls of the just, whom He had liberated from Limbo.

"Ascending on high, He led captivity captive." (Eph. 4, 8.)

3. For what purpose did Christ ascend into Heaven?

1. To take possession of His glory as conqueror of death and hell; (Phili. 2, 8—11.) 2. To be our Mediator and Advocate with His Father; (Hebr. 9, 24.) 3. To send the Holy Ghost to His Disciples (John 16, 7.); and 4. To open Heaven, and to prepare a place for us also. (John 14, 2.)

4. What means, "Sitteth at the right hand of God?"

It means that Christ, as Man also, is exalted above all created things, and participates in the power and glory of the Divine Majesty.

"He hath raised Him up from the dead, and set Him on His right hand in the heavenly places, above all principality, and power, and virtue, and dominion, and every name that is named, not only in this world, but also in that which is to come. And He hath subjected all things under His feet, and hath made Him Head over all the Church." (Eph. 1, 20—22.

5. Is Christ then not present in all places?

As God, He is everywhere; but as God-Man, He is only in Heaven, and in the Holy Eucharist.

Application.—Consider frequently, especially in your troubles and temptations, that we "*are pilgrims and strangers on the earth,*" and that our true country is Heaven, whither Christ has gone to prepare a place for you also. "*Be therefore not wearied, fainting in your minds,*" but "*look on Jesus who endured the cross, and now sitteth on the right hand of the throne of God.*" (Hebr. 11, 13. and 12, 2. 3.)

THE SEVENTH ARTICLE.

"From thence He shall come to judge the living and the dead."

1. What does the Seventh Article of the Creed teach us?

That Jesus Christ, at the end of the world, shall come again with great power and glory to judge all men, both the good and the wicked. (Acts 1, 11.)

2. What do you call this judgment?
The *general* judgment, the last judgment, or the judgment of the world.

3. When will the day of the judgment of the world come?
"Of that day and hour no one knoweth, no, not the Angels of Heaven." (Matt. 24, 36.)

Nevertheless, Christ and His Apostles have foretold us many things which shall come to pass on the earth before the end of the world (Matt. 24, Mark 13, and 2 Thess. 2.), that the faithful may be on their guard, and not be seduced to fall away. "For there will rise up false Christs and false Prophets, and they shall show signs and wonders, to seduce (if it were possible) even the elect." (Mark 13, 22.)

4. How shall we be judged?
We shall be judged according to all our thoughts, words, works, and omissions.

"I say unto you, that every idle word that men shall speak, they shall render an account for it in the day of judgment." (Matt. 12, 36.)

5. How will the last judgment be held?
1. Christ will come in the clouds of heaven, and gather all nations together before His throne, placing the good on His right hand, and the wicked on His left. (Matt. 24 and 25.) 2. He will then make manifest the good and the evil that every man has done, even his most secret thoughts, and also the graces which He has given to each one; and finally He will pronounce judgment upon all. (2 Cor. 5, 10.)

"And I saw the dead, great and small, standing in the presence of the throne, and the books were opened; and the dead were judged by those things which were written in the books, according to their works." (Apoc. 20, 12.)—"For there is nothing covered, that shall not be revealed; nor hidden, that shall not be known." (Luke 12, 2. and Mark 4, 22.)—"The Lord will bring to light the hidden things of darkness, and will make manifest the counsels of the hearts." (1 Cor. 4, 5.)

6. What will be the sentence, and the end of the last judgment?

Christ will say to the good: "Come, ye blessed of My Father, possess you the kingdom prepared for you from the foundation of the world." But to the wicked He will say: "Depart from Me, you cursed, into everlasting fire, which was prepared for the devil and his angels. And these shall go into everlasting punishment: but the just into life everlasting." (Matt. 25.)

7. Is there not, besides the general, another judgment?

Yes, there is also the *particular* judgment, in which every man shall be judged immediately after his death.

Therefore the Holy Scripture says: "It is easy before God in the day of death to reward every one according to his ways." (Ecclus. 11, 28.)

8. Why will there be a general judgment besides the particular?

For three principal reasons: 1. That God's wisdom and justice may be acknowledged by all men; 2. That Jesus Christ may be glorified before the whole world; and 3. That the good may receive the honour due to them, and the wicked, the dishonour they have deserved.

1. "And the Heavens shall declare His justice; for God is judge." (Ps. 49, 6.)—2. "They shall see the Son of Man coming in the clouds of Heaven with much power and majesty." (Matt. 24, 30.)—3. "Then shall those that have afflicted them, be amazed at the suddenness of their unexpected salvation, saying within themselves, repenting, and groaning for anguish of spirit: These are they, whom we had some time in derision, and for a parable of reproach. We fools esteem their life madness, and their end without honour. Behold how they are numbered among the children of God, and their lot is among the Saints;" etc. (Wisd. 5, 1—5.)

9. Whither does the soul go after the particular judgment?

Either to Heaven, or to Hell, or to Purgatory.

10. Who go to Purgatory ?

1. Such souls as have departed this life, not in mortal, but in venial sin; and 2. Such also as have died without any sin, but have still to suffer the punishment deserved for their past sins.

11. How do we know that there is a Purgatory ?

1. From the Holy Scripture,[1] and from the Tradition of the Church.[2]

[1] In the *Holy Scripture*—namely, the *Old* Testament, it is said (2 Mac. 12, 46): "It is a holy and wholesome thought to pray for the dead, that they may be loosed from sins." In the *New* Testament, Christ speaks (Matt. 12, 32.) of sins which shall be forgiven in the world to come; and (Matt. 5, 26.), of a prison in the other world, from which there shall be no release till the last farthing has been paid. And St. Paul speaks (1 Cor. 3, 12—15.) of such, as on the day of judgment "shall be saved, yet so as by fire."

[2] That *Tradition* teaches it, follows from the constant practice of the Church to pray for the dead, as well as from the unanimous testimony of the Holy Fathers, and of the Councils.

2. Also in some measure from Reason; for as no one goes to Heaven, except those who are perfectly undefiled, (Apoc. 21, 27.) and no one to Hell, but those who die in mortal sin: we cannot but admit a place between Heaven and Hell, where those souls that are not quite clean, but nevertheless died in the state of grace, suffer until they are worthy of entering Heaven.

12. Will there still be a Purgatory after the general judgment ?

After the general judgment there will be only Heaven and Hell.

Application.—Never imagine that you are in the dark, or that nobody sees the evil you are doing. For nothing escapes the eye of God, "And all things that are done, God will bring into judgment for every error, whether it be good or evil." (Eccles. 12, 14.)

The Eighth Article.
"I believe in the Holy Ghost."
(See Short Hist. of Rel. §. 28.)

1. By whom is the fruit or grace of the Divine Redemption communicated to us?
By the Holy Ghost.

2. Where is this grace communicated to us?
It is communicated to us in the Catholic Church, to which Christ has, for that very purpose, promised and sent the Holy Ghost.

3. Who is the Holy Ghost?
The Holy Ghost is the Third Person of the Blessed Trinity, true God with the Father and the Son.

Thus the *Holy Scripture* teaches. 1. It calls the Holy Ghost *God*, one with the Father and the Son: "Why hath Satan tempted thy heart, that thou shouldst lie to the Holy Ghost? Thou hast not lied to men but to God." (Acts 5, 3. 4.) —"The Father, the Word, and the Holy Ghost, and these three are one." (1 John 5, 7.) It attributes *Divine Perfections* to Him: Omnipotence, Omnipresence, Omniscience, Eternity, etc. (1 Cor. 12, 8—11. Ps. 138, 7—10. and 1 Cor. 2, 10. 11. etc.)—It attributes *Divine Works* to Him: The Creation, Regeneration, Sanctification, the Communication of all spiritual gifts, &c. (Ps. 103, 30. John 3, 5. 1. Cor. 6, 11. Rom. 5, 5. Acts 2, 4. 17. etc.)

2. It represents the Holy Ghost as a *Person distinct* from the Father and from the Son: "I will ask the Father, and He shall give you another Paraclete, that He may abide with you for ever, the Spirit of Truth." (John 14, 16. 17.)—"The Holy Ghost descended in a bodily shape, as a dove upon Him; and a voice came from Heaven: Thou art My beloved Son." (Luke 3, 22. and elsewhere.)

Thus also the *Catholic Church* teaches, and has always taught. As early as in the General Council of Constantinople (A.D. 381.), she unanimously condemned the heresy of Macedonius, who denied the Divinity of the Holy Ghost, and she expressly declared, "That the Holy Ghost, the Lord and Giver of life, is adored and glorified together with the Father and the Son."

4. From whom does the Holy Ghost proceed?

The Holy Ghost proceeds from the Father and the Son, as from one source.

"I will send you the Spirit of truth, who proceedeth from the Father."—"He shall receive of *Mine*." (John 15, 26. and 16, 15.)

5. Why is the *Third* Person of the Blessed Trinity in particular named the "*Holy Spirit*," since the appellation of "*Spirit*" and "*Holy*" equally belongs to the *First* and the *Second* Person?

The Third Person is in particular called the "*Holy Spirit*," because it is He to whom is especially ascribed the work of our *Sanctification*, and who imparts to us the *spiritual* life of grace.

Hence the Third Person is also called the "*Sanctifier*" and "*Giver of Life*." Divines see a still deeper reason why the Third Person of the Trinity is called "Spirit," in the peculiar and mysterious manner, in which He proceeds from the Father and the Son.

6. Why is the work of our Sanctification especially ascribed to the Holy Ghost?

Because He, as the Spirit of Love, is the Author of all inward sanctity, and the Dispenser of all supernatural gifts and graces, whereby we are *sanctified*.

It is true, the work of our Sanctification is common to all the three Divine Persons; nevertheless, as a work of love, it has a special relation to the Holy Ghost—the Spirit of Love.

7.* But is not Jesus Christ, as our Redeemer, the Author of our sanctification?

Jesus Christ is the Author of our Sanctification, inasmuch as He has merited and prepared for us the grace of Sanctification; but the Holy Ghost, inasmuch as He, through the merits of Christ, actually sanctifies us, that is, cleanses us from sin, and makes us just and pleasing to God.

"You are washed, you are sanctified, you are justified in the name of our Lord Jesus Christ, and by the Spirit of our God." (1 Cor. 6, 11.)

8. How does the Holy Ghost sanctify us?

He sanctifies us by means of the supernatural grace which He ordinarily infuses into our souls through the Sacraments.

9. What are in particular the Gifts of the Holy Ghost?

These seven: 1. Wisdom; 2. Understanding; 3. Counsel; 4. Fortitude; 5. Knowledge; 6. Godliness or Piety; and 7. The Fear of the Lord. (Isai. 11, 2. 3.)

10. When did Christ send down the Holy Ghost upon His Church?

Christ sent down the Holy Ghost in a visible manner upon her on Whit-Sunday, when He descended upon the Apostles in the form of fiery tongues.

11. For what purpose was the Holy Ghost sent upon the Church?

That He might perpetually teach her, sanctify her, and direct her in an invisible manner; and, in general, that He might impart to her those abundant graces which Christ has merited for her.

By virtue of the Holy Ghost, the Church teaches, (John 14, 26.) cleanses from sin, and sanctifies, (John 20, 22. etc.) guides and rules. (Acts 20, 28. and 15, 28.)

12. Is the Holy Ghost still sent at the present time?

He is still sent at the present time in an invisible manner, as often as He enters with His sanctifying grace into our souls in order to dwell there.

"Know you not, that you are the temple of God, and that the Spirit of God dwelleth in you?" (1 Cor. 3, 16.)

13. How long does the Holy Ghost remain in the soul?

As long as she is free from any grievous sin.

14. Does sin, then, drive the Holy Ghost from the soul?

Yes, mortal sin drives away the Holy Ghost, and profanes the temple of God.

"But if any man violate the temple of God, him shall God destroy; for the temple of God is holy, which you are." (1 Cor. 3, 17.)

15. But is not the Holy Ghost everywhere?

As God, He is everywhere; but as the Author and Dispenser of grace, He is especially with the Catholic Church, and in the souls of the just.

Application.—Strive most earnestly, by avoiding sin, to preserve the Holy Ghost in your heart, and to correspond faithfully with His inspirations. "Wisdom will not enter into a malicious soul, nor dwell in a body subject to sins; for the Holy Spirit will flee from the deceitful." (Wisd. 1, 4. 5.)

THE NINTH ARTICLE.
"The Holy Catholic Church; the Communion of Saints."

§. 1. *On the Church and the Form of her Government.*

1. What did the Apostles do, after they had received the Holy Ghost on Whit-Sunday?

They went forth into the whole world preaching and baptizing, and gathered all those who believed and were baptized into congregations. (Short Hist. of Rel. §§. 28. 29.)

2. What arose from these congregations of believers?

There arose in many places communities of Christians,† whose rulers were the Apostles.‡ (Short Hist. of Rel. §. 30.)

---

† See Acts of the Ap. 2, 41. 44. and 4, 32.—‡ The whole Book of The Acts of the Apostles, and all their Epistles bear witness that they did not only preach and baptize, but also rule their communities in every way. They made regulations and laws, threatened, judged, and punished; they excluded the unworthy from the community of the faithful, (1 Cor. 5, 5. and 1 Tim. 1, 20.) and received them again when they repented. (2 Cor. 2, 10. and elsewhere.)

3. What further did the Apostles do, when the communities of Christians increased?

They chose elders from amongst them, ordained them Bishops, and appointed them every where as rulers of the new Christian communities, with the commission that they should likewise ordain and appoint others. (Short Hist. of Rel. §. 31.)

"And when they had ordained to them Priests (or Elders, *i.e.* Bishops and Priests) in every church, and had prayed with fasting, they commended them to the Lord, in whom they believed." (Acts 14, 22.) "For this cause I left thee in Crete, that thou shouldest ordain Priests (Elders) in every city, as I also appointed thee." (Titus 1, 5.)

4. Were all these several communities united with one another?

Yes, they were all closely united with one another: they professed the same faith, partook of the same Sacraments, and formed all together one great Christian community under one common Head, St. Peter. (Short Hist. of Rel. §. 31.)

5. What did they call this great community of Christians under one Common Head?

The *Catholic, i.e.* the universal *Church*, or in one word, *the Church*.

6. What, then, is the Church even at the present time?

The *Church* is the community of all those Christians upon earth, who, by professing the same faith, and by partaking of the same Sacraments, are united under one common Head, the Pope, (as the Successor of St. Peter,) and under the Bishops subjected to him, (as the Successors of the other Apostles).

7. Was the Church thus organized by the Apostles?

No; she was thus organized by Jesus Christ, her Founder; the Apostles were only the instruments by which He accomplished His will.

8. How did Jesus Christ thus organize His Church?

By conferring His own power upon the Apostles, and sending them forth, every where, 1. To preach, 2. To baptize, and 3. To govern those who were baptized, under the supremacy of St. Peter.

Before Christ ascended into Heaven, He said to His Apostles: "All power is given to Me in Heaven and in Earth. Going therefore, teach ye all nations; baptizing them in the name of the Father, and of the Son, and of the Holy Ghost. Teaching them to observe all things whatsoever I have commanded you: and behold, I am with you all days, even to the consummation of the world." (Matt. 28, 18—20.)—And even previously to that, He said to them: "As the Father hath sent Me, I also send you. Whose sins you shall forgive, they are forgiven them; and whose sins you shall retain, they are retained." (John 20, 21. 23.)—"Amen I say to you, whatsoever you shall bind upon earth, shall be bound also in Heaven; and whatsoever you shall loose upon earth, shall be loosed also in Heaven." (Matt. 18, 18.)—"He that heareth you, heareth Me; and he that despiseth you, despiseth Me." (Luke 10, 16. and elsewhere.)

9. What do you call the threefold office which, together with His power, Christ conferred upon the Apostles?

The Teaching—the Priestly—and the Pastoral—Office.

10. In what does this threefold Office consist?

The *Teaching-Office* consists in the full power to preach the Divine Doctrine, to condemn heresies, and to decide religious controversies.

The *Priestly-Office*, in the full power to offer the Sacrifice of the Mass, to administer the Sacraments, to consecrate, and to bless.

The *Pastoral-Office*, in the full power to rule the Church, consequently also, to make laws, and inflict punishments.

11. Why were the Apostles not to exercise their Office but under the supreme authority of St. Peter?

Because Christ, in order to maintain unity and

union, appointed St. Peter to be His Representative upon earth, and the visible Head of the whole Church.

12. Is not, then, Christ Himself the Head of the Church?
Christ is undoubtedly the Head of the Church, but the *invisible Head*.

13. Why was it necessary that the Church should have also a *visible* Head together with the invisible One?
Because the Church is a visible community or body, and a visible body must also have a visible Head.

Thus no Kingdom can exist without a visible government, although all Kingdoms in the world are governed by God in an invisible manner.

14. From what do we learn that Christ has appointed St. Peter to be the Supreme Head of His Church?
We learn it from this, 1. That Christ built His Church upon Peter, as upon the true foundation-stone; 2. That He gave him in particular the keys of the Kingdom of Heaven; and 3. That He commissioned him alone to feed His *whole* flock.

1. " Thou art Peter (a rock), and upon this rock I will build My Church, and the gates of hell shall not prevail against it." (Matt. 16, 18.)—Because Peter was to be the foundation-stone of the Church, Christ prayed particularly for him, that "*his faith might not fail,*" and commissioned him "*to confirm once his brethren.*" (Luke 22, 32.)—2. "And I will give to thee the keys of the Kingdom of Heaven. And whatsoever thou shalt bind upon earth, it shall be bound also in Heaven; and whatsoever thou shalt loose on earth, it shall be loosed also in Heaven." (Matt. 16, 19.)—3. " Feed My lambs, feed My sheep." (John 21, 15—17.)—Christ, it is true, made His Apostles collectively the foundation of His Church, and gave them all collectively the power of binding and loosing, and of governing the Church; but what He promised and gave to the Apostles in common, this He first promised and gave to Peter in particular. Thus Peter received the full and independent, the Apostles, on the contrary, only a subordinate power.

15. What facts are there to confirm us in our belief, that Peter was appointed by Christ to be the Supreme Head of the Church?

These, that after Christ's Ascension into Heaven Peter 1. Really exercised the office of Head of the Church; and 2. That he likewise was always acknowledged by the Church as the Head of the Apostles, and the Pastor of the whole flock of Christ.

1. As often as something of importance was to be decided or executed, Peter arose first, and acted as the Head of the rest; as for instance, at the election of Matthias, on the Feast of Pentecost, at the contention about receiving the Heathens into the Church, at the Council of the Apostles in Jerusalem, &c. (Acts 1. 2. 11. 15.)—2. Even the Evangelists, when enumerating the Apostles, always put St. Peter the first, although he was neither the oldest of them, nor had been called to the Apostleship before all the others. St. Matthew expressly says: "The names of the twelve Apostles are these: The *First*, Simon who is called Peter," &c. (Matt. 10, 2.)—The Fathers at the General Council of Ephesus (A.D. 431.) considered it as "A fact, questioned by no one, and known in all ages, that St. Peter was the Prince and the Head of the Apostles, the Foundation-stone of the Catholic Church," &c

16. Was the Supremacy of a Head of the Church to discontinue after the death of St. Peter?

No; for 1. If the Church was to continue as Christ had established it, the Rock also on which He had built it, and the Supremacy of a Head which He Himself had ordained to govern it, were to continue; and 2. If a visible Head was necessary, when the Church was still small, and there were none, or but few, heresies; it was so much the more indispensable afterwards, when the Church was spread, and heresies and schisms were multiplied.

17. Who has been the visible Head of the Church since the death of St. Peter?

The Holy Father, the Pope, who is the legitimate Successor of St. Peter in the Episcopal See of Rome, and therefore, has always been acknowledged as the visible Head of the Church, and the Vicegerent of Christ. (Short Hist. of Rel. § 31.)

The Councils, as well as the Fathers of all ages individually, have unanimously and most decidedly, by word and deed, acknowledged in the Roman Popes the Primacy and Supremacy of St. Peter. The Œcumenical Council of Florence (1438) referred to "the Decrees of the General Councils, and the Ecclesiastical Statutes," when it declared, "That the Bishop of Rome (the Pope) possessed the Primacy over the whole universe; that he was the Successor of the Prince of the Apostles, St. Peter, and the true Vicegerent of Jesus Christ, the Head of the whole Church, the Father and Teacher of all Christians; and that he, in the person of St. Peter, had received from our Lord, Jesus Christ, the full power of feeding, guiding, and governing the whole Church." No General Council was ever held, at which the Pope, or his Legates, did not preside; and there never was a decision of the Church universally received, before it had been confirmed by the Pope; and whosoever refused to recognise the Pope as the Head of the Church, was at all times considered by all the faithful as an apostate.

In the course of time, the Successor of St. Peter gained also, by Divine dispensation, possession of a secular territory of considerable extent, called the Ecclesiastical States; that he might exercise his spiritual power all the more freely, and be dependent, not on any human favour or force, but on God alone.

18. Was the threefold Office which was common to all the Apostles, to continue at all times?

Yes; according to the appointment of Christ, it was to pass over from the Apostles to their Successors, and to continue in them, without interruption, to the end of the world.

19. How do we know this appointment of Christ?

From the words which He spoke, when he conferred the Office upon them: "And behold, I am with you all days, even to the consummation of the world;" (Matt. 28, 20.) which evidently cannot be understood to have been said to the Apostles alone, since they, of course, were not to live to the end of the world.

20. Who are the Successors of the Apostles?
The Bishops who are rightly consecrated, and are in communion with the Head of the Church, the Pope, *i.e.*, the Bishops of the Catholic Church.

21. Why can no one be a Successor of the Apostles, who is not in communion with the Head of the Church?
1. Because He who is separated from the *Head*, cannot even be a *Member* of the Church;† and 2. Because no power has been conferred on the Apostles and their Successors, except when united with him to whom Christ has delegated the supreme and full power over the whole Church.

† Hence the general rule: "Where Peter (*i.e.* the Pope) is, there is the Church." (St. Ambrose, Doctor of the Church.)

22. Has, by Divine appointment, the Pope alone to govern the Church?
The Bishops also have, by Divine appointment, to govern the Church, but only with, and under, their Head, the Pope.

"Take heed to yourselves, and to the whole flock, wherein the Holy Ghost hath placed you Bishops, to rule the Church of God." (Acts 20, 28.)

23. In what manner do the Bishops rule the Church?
They rule it in this manner: 1. Each Bishop governs the Diocese or Bishopric, assigned to him by the Pope; and 2. They occasionally assemble, in order to confer with one another about the general welfare of the Church, and to make decrees and regulations in common with the Pope.

24. Through whom do the Bishops exercise their Office in the particular Congregations (Parishes) of their Diocese?

Through the Priests, or Pastors, sent by them.

25. When then may a Priest discharge the duties of the Priesthood?

When he has been expressly sent, or authorized, for that purpose, by his lawful Bishop.

The Priest receives his ordination and mission, not from the faithful, but from God through a lawful Bishop. All and every one, who have thus been ordained and sent, are "Ambassadors for Christ, God as it were exhorting by them" (2. Cor. 5, 20.); and to all of them, is said what Jesus Christ said to His Disciples when sending them: "He that heareth you, heareth Me; and he that despiseth you, despiseth Me; and he that despiseth Me, despiseth Him that sent Me." (Luke 10, 16.)

26. By what means are unity and good order maintained in the whole Church?

By this, that all those who are not Priests, always continue, with ready obedience, subordinate to the Priests, the Priests to the Bishops, and the Bishops to the Pope.

Consequently, Christ has not given to all the members of the Church the same right and the same power, but "hath set the members every one of them in the body (of the Church) as it hath pleased Him. . . . And He gave some Apostles, and some Prophets, and other some Evangelists, and other some Pastors and Doctors, for the perfecting of the saints, for the work of the ministry. . . . Are all Apostles? Are all Prophets? Are all Doctors?" (1. Cor. 12, 18. 29. Eph. 4, 11. 12.)—Therefore St. Clement, the Disciple and Successor of St. Peter, compares the Church to an army, in which the privates are subordinate to the captains, the captains to the colonels, and these again to the General.

Application.—Always cherish in your heart a profound reverence, and an humble submission, to the Holy Father, the Pope, and to the Bishops and Priests, united with him; for they are set over you in the place of God, and it is their duty to instruct you in the name of God, to make you partake of the Divine graces, and to lead you to eternal salvation. Woe to them who despise the Clergy, and create Schisms! "They have gone in the way of Cain, and have perished in the contradiction of Core. . . . These are wandering stars, to whom the storm of darkness is reserved for ever." (Jude 1, 11. 13.)

§. 2. *On the Marks of the Church.*

27. Has Christ established one Church, or more than one?

Christ has established but one Church, as He has taught but one Faith, instituted one Baptism (Eph. 4, 5.), and ordained one Teaching—and Pastoral Office for all nations.

Christ said: "Upon this rock I will build My Church" (not Churches). (Matt. 16, 18.)—"There shall be one fold and one shepherd." (John 10, 16.)—And the Apostles call the Church the body of Christ (1. Cor. 12, 27. and elsewhere). Now, Christ has only one body; therefore, He has also established only one Church.

28. Is it easy to know this one Church, established by Christ?

Yes; for Christ has established a visible Church with perceptible marks, so that it is easy to find her; † otherwise, He could not have commanded us, under pain of eternal damnation, to apply to the Church, and to hear her.‡

† "Neither do men light a candle and put it under a bushel, but upon a candlestick, that it may shine to all that are in the house." (Matt. 5, 15.)—‡ "If thy brother shall offend against thee, go, and tell the Church; and if he will not hear the Church, let him be to thee as the Heathen and Publican." (Matt. 18, 17.)

29. How is the Church of Christ visible?

The Church of Christ is visible, 1. In her Superiors

and members; 2. In the promulgation and profession of her doctrine; and 3. In the Sacrifice of the Mass, and in the administration of the Sacraments.

If the Church were not visible in this manner, how would it then be possible, according to the direction of Christ and the Apostles (Hebr. 13, 17; Mark 16, 15. 16. and elsewhere), to "obey the Prelates" (Bishops and Priests) of the Church, to hear her Teachers, to participate in her Sacrifice and Sacraments, or, in general, in her Divine Service?

30. By what marks may the true Church of Christ be known?

The true Church of Christ may be known by these four marks: 1. She is *One;* 2. She is *Holy;* 3. She is *Catholic;* and 4. She is *Apostolic.*

As early as A.D. 325, it was pronounced in the Nicene Creed: "I believe in *One, Holy, Catholic,* and *Apostolic* Church."

31. Why must the true Church of Christ be One, Holy, Catholic, and Apostolic?

She must be, 1. *One,* because no kingdom can stand "that is divided against itself" (Luke 11, 17); 2. *Holy,* because her Founder is holy, and her object is to lead all men to holiness; 3. *Catholic* or Universal, because she has been established for all nations, and for all times (Matt. 28, 19.), and is, according to the promise of Christ and of the Prophets, to be spread over the whole universe;* and 4. *Apostolic,* because her origin and her doctrine are Apostolic (Eph. 2, 20.), and her Rulers must be legitimate Successors of the Apostles. (Page 135. Quest. 18—21.)

32. Which Church has all these four marks?

It is evident that no Church has these four marks except the *Roman Catholic,* namely, that Church which acknowledges the Pope in Rome as her Head.

33. Why is the Roman Catholic Church evidently *One?*

---

* See Page 107. Quest. 17. and Page 111. Quest. 31.

Because she has at all times, and in all places, 1. The same Faith; 2. The same Sacrifice and the same Sacraments; and 3. A common Head.

34. Why is the Roman Catholic Church evidently *Holy?*

1. Because her Founder is holy, and she teaches a holy doctrine; 2. Because she faithfully preserves and dispenses all the means of sanctification, instituted by Christ; and 3. Because there were in her at all times Saints, whose holiness God has also confirmed by miracles and extraordinary graces. (Short Hist. of Rel. §§. 37. 41. 46.)

Abuses, and failings of individual members, cannot be imputed to the Church herself, because they did not arise from her doctrine, or organization, and were never approved of by her. If a Church were no longer to be the true Church on account of abuses and scandals met with in her, why then did Christ Himself compare His Church to a field in which wheat and cockle grow together, and to a net that contains both good and bad fishes? (Matt. 13.) And where then was the true Church in the days of the Apostles? for even then there were scandals (1. Cor. 11.), and also blameworthy Bishops, in the Church. (Apoc. 2. and 3.)

35. Why is the Roman Church evidently *Catholic* **or** *Universal?*

1. Because from the time of Christ she has continually existed with the same Teaching—the same Priestly—and the same Pastoral—Office, as at the present time; 2. Because she is spread over the whole universe; and 3. Because she is constantly spreading in accordance with the Divine commission: "Go ye into the whole world, and preach the Gospel to every creature." (Mark 16, 15.)

Therefore, the Roman Church was always called *Catholic*, even by Apostates and Infidels, as St. Augustin testifies; and up to this day she is called throughout the world the *Catholic Church*.

36. Why is the Roman Catholic Church evidently *Apostolic?*

1. Because her origin is unquestionably traced back to the Apostles; 2. Because her doctrine is grounded on Apostolic Tradition;† and 3. Because her Rulers, the Pope and the Bishops, are legitimate Successors of the Apostles. (Page 136. Quest. 20.)

† It is an undisputed fact that Innovators, as, for instance, the Puseyites, approach the nearer to the Catholic Church, the more diligently and sincerely they search in the writings of the Holy Fathers for the Apostolic Traditions.

37.* But are not the other non-Catholic Religious Societies also One?

No; they are not, and cannot be, One, 1. Because they have no common Head; and 2. Because every one of their members has a right to interpret and believe the Holy Scripture as he likes.

Therefore "they are children tossed to and fro, and carried about with every wind of doctrine." (Eph. 4, 14.)

38.* And why can none of them be called Holy?

1. Because their founders were not holy; 2. Because they have rejected many articles of faith, and means of sanctification, as for example, the Sacrifice of the Mass, and most of the Sacraments; and have, on the contrary, established principles which are directly opposed to sanctity (Short Hist. of Rel. §. 43.); and 3. Because they cannot produce from among themselves one Saint, confirmed as such by his miraculous power.

39.* Why can none of them be called Catholic?

Because they arose only in later years, and have not ceased to split again into numerous Sects, none of which is universally spread, or continually spreading in the manner ordained by Christ. (Short Hist. of Rel. §§. 43 and 47.)

40.* And why can none of them be called Apostolic?

1. Because they did not come into existence till long after the time of the Apostles, and that, by separating

themselves from the old Apostolic Church; 2. Because doctrine ever wavering and ever changing, as theirs is, cannot certainly be Apostolic; and 3. Because they have no lawful Successors of the Apostles, and, therefore, neither Teachers nor Pastors, sent by Christ.

41. If then none but the Roman Catholic Church has the marks of the *one* Church of Christ, what follows from this?

That the Roman Catholic Church *alone* is the true Church, established by Jesus Christ.

Application.—Pray frequently for the peace and exaltation of the Catholic Church, and for the conversion of the Heretics and Infidels. "Blessed are all they that love thee (the Church), and that rejoice in thy peace." (Tob. 13, 18.)

§. 3. *On the End of the Church, and on her Qualities resulting from this End.*

42. For what end did Christ establish the Church?

Christ established the Church, that by her He might lead all men to eternal salvation.

43. What has the Church to do, in order to lead men to salvation?

She has 1. To preach the doctrine of Christ to them; 2. To administer to them the means of grace, instituted by Christ; and 3. To guide and govern them in the way to eternal life.

44. How has Christ enabled the Church to do all this in a proper manner?

He has 1. Intrusted the Church with His doctrine, His means of grace, and His powers, by conferring upon her His Teaching—His Priestly—and His Pastoral Office; and 2. He has given her the assistance of the Holy Ghost, in order that she might also perpetually preserve the Divine doctrine uncorrupted, rightly administer the means of grace, and exercise her powers for the salvation of mankind.

a, *On the Infallibility of the Church.*

45. By whom is the Divine doctrine always preserved pure and uncorrupted in the Church?
By the *Infallible* Teaching Body of the Church.

46. Who composes this Infallible Teaching Body?
The Pope, and the Bishops united with him.

They are also called the *Teaching Church*, or simply, the *Church* (Matt. 18, 17.), in contradistinction to the rest of the faithful, who are called the *Hearing Church*.

47. Why is the Teaching Church called infallible?
Because, by the assistance of the Holy Ghost, she is secured against erring both in matters of faith and of morals.

48. Who assures us that the Church cannot err?
Christ Himself, who has promised us,
1. That " He will be with her all days, even to the consummation of the world;" (Matt. 28, 20.)
2. That " The Spirit of Truth shall abide with her for ever;" (John 14, 16. 17.)
3. That " The gates of hell shall not prevail against her."† (Matt. 16, 18.)

† Were it possible that the *Teaching Church* might err, the *Hearing Church* would likewise fall into error, as she is to be instructed and guided by the former; and then the *whole Church* would, contrary to the promise of Christ, be prevailed against by the spirit of lies, or the powers of hell.

49. What does St. Paul call the Church on account of her Infallibility?
St. Paul calls the Church " The pillar and ground of the truth." (1 Tim. 3, 15.)

50. But have there not also been in the Catholic Church some individual teachers who have fallen into error?
Yes; but this happened, only because they taught

differently from the whole Teaching Body; for Infallibility is not granted to each one individually, but to the Teachers (Bishops) collectively, when united with the Pope.

If non-Catholics pretend to say that the whole Catholic Church has, in the course of time, departed from the Divine doctrine, and fallen into errors; 1. They manifestly contradict the promises of our Divine Saviour; 2. They condemn all the Holy Fathers of the Church, who taught exactly the same as the Catholic Church teaches; 3. They set themselves at variance with one another, since they have always disagreed among themselves about what properly is Divine doctrine, and what is not; and 4. They must, if the nations had been deceived by the Teaching Church, lay the fault on God, who continually accredited the Catholic Church together with her Teachers, and confirmed her authority by evidently protecting her at all times, by spreading her over the whole world, by illustrating her by innumerable miracles, and blessing her labours with the most glorious success (Short Hist. of Rel. Conclud. Remarks, §.§. 6. 7. 8); whereas, on the other hand, the Sectarians never could corroborate their pretended mission by any miracle, but, on the contrary, fell into many manifest contradictions and pernicious errors, by which the world was only more and more corrupted. (Short Hist. of Rel. §.§. 43. 47.)

51. If then differences arise in matters of faith, what are we to do?

We must adhere to the decisions of the Church.

"And He gave some Apostles. . . . . and other some Pastors and Doctors, ... that henceforth we be no more children tossed to and fro, and carried about with every wind of doctrine by the wickedness of men, by cunning craftiness, by which they lie in wait to deceive." (Eph. 4, 11. 14.)

52. By whom are the decisions of the Church given?

Either by the Supreme Head of the Church, the Pope, or by a Council confirmed by the Pope. (Short Hist. of Rel. §. 36.)

53. Are all Christians bound to submit to the decisions of the Pope?

Yes, as often as he decides as Head and Teacher of the whole Church.

54. How does the Church decide, when differences arise in matters of faith?

She decides conformably to the tenor of Holy Scripture and Tradition.

55. Does the Church then teach nothing new, when, in such differences, she decides what is to be believed?

No; she only explains the Word of God intrusted to her in Holy Scripture and Tradition, and condemns the opposite errors and innovations.

The doctrine of the Catholic Church is no other than the doctrine of Christ and the Apostles, which she has been intrusted with, in order that she may faithfully preserve and preach it. The Church, therefore, perpetually adheres to the old doctrine, inherited from the Fathers, and cries out with the Apostle to all: "Keep that which is committed to thy trust, avoiding the profane novelties of words, and oppositions of knowledge falsely so called." (1 Tim. 6, 20. and 2 Tim. 1, 14.)—"But evil men and seducers shall grow worse and worse: erring, and driving into error. But continue thou in those things which thou hast learned, and which have been committed to thee." (2 Tim. 3, 13. 14.)—"If any one preach to you a Gospel, besides that which you have received, let him be anathema." (Gal. 1, 9.)—"What has been believed in all places, at all times, and by all people, that is really and truly *Catholic*." (Vincent of Lerins; d. 450.)

b, *On Salvation in the true Church of Christ alone.*

56. If the Catholic Church is to lead all men to eternal salvation, and has, for that purpose, received from Christ her doctrine, her means of grace, and her powers; † what, for his part, is every one obliged to do?

---

† Compare Page 142. Q. 42—44.

Every one is obliged, under pain of eternal damnation, to become a member of the Catholic Church, to believe her doctrine, to use her means of grace, and to submit to her authority.

57. Who teaches us this obligation?
Jesus Christ Himself in these words (Matt. 18, 17.): "If he will not hear the Church, let him be to thee as the Heathen and Publican;" and (Mark 16, 16.): "He that believeth not (the Apostles and their lawful Successors,)‡ shall be condemned."

Hence the Catholic Church is justly called the *only saving* Church. To despise her, is the same as to despise Christ; namely, His doctrine, His means of grace, and His powers; to separate from her is the same as to separate from Christ, and to forfeit eternal salvation. Therefore, St. Augustine, and the other Bishops of Africa, pronounced, A.D. 412, at the Council of Zirta, this decision: "Whosoever is separated from the Catholic Church, however commendable in his own opinion his life may be, he shall for this very reason, because he is at the same time separated from the Unity of Christ, *not see life, but the wrath of God abideth on him.*" (John 3, 36.)

58. Who is a member of the Catholic Church?
Every one who is baptized, and has neither voluntarily separated himself, nor has been excluded, from her.

59. Who have voluntarily separated themselves from the Church?
1. All those who, by their own fault, are *Heretics*, i.e., who profess a doctrine that has been condemned by the Church; or, who are *Infidels*, that is, who no longer have, nor profess, any Christian faith at all; and

2. All those who, by their own fault, are *Schismatics*, that is, who have renounced, not the doctrine

---

‡ Compare Page 135.. Q. 18 and 19.

of the Church, but their obedience to her, or to her Supreme Head, the Pope.

60. Who are excluded from the Catholic Church?

Excommunicates, that is, those who, as degenerate members, have been expelled from the communion of the Church.

61. Are not those also who are Heretics without their own fault, separated from the Catholic Church?

Such as are Heretics without their own fault, but sincerely search after the truth, and in the meantime do the will of God to the best of their knowledge, although they are separated from the body, remain, however, united to the soul, of the Church, and partake of her graces.

Even those who are Heretics without their own fault, are deprived, though not of all, at least, of many graces and blessings of our holy religion; as for instance are, the Holy Sacrifice of the Mass, the *true* Lord's Supper, Sacramental Absolution, the Holy Sacraments administered to the dying, etc.—Therefore, we should fervently pray for Heretics, and by sincere charity, and an edifying life, contribute towards their conversion.

62.* Who is a Heretic by his own fault?

A Heretic by his own fault is,

1. He who knows the Catholic Church, and is convinced of her truth, but does not join her; and

2. He who could know her, if he would candidly search, but, through indifference and other culpable motives, neglects to do so.

63.* Does it become us to judge whether such a one is a Heretic by his own fault, or not?

No; for such judgment belongs to God, who alone "is the searcher of hearts and reins" (Ps. 7, 10.), and "judges the secrets of men." (Rom. 2, 16.)

"Judge not before the time, until the Lord come, who both will bring to light the hidden things of darkness, and will make manifest the counsels of the hearts." (1 Cor. 4, 5.)

64. Is it sufficient for obtaining eternal salvation, to be a member of the Catholic Church?

No; for there are also rotten and dead members (Apoc. 3, 1.) who, by their sins, bring upon themselves eternal damnation.

65. What then do we profess to believe by these words of the Creed, "I believe in the Holy Catholic Church?"

We profess to believe that Jesus Christ has established a visible Church, endless in her duration, and infallible in her doctrine, which we must believe and obey without reserve, if we would obtain eternal salvation; and that this is no other but the *Roman Catholic Church*.

Application.—It is but just that we call the Catholic Church our mother; for 1. She has regenerated us in a spiritual manner in Baptism, and has made us children of God; 2. She feeds us with the Word of God, and with the Bread of Angels; 3. She brings us up in the fear of the Lord; and 4. She kindly prays for us, comforts us, and assists us, as long as we live here below, and even after we have departed this life. Honour and love, therefore, the Church as your mother; listen diligently to her instructions, and humbly submit to all her laws and directions; for "He shall not have God for his Father, who will not have the Church for his Mother." (St. Cyprian, Bishop and Martyr; d. 258.)

§. 4. *The Communion of Saints.*

66. Are only the faithful on earth united together as one Church?

With the faithful on earth are also spiritually united the Saints in Heaven, and the souls in Purgatory.

The faithful on earth who are members of the Catholic Church, constitute the Church *Militant;* the souls in Purgatory, the Church *Suffering;* and the Saints in Heaven, the Church *Triumphant;* yet, these three Churches are, properly speaking, but one in different states.

67. In what does this spiritual union consist?
This spiritual union consists in this, that *all* are members of one body, whose Head is Christ Jesus, and that, therefore, the different members participate in one another's spiritual goods.

"As in one body we have many members, so we being many, are one body in Christ, and every one members one of another." (Rom. 12, 4. 5.)—"He (Christ) is the Head of the body, the Church." (Col. 1, 18.)

68. What is this spiritual union called?
The Communion of Saints.

69. Why are all the members of this Communion styled *Saints*?
Because all are called *to be* Saints (1 Thess. 4, 3.), and have been sanctified by Baptism; and many of them have already arrived at perfect sanctity.

70. What benefit do we reap from the communion with the Saints in Heaven?
We partake of the merits which they acquired while here below, and are assisted by their intercession with God in our behalf.

71. But does not death dissolve all union between the living and the dead?
No; no more than it dissolves their union with Christ, their Head.

72. What benefit do the souls in Purgatory receive from our communion with them?
We come to the assistance of these our suffering brethren, in order that their pains may be mitigated and shortened.

73. By what means can we assist the poor souls in Purgatory?
By prayers, alms-deeds, and other good works, especially by the Holy Sacrifice of the Mass, and the application of Indulgences.

"Judas (Machabeus) sent twelve thousand drachms of silver to Jerusalem for sacrifice to be offered for the sins of the dead. It is, therefore, a holy and wholesome thought to pray for the dead, that they may be loosed from sins." (2. Mach. 12, 43. 46.)—That the Church has at all times prayed for the dead, and that the Apostles themselves ordained to remember them at the Holy Sacrifice of the Mass, is testified by the most ancient Fathers of the Church. (All-Souls-day).

74. What profit do we derive from the mutual communion with the faithful on earth?

We participate in all the Masses, prayers, and good works of the Catholic Church, and in general, in all her spiritual goods.

"God hath tempered the body together. . . . that the members might be mutually careful one for another. . . . Now, you are the body of Christ, and members of member." (1. Cor. 12, 24—27.)

75. Do sinners, as long as they are not cut off from the Church, also participate in this communion?

Sinners, as dead members, forfeit, in deed, most of the spiritual goods; nevertheless, in virtue of their union with the Church, they still receive various blessings and graces, which help to their conversion.

Application.—Every day pray for your fellow-christians who are either combating on earth, or suffering in Purgatory, and recommend yourself every morning and night to the protection of the Saints in Heaven.—Above all, strive to lead a holy life; for we are "fellow-citizens with the Saints, and the domestics of God." (Eph. 2, 19.)

The Tenth Article.
"*The Forgiveness of Sins.*"

1. What does the Tenth Article of the Creed teach us?

That in the Catholic Church we can receive, through the merits of Jesus Christ, forgiveness of sins and of the punishment due to them.

"Blessed be the God and Father of our Lord Jesus Christ, in whom we have redemption through His blood, the remission of sins, according to the riches of His grace." (Eph. 1, 3. 7.)

2. What sins can be forgiven in the Catholic Church?
All sins without exception.

3. What must the sinner do in order to obtain forgiveness of his sins?
1. He must truly repent; for Christ says, "Unless you shall do penance, you shall all perish;" (Luke 13, 3.) and 2. He must worthily receive the Sacraments instituted by Christ for the remission of sins.

4. Which Sacraments were instituted by Christ for the remission of sins?
The Sacraments of Baptism and Penance.

5. Who has power to forgive sins in the Sacrament of Penance?
The Bishops of the Catholic Church, and the Priests commissioned by them; for it was to them only, that Christ said, "Whose sins you shall forgive, they are forgiven them." (John 20, 23.)

Application.—Give hearty thanks to God for having promised you forgiveness of your sins, and go willingly and frequently to confession; but first prepare yourself well for it, that it may be said to you also, "Be of good heart, son, thy sins are forgiven thee." (Matt. 9, 2.)

THE ELEVENTH ARTICLE.
"The Resurrection of the Body."

1. What happens to man at his death?
The soul separates from the body, and appears before the judgment-seat of God; but the body returns into the earth. (Eccles. 12, 7.)

2. Why must all men die?

Because all have sinned in Adam.

"By one man sin entered into this world, and by sin death." (Rom. 5, 12.)

3.* Why has God hidden from us the time of our death?

1. That we may so much the more honour and fear Him as the Supreme Lord of life and death; 2. That we may keep ourselves every moment prepared for death; † and 3. That the dread, with which we are seized when we think of our imminent dissolution, may be moderated.

† "Be you then also ready; for at what hour you think not, the Son of man will come." (Luke, 12, 40.) —Parable of the Ten Virgins. (Matt. 25.)

4. How are we to keep ourselves prepared for death?

We should carefully avoid sin, and lead a godly life.

5. How long will the body remain in the earth?

The body will remain in the earth till the day of judgment, when God will raise it again to life, and reunite it for ever to the soul, from which death had separated it.

"The hour cometh, wherein all that are in the graves shall hear the voice of the Son of God. And they that have done good things, shall come forth into the resurrection of life; but they that have done evil, unto the resurrection of judgment, *i.e.*, to hear the sentence of condemnation." (John 5, 28. 29.)

6. What do we call this raising of the bodies to life?

The Resurrection of the Flesh or Body.

7. But how can the bodies, when reduced to dust, rise again?

By the Omnipotence of God our bodies, reduced to dust, can as easily be raised again to life, as they were once made out of nothing.

Parable of the grain of wheat. (1. Cor. 15, 35. etc.)

8. Why shall our bodies rise again?

1. That, as the body was a partner with the soul in the performance of good or evil works, so it may also be a partaker of the reward or punishment (2. Cor. 5, 10.); and 2. That the victory of Christ over death may be perfect.

"When this mortal hath put on immortality, then shall come to pass the saying that is written, "Death is swallowed up in victory; O death, where is thy victory?" (1. Cor. 15, 54. 55.)

9. Shall all men rise from the dead?

Yes, all men, the good as well as the wicked. (John 5, 28. 29.)

10. Will the bodies, when raised to life, be all alike?

No; the bodies of the bad shall be hideous and miserable, but those of the good shall be glorious, and like to the glorified Body of Christ.

" We shall all indeed rise again, but we shall not all be changed," (*i.e.* glorified). (1. Cor. 15, 51.)—" Our Lord Jesus Christ will reform the body of our lowness, that it may be made like to the body of His glory." (Phili. 3, 21.) —Hence the honour we pay to the bodies of the deceased. (Funerals; blessed Burying-grounds.)

According to 1. Cor. 15, 42—44, we distinguish four qualities of the glorified bodies: 1. "It (the body) is sown (*i.e.* buried) in corruption, it shall rise in incorruption" *(incorruptible* and *impassible, i.e.* incapable of corruption, and of any suffering). 2. "It is sown in dishonour, it shall rise in glory" *(bright, i.e.* shining with glory, without spot or blemish). 3. "It is sown in weakness, it shall rise in power," *(agile, i.e.* capable of transporting itself with the soul in an instant from one place to another). 4. "It is sown a natural body, it shall rise a spiritual body" *(subtile, i.e.* spiritualized, or capable of penetrating any corporeal substance, like our Saviour's Body after His Resurrection).

11. What impression should our belief in the resurrection of the body make upon us?

It should incite us, 1. To honour our body, and never to abuse it by sinning; 2. Patiently to suffer all bodily pains, and even death; and 3. To console ourselves at the death of our friends.

1, "Glorify and bear God in your body." (1. Cor. 6, 20.) —2. Examples: Job 19, 25—27. "In the last day I shall rise out of the earth, and I shall be clothed again with my skin, and in my flesh I shall see my God. This my hope is laid up in my bosom." The Machabean Brothers, 2. Mach. 7, 9—14.—3. "We will not have you ignorant, Brethren, concerning them that are asleep, that you may not be sorrowful, even as others who have no hope;" etc. (1. Thess. 4, 12—17.)

Application.—Never abuse your eyes, tongue, ears, hands, nor your other senses or members, by doing evil, but "yield them to serve justice, unto sanctification" (Rom. 6, 19); that you may one day rise to everlasting glory, and not to everlasting damnation.

THE TWELFTH ARTICLE.
"And life everlasting. Amen."

1. What does the Twelfth Article of the Creed teach us?

1. That after this life there is another, which will last for ever; and 2. That the just shall enjoy eternal happiness in it.

"The just shall go into life everlasting," that is, into eternal glory. (Matt. 25, 46.)

2. In what does the eternal happiness of the just consist?

1. They see God as He is, and are united with Him in the most intense love; and 2. With this sight and love of God, is combined the possession of all good things, eternal joy and glory in the company of all the Angels and Saints.

1. "We see now through a glass in a dark manner; but then face to face." (1. Cor. 13, 12. Comp. 1. John 3, 2.)—2. "God shall wipe away all tears from their eyes;

and death shall be no more, nor mourning, nor crying, nor sorrow." (Apoc. 21, 4.)—" They shall be inebriated with the plenty of Thy house, (O God!) and Thou shalt make them drink of the torrent of Thy pleasure." (Ps. 35, 9.—" They shall receive a kingdom of glory, and a crown of beauty at the hand of the Lord." (Wisd. 5, 17.)

3. Can we conceive this eternal happiness?

No; the happiness in Heaven is so great, that it exceeds all that can be said or imagined.

For "Eye hath not seen, nor ear heard, neither hath it entered into the heart of man, what things God hath prepared for them that love Him." (1. Cor. 2, 9.)

4. Will all be equally happy?

No; for "Every one shall receive his own reward according to his own labour," *i.e.* according to his deserts. (1 Cor. 3, 8.)

"He who soweth sparingly, shall also reap sparingly; and he who soweth in blessings, shall also reap blessings." (2 Cor. 9, 6. Comp. 1. Cor. 15, 41. 42.)

5. What will be the life of the wicked through all eternity?

A life without any grace or joy, a life full of pains in Hell.

"Such a life is called in the Holy Scripture the *second* (eternal) death. "The fearful, and unbelieving, and the abominable, and murderers, and whoremongers, and sorcerers, and idolaters, and all liars, they shall have their portion in the pool burning with fire and brimstone, which is the *second* death." (Apoc. 21, 8.)

6. What is Hell in the words of Christ?

"A place of torments " (Luke 16, 28.); " an everlasting punishment " (Matt. 25, 46.); " an unquenchable fire" (Mark 9, 44.); "the exterior darkness, where there shall be weeping and gnashing of teeth." (Matt. 8, 12.)

7. Who shall be condemned to the torments of Hell?

Every one who dies an enemy of God, that is, in mortal sin.

"He that committed sin, is of the devil" (I. John 3, 8.); therefore, he also deserves to be punished like the devil. (Comp. Matt. 25, 41.)

8.* What sort of pains shall the souls of the damned suffer?

1. Internal torture and despair at the thought of all the evil they have done, and of the many graces they have abused; (Wisd. 5, 1—15. Matt. 8, 12.)

2. Unspeakable sadness and misery, because they have, by their own fault, forfeited eternal happiness in Heaven; (Luke 13, 25—28.)

3. Perpetual horror of the dismal company of the devils, and of all the damned; (Matt. 25, 41.) and

4. The most intolerable torments and pangs without any hope of a relief or end; for their fire shall not be extinguished, and their worm shall not die. (Mark 9, 45. Apoc. 20, 9. 10.)

"And the rich man also died, and he was buried in Hell. And lifting up his eyes when he was in torments, he saw Abraham afar off, and Lazarus in his bosom; and he cried, and said: Father Abraham, have mercy on me, and send Lazarus, that he may dip the tip of his finger in water, to cool my tongue; for I am tormented in this flame," etc. (Luke 16, 22—24.)

9. Whence do we know that the pains of the damned are eternal?

1. From the clear testimony of Christ and the Apostles;† and 2. From the express doctrine of the infallible Church, which has solemnly condemned the erroneous opinion of those Heretics, who taught that the pains of the devils, and of the damned, would in time have an end.

† "Depart from Me, ye cursed, into *everlasting* fire . . . . . . and they shall go into *everlasting* punishment." (Matt. 25, 41. and 46.)—"It is better for thee to enter lame into life everlasting, than having two feet, to be cast into the

hell of *unquenchable fire*; where their worm *dieth not*, and the fire is *not extinguished*." (Mark 9, 44. 45.)—" And the smoke of their torments shall ascend up *for ever and ever*." (Apoc. 14, 11. and elsewhere.)

10. Why are the pains of the condemned souls eternal?

1. Because the offence against the *infinite* Majesty of God demands of His justice a punishment without end;

2. Because all who die in sin, remain eternally obdurate in sin; †

3. Because God, in virtue of His Holiness, hates evil no less than he loves what is good, and, therefore, punishes vice eternally, as He eternally rewards virtue; and

4. Because only the everlasting pains of Hell are a sufficient means to deter man, even in secret, from evil. ‡

† Sin remains as a propensity to sin, though it can no more be committed in deed. (Innocent III.)—‡ God showed also mercy to us, when He created Hell, whereby He will prevent us from being wicked. (St. John Chrysost.)

11. Will the pains of all the damned be equal?

No; for each one shall have to suffer in proportion to his sins, and to the ill use he has made of the graces bestowed upon him.

"As much as she (the city of Babylon) hath glorified herself, and lived in delicacies, so much torment and sorrow give ye to her." (Apoc. 18, 7.)—"Unto whomsoever much is given, of him much shall be required." (Luke 12, 48.)

12. Will all those who are condemned to eternal Hell-fire be condemned by their own fault?

Yes; for all men may be eternally happy, provided they will avail themselves of the abundant graces which God gives them.

"God will have all men to be saved, for there is one mediator of God and men, the Man Christ Jesus, who gave Himself a redemption for all." (1. Tim. 2, 4—6.)—"Before man is life and death; that which he shall choose, shall be given him." (Ecclus. 15, 18.)

13. What do you understand by the *Four Last Things* of man?

I understand by the four last things, *Death, Judgment, Hell,* and *Heaven.*

14. Of what use is the frequent remembrance of the four last things to us?

It is, as the Holy Ghost testifies, an effectual means to avoid sin, and consequently, to escape eternal damnation.

"In all thy works remember thy last end, and thou shalt never sin." (Ecclus. 7, 40.)

15. With what word do we conclude the Apostles' Creed?

With the word "*Amen*," which means, "So it is," or, "So be it."

16. Why do we conclude the Apostles' Creed with this word?

In order to declare, that we firmly believe all that is contained in the twelve Articles of the Creed, and that we are determined to live according to this belief, and to die in it.

Application.—Often consider, especially at the hour of temptation, this serious truth: "Once lost, lost for ever;" or this one: "Momentary joy brings on eternal pain; but short pain, eternal joy;" and these words of Jesus Christ: "The kingdom of Heaven suffereth violence, and the violent bear it away." (Matt. 11, 12.)

PART II.

ON THE COMMANDMENTS.

1. Is it sufficient for obtaining eternal salvation, that we believe all that God has revealed?

No; we must also keep His Commandments: "If thou wilt enter into life, keep the commandments." (Matt. 19, 17.)

"Not every one that saith to Me, Lord, Lord, shall enter into the kingdom of Heaven; but he that doth the will of My Father who is in Heaven, he shall enter into the kingdom of Heaven." (Matt. 7, 21.)

2. But are we able to keep the Commandments of God?

Yes, with the assistance of God's grace, which He refuses to no one who asks for it.

"His commandments are not heavy." (1. John 5, 3.)—"My yoke is sweet, and My burden light." (Matt. 11, 30.)

3. How do we know that we are able to keep the Commandments?

We know it, 1. Because God inflicts eternal punishment upon those who break them; and 2. Because there were at all times Saints who faithfully observed them.

1. "And that servant who knew the will of his lord, and did not according to his will, shall be beaten with many stripes." (Luke 12, 47.)—2. It is written of Zachary and Elizabeth: "And they were both just before God, walking in all the commandments and justifications of the Lord without blame." (Luke 1, 6.)

On the Chief Commandment.

4. Which is the Chief Commandment that includes all the others?

The Commandment of *Charity*, *i.e.* the Commandment of the *Love of God*, and *of our Neighbour*.

5. How is this Commandment of Charity expressed?

It is expressed in these terms: "Thou shalt love the Lord thy God, with thy whole heart, and with thy whole soul, and with thy whole mind, and with thy whole strength. This is the greatest and the first Commandment. And the second is like to this: Thou shalt love thy neighbour as thyself." (Mark 12, 30. 31; Matt. 22, 37—40.)

§. 1. *On the Love of God.*

6. What is the Love of God?

It is a virtue infused by God into our soul, by which we give ourselves up with all our heart to Him, the Sovereign Good, in order to please Him by fulfilling His will, and to be united with Him.

7. What qualities must our Love of God have?

It must be, 1. *Supernatural*; 2. *Sovereign*; and 3. *Active*.

8. When is our Love *supernatural*?

Our Love is supernatural, when, with the help of God's grace, we love Him as we know Him, not only by our reason, but by our faith.

"Now the end of the commandment is charity, from a pure heart, and a good conscience, and an unfeigned faith. From which things some going astray, are turned aside unto vain babbling." (1 Tim. 1, 5. 6.)—"My just man liveth by faith; but if he withdraw himself, he shall not please my soul." (Hebr. 10, 38.)—By faith we know God not only as the Creator of the world, and the Giver of all natural goods, which we can likewise perceive by our reason; but also as the Author and Giver of the supernatural graces and benefits: as the most merciful Father, who has most graciously adopted us, and has given His own Son, in order to save us, to sanctify us, and to make us one day eternally happy in the kingdom of His glory.

9. When is our Love of God *sovereign*?

Our love of God is sovereign, when we love Him more than all other things, so that we are willing to lose all, rather than separate ourselves from Him by sin.

"I am sure that neither death, nor life, nor things present, nor things to come, ... nor any other creature, shall be able to separate us from the Love of God." (Rom. 8, 38. 39.)—This degree of Love, by which we are actuated to lose all, rather than commit a grievous sin, is absolutely necessary to salvation; but this is not the highest degree. For a higher degree is this, when we are not only determined not to commit any grievous sin, but not even the least sin; and there is a higher degree still, when we are resolved always to do what is most perfect, or most pleasing to God.

10. When is our Love *active*?

Our Love is active, when we do what is acceptable to God; that is, when we keep His Commandments.

"He that hath My Commandments, and keepeth them; he it is that loveth Me." (John 14, 21.)—"This is the charity of God, that we keep His Commandments." (1. John, 5, 3.)

11. Why must we love God?

We must love God, 1. Because He is the sovereign and most perfect Good; 2. Because He has loved us first, and has bestowed innumerable blessings upon us in soul and body; and 3. Because He commands us to love Him, and promises us eternal salvation as a reward for it.

12. When is our Love of God *perfect*?

Our Love is perfect when we love God on account of His infinite goodness; that is, when we love Him above all things, because He is both infinitely good in Himself, and infinitely good to us.

"Let us, therefore, love God, because God first hath loved us." (1 John 4, 19.)—Of this perfect Love it is said: "He that abideth in Charity, abideth in God, and God in Him;" and, "Every one that loveth, is born of God." (1. John 4, 16. 7.)—Example: Mary Magdalen: "Many sins are forgiven her, because she hath loved much." (Luke 7, 47.)

13. When is our Love *imperfect*?

Our Love is imperfect, when we love God chiefly because we expect good things from Him.

Example: The Prodigal Son: "How many hired servants in my father's house abound with bread, and I here perish with hunger! I will arise, and will go to my father." (Luke 15, 17. 18.)

14. By what means is the Love of God increased and perfected in us?

1. By frequently and worthily receiving the Holy Sacraments; 2. By meditating on the Perfections and Graces of God, especially on the bitter Passion and Death of Jesus Christ; 3. By self-denial, and patience in afflictions; and 4. By performing good works.

15. How is the Love of God lessened and banished?

By mortal sin the Love of God is banished from our hearts, and, by venial sin, its fervour is lessened.

Application.—Exercise yourself assiduously in the Love of God by these means: Often think of Him, and often pray to Him; delight in hearing and speaking of Him; do and suffer every thing for His sake, and fear nothing so much as to offend Him.

§. 2. *On the Love of our Neighbour.*

16. Whom must we particularly love after God?

Our neighbour; *i.e.* all men without exception.

17. Is it then not enough, if we love God?

"If any man say, I love God, and hateth his brother, he is a liar." (1 John 4, 20.)

18. Why must we love our neighbour?

1. Because Christ, our Lord, commands us to love him, and, by the fulfilment of this Commandment, He will know His true disciples; 2. Because He Himself in His life and death taught us so by His example; and 3. Because every one is a child and an image of God, was redeemed with the blood of Christ, and is called to eternal salvation.

1. "By this shall all men know that you are My Disciples, if you have love one for another." (John 13, 35.)—2. "Be ye, therefore, followers of God, as most dear children; and walk in love, as Christ also hath loved us, and hath delivered Himself for us." (Eph. 5, 1. 2.)—3 "Have we not all one Father? Hath not one God created us? Why then doth every one of us despise his brother?" (Mal. 2, 10.)

19. What qualities must the love of our neighbour have?

It must be, 1. *Sincere*; 2. *Disinterested*; 3. *General*.

20. When is our love *sincere*?

Our love is sincere, when we love our neighbour, not in appearance, but as ourselves?

"My little children, let us not love in word, nor in tongue, but in deed, and in truth." (1. John 3, 18.)

21. When do we love our neighbour as ourselves?

We love our neighbour as ourselves, when we observe the command of Christ: "All things whatsoever you would that men should do to you, do you also to them." (Matt, 7, 12.)

"See thou never do to another what thou wouldst hate to have done to thee by another." (Tob. 4, 16.)

22. When is our love *disinterested*?

Our love is disinterested, when we do good to our neighbour for God's sake, and not that we may be praised or rewarded by men.

"When thou makest a feast, call the poor, the maimed, the lame, and the blind: and thou shalt be blessed, because they have not wherewith to make thee recompense; for recompense shall be made thee at the resurrection of the just." (Luke 14, 13. 14.)

23. When is our love *general*?

Our love is general, when we exclude no one from it, whether he be our friend, or our enemy.

"For, if you love them that love you, what reward shall you have? Do not even the publicans this? And if you salute your brethren only, what do you more? Do not also the heathens this?" (Matt. 5, 46. 47.)—Ex: The Good Samaritan. (Luke 10.)

24. Is it not enough, if we do not revenge ourselves on our enemies?

No; God commands us to love our enemies; *i.e.* to wish them well, and to be ready to assist them in their necessities, as much as lies in our power.

"Love your enemies; do good to them that hate you, and pray for them that persecute and calumniate you; that you may be the children of your Father who is in Heaven, who maketh His sun to rise upon the good and the bad, and raineth upon the just and the unjust." (Matt. 5, 44. 45.)—Ex: St. Stephen.

25. Why must we love our enemies?

1. Because the Lord our God commands us to love them; 2. Because Christ Jesus, our Divine Model, has given us the example of loving our enemies; and 3. Because we also wish to be forgiven by God.

1. "But I say to you, Love your enemies; do good to them that hate you;" etc. (Matt. 5.)—2. Jesus addressed even His betrayer in the kindest manner, saying: "Friend, whereto, art thou come?" (Matt. 26, 50.) and He prayed on the cross for His murderers: "Father, forgive them, for they know not what they do." (Luke 23, 34.)—3. "Forgive us our trespasses, as we" etc.—Parable of the Unmerciful Servant. (Matt. 18, 23—35.)

26. What has he to expect who will not forgive him, by whom he has been offended?

Judgment without mercy.

"Judgment without mercy to him that hath not done mercy." (James 2, 13.)—"But if you will not forgive, neither will your Father that is in Heaven, forgive you your sins." (Mark 11, 26.)

27. What must we do when we have offended some one?

We must go and be reconciled to him. (Matt. 5, 23, 24.)

28. What must we do, when some one has offended us?

We must willingly offer to make peace with him, forgive him from our heart, and suffer injustice rather than return evil for evil.

"To no man render evil for evil. If it be possible, as much as is in you, have peace with all men. Revenge not yourselves, my dearly beloved; for it is written: *Revenge is Mine; I will repay*, saith the Lord." (Rom. 12, 17—19. Comp. Matt. 5, 39—41.) Ex.: Jacob and Esau; David and Saul.

29. What sort of people does Holy Scripture particularly recommend to our love?

The poor, widows, and orphans, and in general, all those who are in corporal and spiritual need.

30. How are we to assist them?

By the Corporal and Spiritual Works of Mercy.

"Blessed are the merciful; for they shall obtain mercy." (Matt. 5, 7.)

31. Which are the *Corporal Works of Mercy*?

The Corporal Works of Mercy are these seven: 1. To feed the hungry; 2. To give drink to the thirsty; 3. To clothe the naked; 4. To harbour the harbourless; 5. To visit the imprisoned; 6. To visit the sick; 7. To bury the dead.

32. Is it also a duty to perform corporal works of mercy?

Yes, it is such an indispensable duty that Christ condemns the unmerciful to everlasting fire.

"Depart from Me, you cursed, into everlasting fire. For I was hungry, and you gave Me not to eat; I was thirsty and you gave me not to drink; I was a stranger, and you took Me not in; naked, and you covered Me not; sick and in prison, and you did not visit Me. . . . Amen I say to you, as long as you did it not to one of these least, neither did you do it to Me. And these shall go into everlasting punishment." (Matt. 25, 41—46.)— With regard to the dead, the Holy Scripture says: " My son, shed tears over the dead, and neglect not his burial." (Ecclus. 38, 16.)

33. What good things are promised to those who give alms?

Temporal blessings, † and especially spiritual graces, in order to obtain forgiveness of their sins, and life everlasting. ‡

† "He that giveth to the poor, shall not want; he that despiseth his entreaty, shall suffer indigence." (Prov. 28, 27.)—Ex. Tobias.—‡ "Alms delivereth from death, and the same is that which purgeth away sins, and maketh to find mercy and life everlasting." (Tob. 12, 9.) —Examples: Zacheus, the Publican; Cornelius, the Centurion.

34. Which are the *Spiritual Works of Mercy?*

The Spiritual Works of Mercy are these seven:— 1. To admonish sinners; 2. To instruct the ignorant; 3. To counsel the doubtful; 4. To comfort the sorrowful; 5. To bear wrongs patiently; 6. To forgive injuries; 7. To pray for the living and the dead.

35. Are we also bound to perform spiritual works of mercy?

Yes; provided we have sufficient knowledge, and an opportunity, to perform them; for the spiritual good of our neighbour should affect us far more than his corporal welfare.

"My brethren, if any one of you err from the truth, and one convert him: he must know that he who causeth a sinner to be converted from the error of his way, shall save his soul from death, and shall cover a multitude of sins." (James 5, 19. 20.)

36.* When are we in general bound to admonish or rebuke our neighbour in a brotherly manner?

When it is necessary, in order to prevent him from committing sin, and there is hope that it will not be in vain.

"If thy brother shall offend against thee, go and rebuke him between thee and him alone." etc. (Matt. 18, 15.)

37.* How is fraternal rebuke to be given?

With all possible prudence, love, and meekness.

"Brethren, if a man be overtaken in any fault, instruct such a one in the spirit of meekness." (Gal. 6, 1.)

Application.—Be peaceable and kind to every one, especially to your brothers and sisters, and to your relations. Bear with the faults and frailties of your neighbour; never render evil for evil; but pray for him who may have offended you.

§ 3. *On Christian Self-Love.*

38. May a Christian love himself also?

Yes, he may, and ought to love himself; for Christ says: "Thou shalt love thy neighbour as *thyself.*"

39. In what does Christian self-love consist?

Christian self-love consists in being, above all things, solicitous for the salvation of our soul.

40. Why must we, above all things, be solicitous for the salvation of our soul?

1. Because the soul has been created to the likeness of God, has been ransomed with the precious blood of Jesus Christ, and sanctified by the grace of the Holy Ghost; and 2. Because on the salvation of the soul depends our eternal welfare. (Matt. 16, 26.)

41. What are we to do in order to secure the salvation of our soul?

1. We must carefully avoid sin, and every occasion of sin; 2. When nevertheless we have sinned, we must not delay to do sincere penance; and 3. We must earnestly endeavour to practise virtue, and to do good works.

1. "They that commit sin and iniquity, are enemies to their own soul." (Tob. 12, 10.)—2. "Delay not to be converted to the Lord, and defer it not from day to day; for His wrath shall come on a sudden, and in the time of vengeance He will destroy thee." (Ecclus. 5, 8. 9.)—3. "Wherefore, brethren, labour the more, that by good

works you may make sure your calling and election." (2. Pet. 1, 10.)

42. May we also love our body, and temporal goods in a Christian manner?

Yes, we may, and are also bound to love, in a Christian and supernatural manner, our body, and temporal goods; as, health, property, and good reputation.

43. When do we love our body in a Christian manner?

When we love it, 1. Because it is the dwelling-place of our soul, and her instrument for the service of God; and 2. Because it also was sanctified in Baptism, and is destined for eternal glory.

He who loves his body in this manner, will constantly subdue its unlawful desires, and thus, according to the admonition of St. Paul, "*Present it a living sacrifice, holy, pleasing unto God.*" (Rom. 12, 1.)

44. When do we love the goods of this world in a Christian manner?

When we love them, 1. As far as all created things have their origin in God, and are His gifts; and 2. As far as they serve us, to promote the honour of God, to assist the needy, and to fulfil the duties of our state of life.

He who loves the goods of this world in this manner, will not turn away his heart from God, in order to seek his happiness in them, but will make such a use of them, that on their account he will not forfeit those of Heaven.

45. What is opposite to Christian self-love?
Inordinate self-love.

46. When is self-love inordinate?

1. When man prefers his own honour and will to the honour and will of God; 2. When he is more solicitous for his body and for temporal things, than for his soul and eternal salvation; and 3. When he seeks his own welfare to the prejudice of his neighbour.

This vicious self-love is the source of all sins. "Men shall be lovers of themselves, covetous, haughty, proud, blasphemers, disobedient to parents, ungrateful, wicked, without affection, without peace, slanderers, incontinent, unmerciful, without kindness, traitors, stubborn, puffed up, and lovers of pleasures more than of God." (2. Tim. 3, 2—4.)

47. * Is every self-love that is not supernatural, vicious and inordinate?

No; there is also a merely natural self-love, by which we may indeed love ourselves, and all that belongs to us, in a lawful manner, though not meritorious for eternity.

Thus also those who are evil, know how to give (through natural love) good gifts to their children. (Luke 11, 13.)

Application.—Oppose in good time that pernicious self-love, by which a person, in all that he thinks, speaks, and does, has not in view the honour of God, or the welfare of his neighbour, but only his own self, and his pretended advantages over others.

On the Ten Commandments of God.

(See Short Hist. of Relig., §. 11.)

1. Where is our duty of loving God and our neighbour more fully contained?

In the Ten Commandments, which God gave to Moses, written on two tables of stone.

2. What are the Ten Commandments?

1. I am the Lord thy God. Thou shalt not have strange gods before Me; thou shalt not make to thyself any graven thing to adore it.

2. Thou shalt not take the name of the Lord thy God in vain.

3. Remember that thou keep holy the Sabbath-day.

4. Honour thy father and thy mother, that it may

be well with thee, and thou mayest live long on the earth.

5. Thou shalt not kill.

6. Thou shalt not commit adultery.

7. Thou shalt not steal.

8. Thou shalt not bear false witness against thy neighbour.

9. Thou shalt not covet thy neighbour's wife.

10. Thou shalt not covet thy neighbour's house, nor his field, nor his servant, nor his hand-maid, nor his ox, nor his ass, nor anything that is his.

3. Why are we Christians also bound to keep these Commandments of the Old Law?

1. Because Christ is not come "To destroy the Law, but to fulfil it" (Matt. 5, 17.), *i.e.* to confirm it, and to teach us, how to observe it perfectly; and

2. Because the Ten Commandments contain that Law which already binds all men, since it is grounded in human nature, and written by God in all hearts. (Rom. 2. 15.)

4. * If the Law is written in all hearts, why did God give it to man, written on tables of stone?

That we may the more surely know the Law of God, and be the more strongly impelled to fulfil it; for our capacity to know, and to will, what is good, has been very much weakened by sin.

5. What in particular ought to induce us, faithfully to keep the Divine Commandments?

1. The reverence, love, and gratitude, which we owe to God; 2. The fear of eternal punishment, and the hope of eternal reward.

The First Commandment of God.

"I am the Lord thy God. Thou shalt not have strange gods before Me; thou shalt not make to thyself any graven thing to adore it."

6. What are we commanded by the First Commandment?

By the First Commandment we are commanded to pay to Almighty God due honour and adoration.

7. How many kinds of honour do we owe to God?

We owe to God two kinds of honour, namely, *interior* and *exterior* honour.

8. How do we honour God *interiorly*?

We honour God interiorly, 1. By faith, hope, and charity; 2. By reverence and adoration; 3. By thanksgiving for all His blessings; 4. By zeal for His honour; and 5. By obedience and resignation to His holy will.

9. How do we sin against faith?

1. By infidelity, heresy, and scepticism; 2. By impious and profane language, or by wilfully listening to it; likewise, by reading or spreading irreligious books and writings; and 3. By indifference in matters of faith, or by actually denying it.

10. When do people become guilty of indifference in matters of faith?

1. When they do not care for any religion, or when they consider all equally good; 2. When they stand in need of being instructed, and neglect to attend the Christian Doctrine; and 3. When parents or guardians allow their children to be brought up in an erroneous belief.

11. How do we sin against hope?

1. By despair, or by distrust; and 2. By presumption, or by false confidence.

12. When do we sin by despair or by distrust?

When we either do not hope at all for that which we ought to hope for from God; † or when we do not hope for it with confidence in Him.‡

Examples: † Cain and Judas. ‡ Moses and the Israelites in the desert.

13. What are we to hope for from God?

We are, above all, to hope for life everlasting, and for that which is necessary and conducive to it; as, the forgiveness of our sins, and the grace of God.

14. Why are we to hope for these things?

Because God, who is infinitely powerful, merciful, and faithful, has promised them to us, and Jesus Christ has merited them for us.

15. What, then, is Christian Hope?

Christian Hope is a virtue infused into our souls, by which we most confidently expect all the things, which God has promised us through the merits of Jesus Christ.

16. May every sinner hope for pardon?

Yes, every sinner, even the greatest, may and ought to hope for pardon, provided he will be converted with all his heart, and do penance.

"If the wicked do penance for all his sins which he has committed, and keep all My Commandments, living he shall live, and shall not die." (Ez. 18, 21.)—Examples: The Ninivites, Mary Magdalen, the Thief on the Cross, and others. Parable of the Lost Sheep, and of the Prodigal Son. (Luke 15.)

17. How far may we also expect temporal goods from God?

As far as they help us, or at least do not hinder us, to obtain eternal salvation.

18. When do we sin by presumption and false confidence?

1. When, relying on the mercy of God, we continue to sin without fear, or delay our repentance to the end of our life; 2. When we rashly expose ourselves to a danger from which we confidently expect God will extricate us.

19. Is Christian hope also consistent with fear?

Confidence in God does not exclude diffidence in ourselves; † therefore, we should neither be excessively uneasy about our salvation, nor should we throw off all sense of fear and solicitude for it. ‡

† "Wherefore he that thinketh himself to stand, let him take heed lest he fall." (1. Cor. 10, 12.)—"I am not conscious to myself of anything, yet am I not hereby justified; but He that judgeth me, is the Lord." (1. Cor. 4, 4.)—"Justify not thyself before God, for He knoweth the heart." (Ecclus. 7, 5.)—‡ "With fear and trembling, work out your salvation." (Phili. 2, 12.)—"I chastise my body, and bring it into subjection; lest perhaps, when I have preached to others, I myself should become a castaway." (1. Cor. 9, 27.)

20. What sins are chiefly opposed to the love of God?

In general, all mortal sins; but in particular, 1. Indifference, and aversion to God and Divine things; and 2. Hatred and repugnance to Him and His paternal dispensations.

21. How do we honour God also *exteriorly?*

We honour God also exteriorly, when we manifest our interior respectful sentiments towards Him by exterior actions; as, common prayer, genuflections, joining our hands, etc.

22. Why are we also commanded to honour God exteriorly?

1. Because the body has been created by God as well as the soul, and, therefore, both should pay Him honour and homage; 2. Because it is quite natural to man to manifest his interior worship of God also exteriorly; 3. Because the interior worship is increased by the exterior; and 4. Because the exterior worship is conducive and necessary for our mutual edification, for fortifying ourselves in our faith, and for preserving and propagating our religion.

Example: Daniel who chose to be cast into the den of the lions rather than to give up the exterior adoration of God as prescribed by the Law. (Dan. 6.)

23. How do we sin against the exterior worship of God?

By neglecting to attend Divine Service, or by behaving irreverently, when we are present.

Punishment of the men of Bethsames, because they approached the Ark of the Lord in an irreverent manner. (I. Kings 6, 19.)

24. May we sin in any other way against the reverence due to God?

Yes, we sin also against it by idolatry, superstition, witchcraft, sacrilege, and simony.

25. When does a person commit idolatry?

He commits idolatry (worship of images), when he pays Divine honour to any creature or thing, as the Heathens did.

26. When do we sin by superstition?

1. When we honour God or the Saints in a manner contrary to the doctrine or practice of the Church;

2. When we attribute to things a certain power which they cannot have either by nature, or by the prayers of the Church, or by virtue of Divine dispensation.

For inst.: When we consult fortune-tellers, and make them tell us our fortune by cutting cards, or by inspecting our hands; or when we have recourse to the interpretation of dreams, or to vain and foolish signs and practices, in order to know hidden things, or to obtain luck or health; and when, for that purpose, we abuse even holy names and blessed things; etc.

27. Is such superstition a grievous sin?

It is generally a very grievous sin, because he who practises such things, mostly expects the assistance of the evil spirit, if not openly, at least secretly, but, at all events, puts that confidence which he ought to place in God alone, in idle or delusive things.

28.* Is it also superstitious to wear on our persons images (medals) of the Saints, or blessed things?

On the contrary, it is praiseworthy, if it is done with a pious intention, that is to say, with confidence in God, in the intercession of the Saints, or in the prayer and blessing of the Church.

29. How do people become guilty of witchcraft?

When they try, with the help of the evil spirits, to find hidden treasures, to injure others, or to work wonderful things.

Thus one day that wicked one, Antichrist, will do, "Whose coming is according to the working of Satan, in all (deluding) power, and signs, and lying wonders, and in all seduction of iniquity to them that perish." (2. Thess. 2, 9. 10.)—This God will permit for the just punishment of those who rejected the Christian truth, and the Divine miracles.

30. What is sacrilege?

Sacrilege is a profanation of holy things, holy persons, or holy places; for inst.: The unworthy receiving of a Sacrament, the ill-treatment of an Ecclesiastic, the desecration of a Church, or of sacred Vessels, &c.

Examples: Punishment of King Baltassar (Dan. 5.), of Heliodorus (2. Mac. 3.). How Christ cast the sellers out of the temple, see John 2, 15.

31. When does a person commit simony?

When he buys or sells spiritual things, preferments, and the like, for money or money's worth; as Simon, the Magician, intended to do. (Acts 8.) This sin has been forbidden by the Church under the most severe penalties, even under pain of excommunication.

Application.—Make every day Acts of Faith, Hope, and Charity, and never neglect to say your Morning and Evening Prayers. At Church behave with reverence, and pray with attention, on your knees, and with your hands joined. Never use forbidden or suspicious means, in order to cure diseases, or to discover hidden things. Are you in doubt whether the use of certain things is permitted or not, ask the Priest, or your Confessor.

The First Commandment (*Continued*).

On the Veneration and Invocation of the Saints.

32. What does the Catholic Church teach respecting the veneration and invocation of the Saints?

She teaches that it is right and available to salvation to honour and invoke the Saints.

33. But is not the honour which we pay to the Saints against the First Commandment?

By no means; for 1. We pay no Divine honour to the Saints; and 2. We honour and praise in the Saints God Himself, who has shown Himself so powerful and merciful in them.

34. What is the difference between the honour which we show to God, and that which we show to the Saints?

1. We honour and adore God alone as our Sovereign Lord, and the Author of all good things; but we honour the Saints only as His faithful servants and friends. 2. We honour God for His own sake, or on account of the infinite Perfections which He has of Himself; but we honour the Saints on account of the gifts and advantages which they have received from God.

35.* But do we not kneel down when we honour the Saints? Do we not build churches and altars, and offer the Sacrifice of the Mass to them, as to God Himself?

We kneel down, it is true; but we adore the Saints no more than a courtier adores his king, when on his knees he asks a favour of him. We consecrate churches and altars, and offer the Holy Sacrifice of the Mass to God, alone, although, at the same time, we honour the memory of the Saints, and implore their intercession.

From the most ancient times, the Church has approved and cherished such veneration, has instituted festivals, built churches and altars in commemoration of the Saints, and implored their intercession at the Holy Sacrifice; and God often confirmed such devotion by extraordinary graces.

36. What should we have principally in view when we venerate the Saints?

We should imitate their virtues, and strive to become like them, that we may also one day share in their eternal happiness.

37. In what does our praying to God differ from our praying to the Saints?

We pray to God that He may help us by His Omnipotence; but we pray to the Saints that they may help us by interceding with God for us.

38. Is it, then, in the power of the Saints in Heaven to obtain anything from God in our behalf?

It was in their power when they were living on earth; much more must it be so now that they are in Heaven; for death does not dissolve the communion between them and us. (See the Ninth Article of the Creed, Page 149. Quest. 71.)

"Pray one for another, that you may be saved; for the continual prayer of a just man availeth much." (James 5, 16.)—No one but a most obstinate Infidel can deny the miracles which were, and are still, wrought by the intercession of the Saints. (Proceedings of the Church at a Beatification, or Canonization.)

39. * Does the Holy Scripture also testify that the Saints in Heaven pray for us?

Yes, the Holy scripture says, 1. That the Angels pray for man; † 2. That the Prophet Jeremias, long after his death, "prayeth much for the people, and for all the holy city;" (2 Mac. 15, 14.) and 3. That the four and twenty Ancients incessantly offer up the prayers of the Saints at the throne of the Most High. (Apoc. 5, 8.)

† "And the Angel of the Lord answered, and said: O Lord of Hosts, how long wilt Thou not have mercy on

Jerusalem, and on the cities of Juda?" (Zach. 1, 12.)—"When thou didst pray with tears, I offered thy prayer to the Lord," said the Angel Raphael to Tobias. (Tob. 12, 12.)

40. * Do then the Saints in Heaven know anything of us?

If they did not know anything of us, the Archangel Raphael could not have offered the prayer of Tobias to God, nor could there be joy before the Angels of God upon one sinner doing penance, as the Gospel testifies. (Luke 15, 10.)

41. * But is it not a mark of distrust in Jesus Christ, when we address ourselves to the Saints?

No; for 1. We expect grace and salvation from God alone through the merits of Jesus Christ; and 2. If it were a mark of distrust, St. Paul would not have applied to the faithful, saying: "I beseech you, Brethren, through our Lord Jesus Christ, that you may help me in your prayers for me to God." (Rom. 15, 30.)

42. Why does God grant us many graces through the intercession of the Saints?

Because it is the will of God that we should acknowledge our own unworthiness, and the merits of His faithful servants. Therefore, He Himself, in former times, commanded the friends of Job, saying: "Go to My servant Job . . . and My servant Job shall pray for you." (Job 42, 8.)

43. Whom should we in particular honour and invoke above all the Angels and Saints?

Mary, the Blessed Virgin, and Mother of God.

44. Why should we particularly honour and invoke Mary?

1. Because she is the Mother of God, and, therefore, far surpasses all the Angels and Saints in grace and glory;

2. Because, for that very reason, her intercession with God is most powerful.

45. Should we also honour the images of Jesus Christ and of the Saints?

Yes, certainly; for if even a child honours the likenesses of his parents, and a subject the image of his prince; so much the more must we honour the images of our Lord and of His Saints.

How strictly the veneration of holy images was at all times observed in the Church, was shown in the eighth century, when the Heretics, called Iconoclasts (Breakers of Images), arose. Although, supported by the Greek Emperor, they raged most obstinately and furiously against the images, and those who revered them, yet they were not able to abolish the pious practice. The faithful firmly suffered all imaginable ill-treatment, even torture and death; and in the year 787, the new Heresy was solemnly condemned by the Seventh General Council.

46. But does not the Scripture say: "You shall not make to yourself any idol or graven thing?"

True; but it is also immediately added: "To adore it," (Levit. 26, 1.) as the Heathens did. But we Catholics detest the adoration of images.

God Himself commanded Moses to "make two Cherubim of beaten gold on the two sides of the oracle" (Exod. 25, 18.), and also to "make a brazen serpent, and set it up for a sign" (Num. 21, 8.), which was a figure of our Crucified Redeemer.

47. But is it not superstitious to pray before images?

Not at all; for when we pray before the images or Jesus Christ and His Saints, we pray to Jesus Christ and to the Saints, whom they represent.

48. * Does it not prove that we put our trust in images, when we go on pilgrimages to them?

No; for we do not visit holy places because we trust in the images that are honoured there, but because we know that God has been pleased to bestow many graces and benefits in such places, and, therefore, feel ourselves animated to pray there with greater fervour and confidence.

49. What is the use of placing images of Christ and of the Saints in our churches?

They instruct and strengthen us in our faith, and incite us to live in conformity to it, whilst they represent before our eyes the mysteries of our Religion, the history of our Redemption, and the holy lives of the Saints.

50. Why do we honour the Relics of the Saints?

Because their bodies were living members of Jesus Christ, and temples of the Holy Ghost, and will one day rise again from the dead to eternal glory.

At all times, Relics have been kept in honour in the Church. As early as in the second century, the Christians in Antioch and Smyrna, as they testify themselves, honoured the Relics of their Holy Bishops Ignatius and Polycarp, who had suffered death for Jesus Christ.

51. Whence do we know for certain, that the veneration of Relics is pleasing to God?

From this, that God has frequently been pleased to work great miracles through their means, as we read in the Holy Scripture and the History of the Church.

"When the man (whom they were burying) had touched the bones of Eliseus, he came to life, and stood upon his feet." (4. Kings 13, 21.)—"And God wrought by the hand of Paul more than common miracles; so that even there were brought from his body to the sick, handkerchiefs and aprons, and the diseases departed from them, and the wicked spirits went out of them." (Acts 19, 11. 92.)—St. Augustin, St. Ambrose, and others, give us an account of the miracles which were wrought at the graves of St. Stephen, St. Felix of Nola, St. Gervasius, and of many other Saints.

The authenticity of a Relic, which is exposed to the veneration of the faithful, is not a matter of faith, but rests simply on human, but nevertheless credible, testimonies.

Application.—Honour the Blessed Saints in Heaven with great devotion, especially the Most Blessed Virgin, St. Joseph, and your Patron Saint. Diligently read their lives, and faithfully imitate their examples. Keep in your dwelling no immodest, but holy images, and, above all, an image of your Crucified Redeemer. (Feast of All Saints.)

The Second Commandment of God.

"Thou shalt not take the name of the Lord thy God in vain."

1. What does the Second Commandment forbid?

The Second Commandment forbids all profanation of the holy name of God.

2. How do we profane the name of God?

We profane the name of God, 1. By irreverently pronouncing it; 2. By deriding religion; 3. By blasphemy; 4. By sinful swearing, and by cursing; and 5. By breaking vows.

3. How do we sin by irreverently pronouncing God's holy name?

By pronouncing the name of God in jest, or in anger, or in any other careless manner.

This applies also to other names and words worthy of reverence, as, the name of the Blessed Virgin, the Holy Cross, the Holy Sacraments, etc., and to the words of the Holy Scripture, which are never to be abused in jest, or by way of derision.

"The Lord will not hold him guiltless that shall take the name of the Lord his God in vain." (Exod. 20, 7.)

4. How do we sin by deriding religion?

By scoffing at religion, at the rites or ceremonies of the Church, or by turning them into ridicule, in which cases we may also become guilty of blasphemy.

"Knowing this first, that in the last days there shall come deceitful scoffers, walking after their own lusts. . . You, therefore, brethren, knowing these things before, take heed, lest being led aside by the error of the unwise, you fall from your own steadfastness." (2. Pet. 3, 3. 17.)

5. What is meant by blasphemy?

By blasphemy is meant contemptuous and abusive language uttered against God, the Saints, or holy things.

This sin is so great that, in the Old Law, those who were found guilty of it, were put to death. "He that blasphemeth the name of the Lord, dying let him die: all the multitude shall stone him." (Levit. 24, 16.)—How Sennacherib, King of the Assyrians, was punished for blaspheming the Lord, see 4. Kings 19.

6. May we also become guilty of blasphemy by thoughts?

Yes, when we voluntarily think contemptuously of God, or of the Saints.

7. What is swearing or taking an oath?

Swearing or taking an oath is to call the Omniscient God to witness, that we speak the truth, or that we will keep our promise.

We call God also to witness, when we swear by Heaven, by the Holy Cross, or by the Gospel, etc. "Whosoever shall swear by the temple, sweareth by it, and by Him that dwelleth in it; and he that sweareth by Heaven, sweareth by the throne of God, and by Him that sitteth thereon." (Matt. 23, 21. 22.)

8. How do we sin by swearing?

We sin by swearing, 1. When we swear falsely, or in doubt; 2. When we swear, or induce others to swear, without necessity; 3. When we swear to do what is evil, or to omit what is good; and 4. When we do not keep our oath, although we can keep it.

"Thou shalt swear in truth, and in judgment, and in justice." (Jer. 4, 2.)

9. What means swearing falsely, or in doubt?

It means, 1. To assert with an oath that something is true, though we know that it is untrue, or do not know whether it is true or not; 2. To promise with an oath something which we do not intend to perform.

10. What are we to think of perjury, or a false oath?

Perjury, especially in a court of justice, is one of the greatest crimes; because he who commits it, 1. Mocks God's Omniscience, Sanctity, and Justice; 2. Destroys the last means of preserving truth and faith among men; and 3. Almost solemnly renounces God, and calls down His vengeance upon him.

"And the Lord said to me: This flying volume which thou seest, is the curse that goeth forth over the face of the earth; for every one that sweareth shall be judged by it. I will bring it forth, said the Lord of Hosts, and it shall come to the house of him that sweareth falsely by My name, and it shall remain in the midst of his house, and shall consume it, with the timber thereof, and the stones thereof." (Zach. 5, 3. 4. Comp. Ezech. 17.)

11. When a person has sworn to do something evil, or to omit something that is good, is he bound to keep such an oath?

No; for as it was a sin to take such an oath, so it would be another sin to keep it. Ex.: Herod. (Mark 6, 23—28.)

12. What do you mean by cursing?

Cursing means, to wish any evil either to ourselves, or to our neighbour, or to any of God's creatures, whereby the name of God is frequently dishonoured.

Cursing is something very hateful, which betrays a rude, angry temper. From the mouth of a Christian, or Child of God, nothing but "*blessing*" ought to come forth (1. Pet. 3, 9.). Cursing is at the same time an oath, when we call upon God to punish us, if we speak an untruth.

13. What is a vow?

A vow is a voluntary promise made to God, to do something that is agreeable to Him, although there be no obligation to do it.

Accordingly, a vow is, 1. A real *promise*, by which we

deliberately bind ourselves, and not a mere desire, or resolution; 2. A promise *made to God*, because it is to God alone we make vows; and 3. A promise to do something *that is agreeable to God;* therefore, it cannot be anything trifling, sinful, or injurious to others; nor anything good by which something better may be prevented, or higher duties neglected.

14. What does the Church teach with regard to vows?

1. That they please God, because they are voluntary offerings made to Him. Thus God kindly accepted the vows of the Patriarch Jacob, † and of the pious Anna, the mother of Samuel, ‡ and granted their petitions.

† "And Jacob made a vow, saying: If God shall be with me, and I shall return prosperously to my father's house, of all things that Thou shalt give to me, I will offer tithes to Thee." (Gen. 28, 20—22,)—‡ "Anna made a vow, saying: O Lord of Hosts, if Thou wilt be mindful of me, and wilt give to Thy servant a man-child, I will give him to the Lord all the days of his life." (1. Kings 1, 11.)

2. That it is a sacred duty to keep them, unless it be impossible to do so. People should, therefore, be very cautious about making vows, and should, in general, ask advice of their Confessor, or any other prudent Priest.

"If thou hast vowed anything to God, defer not to pay it. It is much better not to vow, than after a vow not to perform the things promised." (Eccles. 5, 3. 4.)

15. Is it sufficient not to dishonour the name of God?

No; we must also honour and revere it; *i.e.*, we must gratefully praise it, devoutly call upon it, steadily confess it, and exert ourselves to promote its honour.

Application.—Carefully avoid the shameful habit of cursing and swearing. "A man that sweareth much, shall be filled with iniquity, and a scourge shall not depart from his house." (Ecclus. 23, 12.) On the contrary, often invoke with devotion the names of Jesus and Mary, especially in temptations against purity.

The Third Commandment of God.

"Remember that thou keep holy the Sabbath-day."

1. What are we commanded by the Third Commandment?

By the Third Commandment we are commanded to sanctify the Lord's day by performing works of piety, and abstaining from servile works.

2. Which is the Lord's day?

In the Old Law, it was the seventh day of the week, or the Sabbath-day (day of *rest*), in memory of God's resting on that day, after He had finished the work of Creation in six days. In the New Law, it is the first day of the week, or the Sunday, in memory of the accomplishment of our Redemption, which is a new spiritual Creation. (Gal. 6, 15.)

"In six days the Lord made heaven and earth, and the sea, and all things that are in them, and *rested* on the seventh day; therefore the Lord blessed the seventh day, and sanctified it." (Exod. 20, 11. Comp. Gen. 2, 2. 3.)

3.* How was our Redemption accomplished on the Sunday?

It was on a Sunday that our Saviour rose from the dead, and it was also on a Sunday that He sent down the Holy Ghost upon His Church.

4. What works of piety should we perform on the Sunday?

1. We are bound to hear Mass, and if possible, we should also attend the other Divine Service, especially the Sermon and Catechetical Instruction; and 2. We should receive the Holy Sacraments, read books of devotion, or meditate on the great truths of our Re-

ligion, and occupy ourselves in works of mercy, either corporal or spiritual. (James 1, 27.)

5. Which works are servile, and forbidden?

All bodily works which are commonly performed by servants, day-labourers, and tradesmen.

Works by which the mind only is exerted, are not numbered amongst the servile ones. But all those noisy, or merely worldly employments, which disturb quiet religious observance, as, lawsuits, buying and selling, etc., are also forbidden.

6. Is it never lawful to do servile work on a Sunday?

It is lawful, 1. When the Pastors of the Church, for weighty reasons, give a dispensation; and 2. As often as the honour of God, † the good of our neighbour, ‡ or urgent necessity, § require it.

Examples: Matt. 12. † Officiating in the temple, v. 5. —‡ Parable of the sheep that falls into a pit. v.v. 11. 12. —§ The Disciples plucking ears of corn. v. 1—4.

7. Are they only guilty, who themselves do forbidden work?

No; those also are guilty, who without any necessity require their inferiors, as, servants, day-labourers, or tradesmen, to do such work, or allow them to do it; for God says: "That thy man-servant and thy maid-servant may rest, even as thyself." (Deut. 5, 14.)

Servants, apprentices, and journeymen are obliged to look out for places where they are allowed to observe the Sundays and Holydays according to the command of God and of the Church.

8. Is the Sunday profaned only by servile work, and staying away from Divine Service?

No; it is likewise profaned by debauchery, intemperance, and extravagant games, sports, and amusements, which make of the Lord's day a day of revelry and public scandal.

9. What should we particularly consider in order to be deterred from profaning the Sunday?

We should consider,

1. The temporal and eternal punishment with which God threatens such as break the Sabbath.

"They grievously violated My Sabbaths; I said therefore, that I would pour out My indignation upon them in the desert, and would consume them." (Ezec. 20, 13.)—"Keep you My Sabbath; for it is holy unto you: he that shall profane it, shall be put to death." (Exod. 31, 14.)

2. That it is an unjustifiable heedlessness, not to devote even so much as one day to the care of our immortal soul, after the body has been taken care of during six days.

3. That the observance of the Sunday is a public profession of our Christian Faith, and consequently, that by its profanation we bring disgrace on our Religion, and give great scandal to our fellow-christians.

Zeal of the Jews in keeping holy the Sabbath-day: 2. Mac. 6, 11.

Application.—Always observe the Lord's day conscientiously, and never be induced to violate it, either by thoughtlessness and excessive fondness for amusements, or by the example of wicked or infidel people. "God be merciful unto us; it is not profitable to us to forsake the law." (1 Mac. 2, 21.)

The Fourth Commandment of God.

"Honour thy Father and thy Mother."

1. What is commanded by the Fourth Commandment?

By the Fourth Commandment children are commanded to show reverence, love, and obedience to their Parents, and inferiors to their Superiors.

2. Why must children reverence, love, and obey their Parents?

Because, next to God, their Parents are their greatest benefactors, and supply His place in their regard.

3. How should children reverence their Parents?

They should venerate their Parents as the representatives of God, and should, therefore, always show them respect in word and deed.

"Honour thy father in work and word, and all patience." (Ecclus 3, 9.)

4. How should children love their Parents?

They should, 1. Be grateful to them, and wish them well from their heart; 2. They should make them happy by their good conduct; 3. They should assist them in their necessities, and take care of them in their old age; and 4. They should bear with their faults and weaknesses.

"With thy whole heart honour thy father, and forget not the groanings of thy mother. Remember that thou hadst not been born but through them, and make a return to them as they have done for thee." (Ecclus 7, 28—30.)—Example of Jesus who, when dying on the cross, still provided for His Mother.

5. How should children obey their Parents?

1. They should do what their Parents command, and not do what they forbid, provided they order nothing bad or unjust; and 2. They should willingly receive, and readily follow, their advice and admonitions.

"Children obey your parents in all things; for this is well pleasing to the Lord." (Col. 3, 20.)—Example of Jesus who, though "God, blessed for evermore," yet was subject to Mary and Joseph.

6. What have children to expect, who faithfully observe the Fourth Commandment?

In this life, they may be sure of God's protection and blessing, and in the other, of eternal happiness.

"Honour thy father and thy mother, which is the first commandment with a promise: That it may be well with thee, and thou mayest be long-lived upon earth." (Eph. 6, 2. 3.)—"Honour thy father, that a blessing may come upon thee from him, and his blessing may remain in the latter end. The father's blessing establisheth the houses of the children, but the mother's curse rooteth up the foundation." (Ecclus 3, 9—11.)—Examples: Sem, Isaac, Ruth, Samuel, young Tobias.

7. When do children sin against the reverence they owe to their Parents?

They sin against the reverence they owe to their Parents, 1. When in their heart they despise and disregard them; 2. When they speak ill of them; 3. When they are ashamed of them; and 4. When they treat them harshly and insolently.

" The eye that mocketh at his father, and that despiseth the labour of his mother in bearing him, let the ravens of the brooks pick it out, and the young eagles eat it." (Prov. 30, 17.)

8. When do children sin against the love they owe to their Parents?

They sin against the love they owe to their Parents, 1. When they wish, or do them evil; 2. When, by their bad behaviour, they give them trouble, and bring disgrace upon them, or otherwise grieve them, and put them in a passion; 3. When they do not assist them in their need or old age; 4. When they do not bear with their failings; and 5. When they do not pray for their Parents, whether living or dead.

"He that striketh his father or mother, shall be put to death. He that curseth his father or mother, shall die the death." (Exod. 21, 15. 17.)—"Son, support the old age of thy father, and grieve him not in his life; and if his understanding fail, have patience with him, and despise him not when thou art in thy strength; for the relieving of the father shall not be forgotten." (Ecclus 3, 14. 15.)

9. When do children sin against the obedience due to their Parents?

They sin against the obedience due to their Parents, 1. When they obey them badly, or not at all; 2. When they do not willingly listen to their admonitions; and 3. When they offer resistance to their corrections.

"If a man have a stubborn and unruly son, who will not hear the commandments of his father or mother, and being corrected, slighteth obedience, they shall take him and bring him to the ancients of the city, and shall say to them: This our son is rebellious and stubborn, he slighteth hearing our admonitions, he giveth himself to revelling, and to debauchery and banquetings: the people of the city shall stone him, and he shall die; that you may take away the evil out of the midst of you, and all Israel hearing it may be afraid." (Deut. 21, 18—21.)

10. What have those children to expect, who do not fulfil their duties towards their Parents?

In this life they have to expect the curse of God, disgrace, and ignominy, and in the life to come, eternal damnation.

"Cursed be he that honoureth not his father and mother, and all the people shall say: Amen." (Deut. 27, 16.)—"Remember thy father and thy mother, lest God forget thee, and thou wish that thou hadst not been born, and curse the day of thy nativity." (Ecclus 23, 18. 19.)—Examples: Cham, Absolon, the Sons of Heli, the Highpriest.

11. What Superiors, besides our Parents, must we honour, love, and obey?

Our Guardians, Tutors, Teachers, Employers, Masters and Mistresses, and all our Spiritual and Temporal Superiors.

12. What are our duties towards our Guardians, Tutors, Teachers, and Employers?

We must consider them as the representatives and assistants of our Parents; and, therefore, our duties towards them are in proportion to those which children owe to their Parents.

13. What are the particular obligations of servants to their Masters and Mistresses?

They should, for the Lord's sake, show them respect, fidelity, love, and ready obedience. (Tit. 2, 9. 10.)

"Servants, obey in all things your masters according to the flesh, not serving to the eye, as pleasing men, but in simplicity of heart, fearing God. Whatsoever you do, do it from the heart, as to the Lord, and not to men; knowing that you shall receive of the Lord the reward of inheritance." (Col. 3, 22—24.) "Servants, be subject to your masters with all fear, not only to the good and gentle, but also to the froward." (1 Pet. 2, 18.)

14. How do servants sin against their Masters and Mistresses?
1. By disobedience, obstinacy, moroseness, and ill-will; 2. By laziness, by pilfering dainties, and by wasting and embezzling their goods; 3. By calumny, detraction, and tale-bearing; and most of all, 4. By teaching evil to their children, by seducing them, by assisting them to do evil, or by conniving at it.

15. What are our duties towards our Spiritual Superiors?
We are bound, 1. To honour and love them as the Representatives of God, and our Spiritual Fathers; 2. To submit to their ordinances; 3. To pray for them; and 4. To provide for their support in the manner established by law and custom.

"With all thy soul fear the Lord, and reverence His priests." (Ecclus 7, 31.)—"Obey your prelates, and be subject to them; for they watch as being to render an account of your souls, that they may do this with joy, and not with grief; for this is not expedient for you." (Hebr. 13, 17.)—"The Lord ordained that they who preach the gospel should live by the gospel." (1. Cor. 9, 14. Comp. Luke 10, 7. and 1. Tim. 5, 17. 18.)—Example of the Christians, when Peter was in prison. (Acts 12. Comp. Gal. 4, 14. 15.)

16. When do we sin against our Spiritual Superiors?
1. When, by word or deed, we violate the reverence due to them, or when, by speaking ill of them, we lower their character; 2. When we oppose them, and thereby may be the cause of schism and scandal; and 3. When, contrary to our duty, we refuse to contribute

towards their support, and to provide for the Divine Service.

"He that despiseth you, despiseth Me." (Luke 10, 16.) "The Lord knoweth how to reserve the unjust unto the day of judgment to be tormented: and especially them who despise government, audacious, self-willed, they fear not to bring in sects, blaspheming. They allure by the desires of fleshly riotousness, those who for a little while escape, such as converse in error: promising them *liberty*, whereas they themselves are the slaves of corruption." (2 Pet. 2.) "Wo unto them, for they have gone in the way of Cain, and have perished in the contradiction of Core." (Jude 11.)—Examples: Core, Dathan, and Abiron swallowed up by the earth (Num. 16.); Forty-two boys torn by two bears. (4. Kings 2, 24.)

17. What are our duties towards our Temporal Superiors?

We are bound, 1. To show to our Temporal Superiors, ordained by God, respect, fidelity, and conscientious obedience, and to suffer any thing rather than raise sedition against them; 2. To pay the taxes imposed by them; and 3. To assist them in their necessities and dangers, and even to sacrifice our property and life for their defence against the enemies of our country.

"Let every soul be subject to higher powers; for there is no power but from God, and those that are, are ordained of God. Therefore, he that resisteth the power, resisteth the ordinance of God; and they that resist, purchase to themselves damnation. Wherefore be subject of necessity, not only for wrath, but also for conscience" sake. Render therefore to all men their dues: tribute to whom tribute is due; custom to whom custom; fear to whom fear; honour to whom honour." (Rom. 13, 1—7.)—Examples: Jesus, and the first Christians. David towards Saul. (1. Kings 24, 7.)

18. How do we sin against our Temporal Superiors?

1. By hatred and contempt; 2. By reviling and blaspheming them; 3. By refusing to pay the taxes due to them; 4. By resistance and rebellion; and 5. By any sort of treason, or conspiracy, against our Sovereign and country.

Of those "who despise dominion, and blaspheme majesty," the Apostle St. Jude says: "These are murmurers, full of complaints, walking according to their own desires, and their mouth speaketh proud things, admiring persons for gain's sake." (Jude v. 8 and 16.)

19. When are Parents, Superiors, and Sovereigns not to be obeyed?

When they command anything unlawful before God.

"We ought to obey God rather than men." (Acts 5, 29.)—Examples: Joseph in the house of Putiphar; Susanna; the three Young Men at Babylon; the seven Machabees; the Apostles before the Council.

20. * How should young people behave towards the aged?

Young people should treat the aged respectfully, listen to their good advice, and, as far as possible, lighten the burden of their old age.

"Rise up before the hoary head, and honour the person of the aged man, and fear the Lord thy God." (Levit. 19, 32.)

Application.—Hearken now to your Parents, Teachers, Pastors, etc., and follow them, "Lest thou mourn at the last, and say: Why have I hated instruction, and my heart consented not to reproof, and have not heard the voice of them that taught me, and have not inclined my ear to masters?" (Prov. 5, 11—13.)

* *The Fourth Commandment (continued).*

21. Does the Fourth Commandment regard Children and Inferiors only?

It includes also the duties of Parents and Superiors.

22. What are the duties of Parents towards their children?

The first and most sacred duty of Parents is, to bring up their children for God, and for eternal life. Therefore, they should 1. Instruct them well themselves, and then get them well instructed, in the Catholic Religion; 2. Train them up, as early as possible, to a pious and virtuous life; 3. Set them good example; 4. Guard them against seduction; and 5. Correct their faults with Christian charity.

"And you, fathers, bring your children up in the discipline and correction of the Lord." (Ephes. 6, 4.)—"The child that is left to his own will, bringeth his mother to shame." (Prov. 29, 15.) "Withhold not correction from a child; for if thou strike him with the rod, he shall not die, and thou shalt deliver his soul from hell." (Prov. 23, 13. 14.)

23. How do Parents sin when they neglect these their duties?

They sin grievously, and, moreover, render themselves accessory to the sins of their children, and often are the cause of their eternal damnation. (Heli.)

24. Have Parents charge of the *eternal* salvation only of their children?

They have charge also of their *temporal* welfare and success; therefore, they sin, 1. When they inconsiderately squander their property; 2. When they do not take proper care of the food, clothing, or health of their children; or 3. When they neglect to accustom them early to labour, and to make them learn something useful.

25. What are the duties of Masters and Mistresses towards their servants?

They should 1. Not treat them harshly, but kindly; 2. Give them their just wages, and sufficient nourishment; 3. Urge them, by word and example, to fulfil their religious duties, and to do all that is right; and 4. Keep them from evil, and all occasions of sin.

"If thou have a faithful servant, let him be to thee as thy own soul: treat him as a brother." (Ecclus 33, 31.)—"Masters, do to your servants that which is just and equal, knowing that you also have a Master in Heaven." (Colos. 4, 1.) "But if any man have not care of his own, and especially of those of his house, he hath denied the faith, and is worse than an infidel." (1 Tim. 5, 8.)

26. What are the obligations of Temporal Superiors to their Inferiors?

Temporal Superiors are ordained by God for the good of their Inferiors; therefore they should 1. Promote their welfare as much as lies in their power; 2. Perform the duties of their office with wisdom and incorruptible justice; 3. Punish evil; and 4. Be to all a pattern of a Christian life.

"The power is God's minister to thee for good." (Rom. 13, 4.)—" And charging the judges, Josaphat said: Take heed what you do; for you exercise not the judgment of man, but of the Lord; and whatsoever you judge, it shall redound to you. There is no iniquity with the Lord our God, nor respect of persons, nor desire of gifts." (2 Paral. 19, 6. 7.) —Therefore, at elections for public offices, it is necessary above all things, to consider piety, judgment, and an honest and energetic will in the person to be elected.

Application.—Always honour your Temporal Rulers as the Ministers of God for your own good, and never listen to those enemies of all lawful order, who " promise liberty, whereas they themselves are the slaves of corruption." (2. Pet. 2, 19.)

The Fifth Commandment of God.

"Thou shalt not kill."

1. What sins does the Fifth Commandment forbid?
The Fifth Commandment forbids all sins by which we may injure our neighbour, or ourselves, whether as to the life of the body, or of the soul.

2. When do we injure our neighbour as to the life of his body?
1. When we kill, strike, or wound him in an unjust manner; and 2. When, by vexation or harsh treatment, we embitter and shorten his life.

3. What sin does he commit who kills his neighbour in an unjust manner?
He commits a heinous sin, a sin that cries to Heaven for vengeance; for 1. He wantonly invades the rights

of God; 2. He undermines the safety of human society; and 3. He plunges his neighbour into the greatest temporal, and often into eternal ruin.

"Whosoever shall shed man's blood, his blood shall be shed; for man was made to the image of God." (Gen. 9, 6.)—How murder is punished, even in this life, by tormenting remorse, and often by an ignominious death, we learn from the Examples of Cain (Gen. 4, 16), of Achab and Jezabel. (3 Kings 21, 22. & 4 Kings 9.)

4. Is it ever lawful to destroy human life?

Yes, it is lawful 1. For the Supreme Authority to do so in the execution of criminals (Rom. 13, 4); and 2. For others, in defence of their country, or, when necessary, in protecting life from unjust attack.

5.* Is it also lawful to send a man a challenge, or to accept his, to a duel in defence of our honour?

No; for such a duel is in any case, even if it be not for life and death, a great crime, which is in direct opposition to all order established by God and man; therefore, all those who are accessary to it, even all voluntary witnesses, incur excommunication.

6. Does the Fifth Commandment forbid only the actual crime of taking away the life of our neighbour?

It also forbids everything that leads and induces to the crime; as, Anger, hatred, envy, quarreling, abusive words, and imprecations.

"Whosoever hateth his brother is a murderer." (1 John 3, 15.) "But I say to you, that whosoever is angry with his brother, shall be in danger of the judgment." (Matt. 5, 22.)

7. When do we injure ourselves as to the life of our body?

1. When we take away our life; and 2. When we impair our health, or shorten our life, by intemperance in eating and drinking, by violent anger, by immoderate grief, &c.

8. What sin does he commit who deliberately makes away with himself?

He commits three horrible crimes: 1. A crime against the Divine Majesty, who alone has power over life and death; 2. A crime against his own soul, which he mercilessly plunges into eternal hell-fire; and 3. A crime against human society, and especially against his relations, on whom he brings inexpressible grief and disgrace.

9. How does the Church, therefore, punish suicide or self-murder?

She refuses Christian burial to the self-murderer, for his own punishment as well as to deter others from doing the same.

10. Are we never allowed to expose our life, or our health to danger?

Never without necessity; but, when a higher duty requires it, we may. (Matt. 10, 28.)

11. May we desire our own death?

No, we may not, when it proceeds from dejection, or despair; but we may, when we ardently desire to offend God no more, and to be united with Him in Heaven.

"I desire to be dissolved and to be with Christ."—(Phili. 1, 23.)

12. When do we injure our neighbour as to the life of his soul?

When we scandalize him; that is, when we deliberately seduce him to sin, or voluntarily influence him, and give him occasion, to commit it.

13.* Who render themselves guilty of this sin?

In general, all those who in any way incite, advise, or help others to do evil, command them to do it, or approve of it; and in particular, those, 1. Who use impious or filthy language, or dress themselves immodestly; 2. Who spread abroad bad books and pictures; 3. Who open their houses to thieves, drunkards, gamblers, or other wicked men, for their unlawful meetings; and 4. Those Superiors who give bad example, or who do not hinder evil, as they are in duty bound to do.

14. What should in particular deter us from giving scandal?

1. The thought, that he who gives scandal is a minister of Satan, destroying those souls which Jesus Christ has ransomed with His blood, by seducing them to sin.

"He (the devil) was a murderer from the beginning." (John 8, 44.)—"Destroy not him, for whom Christ died." (Rom. 14, 15.)

2. The dreadful consequences of seduction, since those who have themselves been seduced, generally seduce others, and thus the sin is continually propagated.

The whole human race corrupted through the descendants of Cain. (Gen. 6.)—Jeroboam's sin and punishment. (3 Kings 12—14.)

3. The awful sentence of Jesus Christ:

"He that shall scandalize one of these little ones that believe in Me, it were better for him that a mill-stone should be hanged about his neck, and that he should be drowned in the depth of the sea. Woe to the world because of scandals! Woe to that man by whom the scandal cometh!" (Matt. 18, 6. 7.)—Example of Eleazar, who chose to die rather than scandalize young men (2 Mac. 6); and of St. Paul. (1 Cor. 8, 13.)

15. What must we do when we have injured our neighbour as to his body or soul?

We must not only repent and confess the sin, but we must also, as far as it is in our power, repair the evil we have done.

16. What are we *commanded* by the Fifth Commandment?

We are commanded, 1. To live in peace and union with our neighbour; 2. To promote, according to our condition, his spiritual, as well as his corporal, welfare;

and 3. To take also reasonable care of our own life and health.

Application.—Never presume to curse, to abuse, or to strike any one; but, as it is becoming to a child of God, be peaceable, kind, and meek. Shun a seducer, as the devil; for he is about to kill your soul, let his words or promises be ever so charming and pleasing. Beware of murdering your neighbour's soul by any scandalous act or word.

The Sixth Commandment of God.

"Thou shalt not commit adultery."

1. What does the Sixth Commandment forbid?

The Sixth Commandment forbids, 1. Adultery and all sins of impurity; as, unchaste looks, words, jests, touches, and whatsoever else violates modesty; and 2. Everything that leads to impurity.

"But fornication and all uncleanness, let it not so much as be named among you, as becometh Saints, or obscenity, or foolish talking, or scurrility." (Eph. 5, 3. 4.)

2. What is it that generally leads to impurity?

1. Curiosity of the eyes; 2. Immodest dress; 3. Flatterers or seducers; 4. Obscene books, and scandalous pictures; 5. Nocturnal interviews, indecent plays and dances; 6. A too free intercourse with the other sex; 7. Drunkenness and revelry; and 8. Idleness and effeminacy.

3. Why must we most carefully guard against impurity?

1. Because no sin is more shameful; and 2. Because none is attended with such dreadful consequences.

4. Why is this sin so shameful?

Because man, who, as the image and temple of God, is called to a pure and holy life, is degraded by it to the level of an impure or unclean animal;

whence it is styled, Sin of *impurity* or *uncleanness*. (Comp. 1 Cor. 3, 17.)

5. What are the consequences of impurity?

1. It robs man of his innocence, and infects his body and soul; 2. It leads him to many other sins and vices, and often to murder and despair; and 3. It plunges him into misery, ignominy, and shame, and finally into eternal damnation.

"He that joineth himself to harlots, will be wicked; rottenness and worms shall inherit him." (Ecclus 19, 3.)—"The whoremongers shall have their portion in the pool burning with fire and brimstone." (Apoc. 21, 8.)

Examples: Impurity led David, Solomon, the two Elders (Dan. 13.), Herod, and Herodias into the greatest crimes. Chiefly on account of impurity, nearly the entire human race was destroyed by the deluge; Sodom and Gomorrha, by a rain of brimstone and fire; twenty-four thousand Israelites were put to death in the desert; and almost the whole tribe of Benjamin perished by the sword.

6.* Is every sin of impurity a grievous sin?

Yes, every sin of impurity which one commits knowingly and willingly either with himself or with others, is a mortal sin; "for know you this and understand," says St. Paul (Ephes. 5, 5.), "that no fornicator, or unclean person, hath inheritance in the kingdom of Christ and of God."

7.* Are all sins of impurity equally grievous?

No; some are more grievous than others, according to the persons with whom the sin is committed; or according as the sin is more heinous and unnatural, and its consequences are more pernicious.

8. What are we to do, when we doubt whether any thing is a sin against purity?

We must consult our Director, and, in the meantime, carefully avoid what we are doubtful of.

9. What are we *commanded* by the Sixth Commandment?

We are commanded to be decent and modest in all our thoughts, looks, words, and actions, and most carefully to preserve the innocence of our soul, as the greatest good, and the most beautiful ornament of man.

10. What means should we employ in order to preserve our innocence?

We should 1. Shun all bad company, and all occasions of sin (Ecclus 3, 27); 2. Carefully guard our senses, especially our eyes (Ps. 118, 37); 3. Often receive the Holy Sacraments; 4. In temptation recommend ourselves to God and to the Blessed Virgin; 5. Think that God sees everything, and that we may die at any moment (Ecclus 7, 40); and 6. We should earnestly exercise ourselves in humility, in the mortification of the flesh, and in self-denial (Gal. 5, 24.)

Application.—Love the innocence of your soul; often meditate on these words of the Holy Scripture: "O how beautiful is the chaste generation with glory! for the memory thereof is immortal, because it is known both with God and with men. It triumpheth crowned for ever, winning the reward of undefiled conflicts." (Wisd. 4, 1. 2.) Therefore, whether you are by yourself or with others, never say or do anything that may not be said or done before people of propriety; and should any one attempt to seduce you, repulse him, or seek for the protection of others. "My son, if sinners shall entice thee, consent not to them. If they shall say: Come with us, my son, walk not thou with them." (Prov. 1, 10—15.)

The Seventh Commandment of God.
"Thou shalt not steal."

1. What does the Seventh Commandment forbid?

The Seventh Commandment forbids us to injure our neighbour in his property by robbery or theft, by cheating, usury, or in any other unjust way.

2. Who are guilty of robbery or theft?

Not only those who are properly called robbers and thieves, but also all those, 1. Who give them advice or assistance; 2. Who buy, sell, hide, or keep, stolen goods; 3. Who do not return the things they have found or borrowed; 4. Who do not pay their debts; and 5. All those who beg without need, and thus defraud the real poor of their alms.

3. Who are guilty of cheating?

1. Those who impose upon their neighbours in their dealings by giving them, for instance, false weight or measure, bad money, or bad articles; 2. Those who ask too much for their labour or merchandize; 3. Those who remove the land-marks of their neighbours; 4. Those who set fire to their property in order to get money at the insurance-office; and 5. Those who counterfeit notes or documents, carry on unnecessary or unjust law-suits, endeavour to bribe judges or witnesses, &c.

4. Who are guilty of usury?

1. Those who ask unlawful interest for the money they lend; 2. Those who purchase corn or other things, in order to raise the prices; and 3. In general, all those who take advantage of their neighbour's necessity or ignorance.

5. In what other ways is the Seventh Commandment broken?

1. When we damage other people's meadows, cornfields, or trees; 2. When we wound or kill their animals; 3. When, by gambling or extravagance, we distress our family; 4. When we neglect the work which we are in duty bound to perform; and 5. When we defame tradesmen or merchants, in order to withdraw their customers from them; and generally, as often as we unjustly injure our neighbour in his property.

6.* How may we also grievously sin against the Seventh Commandment by petty thefts or frauds?

1. When we so often repeat them, that the owner suffers a considerable loss; or, when we have only the intention, thus to repeat them; and 2. When the loss of a thing trifling in itself, causes our neighbour a considerable injury.

7. May servants give alms of the property of their masters?

No; unless their masters know it, and approve of it.

8. What must we do when we are in possession of ill-gotten goods, or have unjustly injured our neighbour?

We must restore the ill-gotten goods, and repair, as far as we are able, the injury done; without which we cannot obtain pardon from God.

9. Who is bound to make restitution or reparation?

1. He who is in possession of the things stolen, or of their value, or who has really done the injury;

2. If he does not do it, the obligation devolves on those who, by counsel or action, were accessary to the sin, or who did not hinder it, although they were able, and their conventional or official duties obliged them to do so.

10.* How much must be restored?

1. If one has *knowingly* and *unjustly* taken or detained his neighbour's goods, he must fully indemnify him.

2. If he did it *unknowingly* and *unwillingly*, he must, as soon as he comes to know that it is another man's property, restore all that is still left, and as much more as his wealth has increased by it.

In the former case, restitution must be made not only of the things stolen, or, if they are gone, of their value, but also of that which, in the meantime, they have produced; the expenses, however, being deducted, which even the owner would not have been able to avoid. And, in general, the owner must be compensated for all the profits which he has been deprived of, and for all the losses he has suffered. In the latter case, we are bound to restore all that which, after deducting the expenses, is still remaining of the ill-gotten goods and of their produce, and, in general, as much as, by their possession and temporary use, we have become the richer.

11. To whom must restitution of the ill-gotten goods be made?

To the owner, or to his heirs; but if this be not possible, they must be given to the poor, or be appropriated to religious purposes.

12. What must they do who cannot immediately make restitution?

They must sincerely have the intention of doing so, as soon as they can; and, in the meantime, they must employ all possible means to enable themselves to perform this duty.

13. What should we bear in mind in order to guard against stealing, or against neglecting to make restitution?

1. That death will eventually wrest the ill-gotten goods from us, and, perhaps, sooner than we expect; 2. That the stolen property will bring us, not happiness and blessing, but misfortune and malediction, uneasiness, and a miserable end;† and 3. That there is no greater foolishness than to forfeit Heaven for the perishable things of this world, and to plunge our soul into unquenchable fire.‡

†. "He who soweth iniquity shall reap evils." (Prov. 22, 8.)—‡ "What doth it profit a man if he gain the whole world, and suffer the loss of his own soul? Or what exchange shall a man give for his soul?" (Matt. 16, 26.)

14. What are we *commanded* by the Seventh Commandment?

We are commanded to give to every one his due, and to be charitable to our neighbour.

Application.—Give to every one his own, and be contented with what you have. "A little, justly gained, is better than much, gained unjustly." Never steal anything, be it ever so little, and mind this true saying: "Small beginnings make great endings." Beware of daintiness, drunkenness, idleness, gambling, vain show, and finery; for all this leads people to robbery and theft, and brings them to ruin.

The Eighth Commandment of God.

"Thou shalt not bear false witness against thy neighbour."

1. What does the Eighth Commandment forbid?
The Eighth Commandment forbids above all to give false evidence; that is, to say in a court of justice what is not true.

"And bringing two men, sons of the devil, they made them sit against him (Naboth); and they, like men of the devil, bore witness against him before the people." (3 Kings, 21, 13.)

2. How are we to give evidence in a court of justice?
We must tell the mere truth, just as we know it, and neither more nor less.

3. What other sins are forbidden by the Eighth Commandment?
1. Lies and hypocrisy; 2. Detraction and calumny or slander; 3. False suspicion and rash judgment; and, in general, all sins by which the honour or character of our neighbour is injured.

4. What is meant by a lie?
To say knowingly and deliberately what is not true.

5. Is it ever lawful to tell a lie?
No; it is never lawful to tell a lie, neither for our own, nor for another's benefit, not even in jest or need; for every lie is essentially opposed to God, who is truth itself.

"A lie is a foul blot in a man." (Ecclus 20, 26.)—"Lying lips are an abomination to the Lord." (Prov. 12, 22.) Ex.: Punishment of Ananias and Saphira. (Acts 5.) Although it is never lawful to tell an untruth, yet we are sometimes bound by charity or official duty to conceal the truth.

6. How do we sin by hypocrisy?
By pretending to be better or more pious than we really are, in order thereby to deceive others.

"Woe to you, Scribes and Pharisees, hypocrites! because you are like to whited sepulchres, which outwardly appear to men beautiful, but within are full of dead men's bones, and of all filthiness. So you also outwardly indeed appear to men just, but inwardly you are full of hypocrisy and iniquity." (Matt. 23, 27. 28.)

7. How do we sin by detraction?
By revealing the faults of others without any necessity?

8. When is it allowed to reveal the faults of others?
We are allowed, and even bound to reveal them, 1. When it is for the good of the guilty person; or 2. When it is necessary for preventing a greater evil.

9. What is to be observed in making such revelation?
1. The revelation must proceed from a pure motive of charity, and be made to such only as are able to remedy the evil; 2. The fault is not to be exaggerated, nor is an uncertain one to be represented as certain.

10. How do we sin by calumny or slander?
By imputing faults to our neighbour which he has not at all, or by exaggerating his real faults.

"If a serpent bite in silence, he is nothing better that backbiteth secretly." (Eccles 10, 11.) Ex.: Aman. (Esth. 13.)

11.* Is every calumny or detraction equally sinful?
No; the sin is the greater, 1. The more important the fault is, and the more considerable the person of whom it is mentioned; 2. The greater the loss and injury is which he suffers by it; 3. The more people there are who hear it; and 4. The worse our intention is in divulging it.

A most injurious and detestable sin is "*Tale-bearing*" or "*Whispering*," i.e. when we relate to a person what another has said of him, and thus create hatred and dissension between them. "The *Whisperer* and the double-tongued is accursed; for he hath troubled many that were at peace." (Ecclus 28, 15.)

12. Is it also a sin, even to listen to detraction or calumny?

Yes, it is a sin, 1. To listen with delight to detraction or calumny; 2. Not to prevent it, when it is in our power; and 3. To occasion and encourage it by asking questions, or by approving of it.

"Hedge in thy ears with thorns, hear not a wicked tongue." (Ecclus 28, 28.)—"The north wind driveth away rain, as doth a sad countenance a backbiting tongue." (Prov. 25, 23.)

13. What is he obliged to do, who, by slander or abusive language, has injured the character of his neighbour?

He is obliged, 1. To retract the slander, or to beg pardon; and 2. To repair all the injury he has done him.

"A good name is better than great riches." (Prov. 22, 1.) Therefore, it is an obligation to restore the former as well as the latter.

14. Must we also retract when we have divulged *true*, but hidden faults?

No; in such a case we should try to excuse our neighbour, and to repair his honour by some other lawful means.

15. When do we sin by false suspicion and rash judgment?

We sin, 1. By *false suspicion*, when, without sufficient reason, we surmise evil of our neighbour; and 2. By *rash judgment*, when, without sufficient reason, we believe the evil to be true and certain.

"Judge not, that you may not be judged. . . . . . Why seest thou the mote that is in thy brother's eye, and seest not the beam that is in thy own eye?" (Matt. 7, 1. 3.)

16. What are we *commanded* by the Eighth Commandment?

We are commanded, 1. To speak the truth in all things; 2. To be solicitous for the honour and reputation of every one; and 3. To bridle especially our tongue.

17. How far should we also be solicitous for our own honour?

As far as the honour of God, the edification of our neighbour, and the duties of our state of life require it.

"We forecast what may be good not only before God, but also before men." (2 Cor. 8, 21.)—Yet we should always be ready, to suffer also reproach and ignominy for our own and our neighbour's salvation, or for the sake of Jesus Christ. In this sense it is said: "If one strike thee on thy right cheek, turn to him also the other;" (Matt. 5, 39) and: "If you be reproached for the name of Christ, you shall be blessed." (1 Pet. 4, 14.) "And they (the Apostles) indeed went from the presence of the Council, rejoicing that they were accounted worthy to suffer reproach for the name of Jesus." (Acts 5, 41.)

18. How are we to be solicitous for our own reputation?

By no other but lawful means, and, above all, by continually leading a Christian life,† and by avoiding, to the best of our power, even the least appearance of evil.‡

† "But with modesty and fear, having a good conscience: that whereas they speak evil of you, they may be ashamed who falsely accuse your good conversation in Christ." (1. Pet. 3, 16.)—‡ "From all appearance of evil refrain yourselves." (1 Thess. 5, 22.)

19.* How may we best guard against the sins of the tongue?

1. By not talking inconsiderately, and by bearing in mind that we have to give an account of every idle word we speak (Matt. 12, 36.); and 2. By keeping our heart free from ambition, envy, hatred, vengeance, &c.

1. "He that keepeth his mouth, keepeth his soul; but he that hath no guard on his speech, shall meet with evils."

(Prov. 13, 3.)—2. "O generation of vipers, how can you speak good things, whereas you are evil? for out of the abundance of the heart the mouth speaketh." (Matt. 12, 34.)

Application.—Detest all lies and falsehoods. Never speak uncharitably of your neighbour, nor grieve him by reproachful words: "The stroke of a whip maketh a blue mark; but the stroke of the tongue will break the bones." (Ecclus 28, 21.) However, do not conceal his faults from those who can correct them.

The Ninth and Tenth Commandments of God.

"Thou shalt not covet thy neighbour's wife."
"Thou shalt not covet thy neighbour's goods."

1. What does the Ninth Commandment forbid?

The Ninth Commandment especially forbids the desire to have another man's wife,† and in general, all impure thoughts and desires.

† "Whosoever shall look on a woman to lust after her, hath already committed adultery with her in his heart." (Matt. 5, 28.)

2. Are impure thoughts and desires always sins?

As long as they displease us, and we endeavour to banish them from our mind, they are not sins.

3. When do we sin by impure thoughts?

We sin by impure thoughts, when we voluntarily represent immodest things, or actions, to our mind, and when we voluntarily take pleasure in them.

As it is a sin against purity, designedly to look at immodest things, so it is also a sin, to represent such things to our mind, or, when such representations are involuntary, willingly to take complacency or pleasure in them.

4. When do we sin by impure desires?

We sin by impure desires, when we voluntarily wish to see, hear, or do, something that is contrary to chastity or purity.

5. What should we do, when we are tempted by impure thoughts and desires?

1. We should, in the very beginning, earnestly resist them, and implore the assistance of God; and 2. When the temptation continues, we should not be discouraged, but persevere, and endeavour to occupy ourselves.

1. "As I knew that I could not otherwise be continent, except God gave it, I went to the Lord, and besought Him with my whole heart." (Wisd. 8, 21.)—2. "Blessed is the man that endureth temptation; for when he hath been proved, he shall receive the crown of life." (James 1, 12.)

6. What are we *commanded* by the Ninth Commandment?

We are commanded to think on such things only, as are modest and holy. (Philip. 4, 8.)

7. What does the Tenth Commandment forbid?

The Tenth Commandment forbids all voluntary desire of our neighbour's goods.

"The desire of money is the root of all evils." (1 Tim. 6, 10.)—Example: Achab. (3 Kings 21.)

8. What are we *commanded* by the Tenth Commandment?

We are commanded to be contented with what is our own, and not to be envious of what belongs to others.

9. * How can a Christian, even in poverty, be easily contented with his own?

By bearing in mind, 1. That a clean conscience is the greatest treasure; 2. That our true home is in the other world; 3. That Christ also has become poor for our sake, and that one day He will magnificently reward all those who patiently suffer poverty for His sake.

10. Why does God forbid not only all evil actions, but also all evil thoughts and desires?

Because evil thoughts and desires defile the heart, and finally lead also to evil actions.

"Man seeth those things that appear, but the Lord

beholdeth the heart." (1 Kings 16, 7.)—"From the heart come forth evil thoughts, murders, adulteries," etc. (Matt. 15, 19.)

Application.—Turn your thoughts towards eternity, and you will have no difficulty to despise all that is temporal. "Walk in the spirit," *i.e.* love God, the Supreme Good, "and you shall not fulfil the lusts of the flesh." (Gal. 5, 16.)—Happy is he who can truly say: "My soul longeth and fainteth for the courts of the Lord; my heart and my flesh have rejoiced in the living God." (Ps. 83, 3.)

On the Six Commandments of the Church.

1. Are there, besides the Commandments of God, any others which Christians are bound to keep?

Yes, the Commandments of the Church.

2. Whence has the Church a right to give Commandments?

From Jesus Christ Himself, who has commissioned His Church to guide and govern the faithful in His name. (Page 142. Quest. 42—44.)

Therefore, to despise the Commandments of the Church, is to despise Christ Himself. "He that heareth you, heareth Me; and he that despiseth you, despiseth Me." (Luke 10, 16.)

3. Has the Church no further right than to give Commandments?

She has also a right to watch over the observance of these Commandments, and to punish those who break them; for instance, to refuse them the Holy Sacraments (Matt. 18, 18.), and finally to exclude them from the Church, and to deprive them of Christian burial when they die. (1 Cor. 5, 3—5.)—(See Page 132, Quest. 10.)

4. Which are the general or chief Commandments of the Church?

These six:

1. To keep certain appointed days holy, with the obligation of resting from servile works.

2. To hear Mass on all Sundays and Holy-days of obligation.

3. To keep the days of fasting and abstinence appointed by the Church.

4. To confess our sins to our Pastor at least once a year.

5. To receive the Blessed Sacrament at least once a year, and that at Easter or thereabouts.

6. Not to marry within certain degrees of kindred, or privately without witnesses, nor to solemnize marriage at the forbidden times.

5. Why has the Church given us these Commandments?

1. To explain the Commandments of God more precisely, and to determine more particularly, how they are to be kept; and 2. To lead us to a religious and penitential life, and thereby to secure our eternal salvation.

6. How do these Commandments of the Church bind us?

They bind us strictly, that is, under pain of grievous sin.

"If he will not hear the Church, let him be to thee as the heathen and publican." (Matt. 18, 17.)—Even in the Old Law God had ordained: "He that will be proud, and refuse to obey the commandment of the Priest, that man shall die, and thou shalt take away the evil from Israel; and all the people hearing it shall fear, that no one afterwards swell with pride." (Deut. 17, 12. 13.)

Application.—Be determined, always humbly and conscientiously to observe the Commandments and Ordinances of the Church, that one day Jesus Christ may own you as a faithful sheep of His flock which He has charged St. Peter and his Successors to feed.

The First Commandment of the Church.

1. What are we commanded by the First Commandment of the Church?

By the First Commandment, we are commanded to keep the Holy-days which the Church has instituted in honour of our Lord and of his Saints, in the same manner as the Sundays.

As in the Old Law, on certain occasions, for instance, after the victory gained by the Jews over Holofernes (Judith 16, 31.), and over Aman (Esther 9.), Festivals were instituted in memory of the blessings received from God; so also has the Christian Church, in different times, most justly commanded, that several Holy-days or Anniversaries should be celebrated in honour of Jesus Christ, of His glorious Mother, and of the Saints, His glorified friends.

2. For what purpose were the Feasts of our Lord instituted?

They were instituted, that we should 1. Devoutly meditate on the mysteries of our Redemption; 2. Thank God for His graces; and 3. Renew our zeal in serving Him, and thus render ourselves worthy of the fruits of Redemption.

In the course of each Ecclesiastical Year, the whole life of Jesus Christ is so represented to us in its principal parts, as if the mysteries, which we commemorate, were renewed before our eyes. Therefore, it is the intention of the Church, that we should every year contemplate with her the life of Christ from its beginning to its end. In Advent, we should, by repentance and longing expectation, prepare the way for the coming of our Redeemer into our hearts; in Lent, we should, by penance and mortification, participate in His sufferings, die to sin, and spiritually rise with Him to a new life at Easter. At the approach of the Feast of Pentecost, we should ardently long for the gifts of the Holy Ghost, and then continually endeavour to co-operate with the grace received.

3. Why were the Feasts of the Saints instituted?

That we may 1. Praise the Lord for the graces which he has bestowed upon them, and through them, upon us also; 2. Represent to our mind their exemplary virtues upon earth, and their eternal bliss in Heaven, and resolve to imitate them; and 3. Implore their intercession with God.

4.* Can the Church also suppress Holy-days?

As she has full power to institute Holy-days, so she has also a right to suppress them again, to transfer them, or to limit them to certain places, when time and circumstances require it.

The doctrine of the Church always is, and must be, one and the same, because it comes from God; but it is not so with her regulations and laws of discipline, which she makes after the lapse of ages, and must adapt to variety of times and places. Therefore, without detriment to the unity of her doctrine, there may be a difference in the celebration of her Festivals.

Application.—Prepare yourself, in conformity with the spirit of the Church, as fervently for every chief Festival of the year, as if it were the last in your life. Beware of profaning the Holy-days of obligation by servile work, by excesses, or sinful amusements.

The Second Commandment of the Church.

1. What are we commanded by the Second Commandment of the Church?

By the Second Commandment, we are commanded to assist, on all Sundays and Holy-days of obligation, at the Holy Sacrifice of the Mass with due attention, reverence, and devotion.

2. Why are we commanded especially to hear Mass on Sundays and Holy-days of obligation?

Because the Sacrifice of the Mass is the most holy and salutary of all Divine Services, and that in which the Most High is honoured in the most worthy manner.

3. Who are obliged to hear Mass on Sundays and Holy-days of obligation?

All who have sufficiently attained the use of reason (which is generally the case about the age of seven), are strictly bound to hear Mass, unless weighty reasons, as illness, nursing the sick, &c., excuse them from it.

4. When do we sin against the Second Commandment of the Church?

1. When, through our own fault, we lose Mass either entirely, or a part of it; and 2. When during Mass we give way to voluntary distractions, look about through curiosity, talk, laugh, or otherwise behave irreverently.

"The Lord is in His holy temple: let all the earth keep silence before Him." (Hab. 2, 20.)

5.* Where should the faithful hear Mass on Sundays and Holy-days?

In the Parish Church when it is possible; but they can also fulfil this obligation in any other public church.

6.* Why does the Church wish that the faithful should attend Divine Service especially in their Parish Church?

Because in the Parish Church the Pastor preaches, and offers the Sacrifice of the Mass principally for his parishioners.

7. Does the Second Commandment of the Church also command us to hear the Sermon?

According to the letter it does not; but according to the spirit, it certainly does; for the hearing of the word of God also belongs to the worthy celebration of the Sundays and Holy-days, and is, in general, an essential duty of a Christian.

In the primitive Church, the Sermon was generally preached at Mass after the Gospel; therefore, the Church which commands us to hear Mass, had no occasion for giving a particular and express Commandment to hear the Sermon.

8. Why are all Christians bound to hear the word of God?

1. Because the word of God is for all a most powerful means of sanctification, ordained by God himself; 2. Because it is indispensable to all, to be repeatedly reminded of the truths of religion, and to be admonished to live up to them; and 3. Because all are obliged to mutual edification, by setting one another an example of Christian piety.

"He that is of God, heareth the words of God; therefore you hear them not, because you are not of God." (John 8, 47.) —It is, therefore, a bad sign, when people neglect to hear the word of God.

9. How should we hear the word of God?

We should 1. Listen to it with earnest attention, and with an ardent desire of working out our salvation; and 2. We should reflect well upon it, apply it to ourselves, and faithfully follow it.

"Blessed are they who hear the word of God and keep it." (Luke 11, 28. Comp. Luke 8, 5—15.)

Application.—Make it a rule, to assist with devotion on Sundays and Holy-days at the Divine Service in the morning and in the afternoon, and to prefer your Parish Church to any other.

The Third Commandment of the Church.

1. What are we commanded by the Third Commandment of the Church?

By the Third Commandment, we are commanded to observe the days of fasting and abstinence appointed by the Church.

2. Which are the days of fasting appointed by the Church?

1. The "*Forty Days of Lent,*" that is, every day from Ash-Wednesday to Easter, the Sundays excepted;

2. The "*Ember-days,*" that is, the Wednesday,

Friday, and Saturday, 1. After the third Sunday of Advent; 2. After the first Sunday of Lent; 3. After Whitsunday; and 4. After the Feast of the Exaltation of the Cross.

3. The "*Vigils*" or Eves of great Festivals.

The *Forty Days of Lent* are ordained in imitation of the forty days' Fast of Jesus Christ, in remembrance of His bitter Passion and Death, and that we may worthily prepare ourselves for the celebration of Easter.—The *Ember-days* are ordained that the faithful may thank God for the blessings they have received in each quarter of the year; that in each season they may be reminded to do penance; and also, that they may obtain of God worthy Priests, these being generally the days of their ordination.—By the *Vigils*, we are to prepare ourselves for the worthy celebration of great Festivals.—In many places most of the Vigils have been abolished, and two Fast-days (Wednesday and Friday) in each week of *Advent*, have been substituted.

3. Is it only commanded to abstain from flesh-meat on these Fast-days?

No; it is also commanded to take but one meal in the day, and that not before noon. However, a small collation at night is not forbidden.

The assertion, that "the fast is not broken by eating little at repeated times," has been condemned by the Church. (Alexand. VII. Propos. 29.)

4. Who is obliged to fast in this manner?

Every Christian who has completed the age of twenty-one, and is not excused by any just cause.

5. Who are excused from fasting?

Those who are sick, convalescent, worn out with age, and such as have either to work hard, or would by fasting be prevented from discharging the duties of their calling.

6. When is it commanded to abstain from flesh-meat?

It is commanded to abstain from flesh-meat, unless a dispensation be obtained, 1. On all Fridays and Saturdays (Christmas-day excepted); 2. On the Sundays of Lent; and 3. On all Fasting-days.

In several Dioceses, however, this has been greatly mitigated; so that on many days, on which, according to the general Precept of the Church, the eating of flesh-meat is forbidden, it is now allowed by a dispensation, which the Bishops, authorized by the Pope, give annually to their diocesans. Every one has to conform himself to the practice approved of by the Ecclesiastical Superior of his Diocese.

7. Who are bound to abstain from flesh-meat?

All Christians who have attained the age of seven, unless a just cause, as illness, poverty, &c., excuse them from it.

8. What ought they to do who cannot well abstain from flesh-meat?

They must, through their Pastor, apply to the Bishop for a dispensation, and perform other good works instead.

9. Why does the Church command fasting?

Because fasting is acceptable to God, and very wholesome to us.

10. Why do we say that fasting is acceptable to God?

1. Because God has often recommended fasting, and shown His favour and mercy to those who practised it;† 2. Because Jesus Christ, the Apostles, and the Saints of all times, have fasted;‡ and 3. Because fasting humbles our pride,§ and moderates our sensual desires.

† "Be converted to Me with all your heart, in fasting, and in weeping, and in mourning." (Joel 2, 12.)—"This kind (of devils) is not cast out but by prayer and fasting." (Matt. 17, 20.)—Examples: Deut. 9, 18. 19. Judith 4, 7—12. II. Paral. 20, 3. &c.—‡ Matt. 4, 2. Acts 13, 3. & 14, 22. So did Moses, Samuel, David, Daniel, Judith, Esther, the Macchabees, the widow Anna, and others.—§ "I humbled my soul with fasting." (Ps. 34, 13.)

11. How is fasting useful and wholesome to us?

1. By fasting, we make satisfaction to God for the sins we have committed, and thus avert the punishment deserved; (The Ninivites. Jonas 3.)

2. We bring our passions into subjection, and thus gain strength not to relapse into sin;

3. Prayer and the practice of virtue are rendered easier to us, and we obtain the more certainly the grace of God and eternal salvation.

12.* Is it not superstitious to abstain from certain kinds of food?

It is superstitious, if we abstain from certain food, as if it were bad and unclean in itself, as some Heretics asserted;† but it is not so by any means, if we do it in the spirit of obedience and penance, as the Catholic Church prescribes.‡

† St. Paul combated this heresy (1 Tim. 4, 1—4); and also the Catholic Church has at all times combated and condemned it.—‡ God Himself forbade certain meats to the Jews (Levit. 11, 2. &c.), and the Apostles to the first Christians. (Acts 15, 29.)—St. John, the Baptist, ate nothing but locusts and wild honey. (Mark 1, 6.)— Eleazar and the seven Machabean Brothers, with their mother, chose to suffer the most painful death, rather than transgress the law of God by eating swine's flesh.— (2. Mach. 6 and 7.)

13. But does not our Saviour clearly say: "Not that which goeth into the mouth defileth a man?"

Yes; but the disobedience which proceeds from the heart defiles him (Matt. 15, 11. 18), as it is proved by the fall of our first parents.

Let, however, no one believe that the breaking of the fast is only then a grievous sin, when it proceeds from a *contempt* of the Commandment, or from a *deliberate* resistance to the Church. This opinion is erroneous, and has been expressly condemned by the Church. (Alexand. VII. Propos. 23.) Nay, it is even a culpable disobedience, when one knowingly and deliberately does what the Church has forbidden, though it be neither attended with obstinacy, nor with contempt of the Commandment.

14. Should we, on Fasting-days, content ourselves with abstaining from food?

No; we should, according to the intention of the Church, spend these days in the spirit of penance, and sanctify them by prayer and good works. (Isai. 58, 6. 7.)

Application.—Respect the Commandment of fasting and abstinence as a Commandment which God Himself has given you through His Church, and consider it an honour to observe it strictly.

The Fourth and Fifth Commandments of the Church.

1. What are we commanded by the Fourth and Fifth Commandments of the Church?

By the Fourth and Fifth Commandments, we are commanded, 1. To confess our sins faithfully, at least once a year, to our Pastor, and 2. To receive Holy Communion worthily at Easter or thereabouts.

2. Who is meant by our Pastor?

Any Priest, authorized by his Bishop to hear confessions.

In former times, the faithful were commanded by the Church to confess their sins once a year to their own Parish Priest, or to ask leave of him, if they wished to confess to another Priest. Hence comes this form of the Commandment, which is still in use in some Dioceses: "Thou shalt confess thy sins once a year to thy Parish Priest, or, with his permission, to another."

3. Where are we to receive Easter Communion?

Conformably to a Precept of the Church, we are to receive it in the Parish Church, if not excused by an impossibility, or by a general or particular permission to do otherwise.

4. At what age are we obliged to go to Confession and Communion?

As soon as we come to the use of reason, and are sufficiently instructed to receive the Holy Sacraments with fruit; which must be left to the decision of our Pastor.

5.* Why has the Church commanded that the Blessed Sacrament should be received in Easter-time?

1. Because Jesus Christ instituted the Holy Eucharist within this time; and 2. Because within this time, He died, and rose again from the dead, and, therefore, we also should die to sin, and lead a new life.

6. Ought we to think it sufficient to receive Holy Communion once in a year?

No; it is the intention and most earnest desire of our holy Church, that we should very often partake of this invaluable grace.

Example of the first Christians. (Acts 2.)

7.* Why then does the Church not command us to communicate oftener?

1. Because the love of God and the care for our souls should alone be sufficient motives to induce us to do so; and 2. Because the Church wishes to prescribe, under pain of excommunication, only what she deems absolutely necessary.

Application.—Make it a rule to go to Confession and Communion at least once a month.

(On the Sixth Commandment of the Church, "Not to marry within certain degrees of kindred, or privately without witnesses, nor to solemnize marriage at the forbidden times," see the Sacrament of Matrimony, Quest. 7, 14, and 15.)

ON THE VIOLATION OF THE COMMANDMENTS.

§ 1. *On Sin in General.*

1. What is sin?
Sin is a wilful violation of the Law of God.

2. In how many ways may we sin?
We may sin, 1. By *bad* thoughts, desires, words, and actions; and 2. Also by the omission of the *good* which we are bound to do.

3. Are all sins equally grievous?

No; there are grievous sins, which are also called *mortal;* and there are lesser ones, which are also called *venial*.

Some sins in the Holy Scripture are compared to *motes*, and others to *beams* (Matt. 7, 3); and it is also written of the just man, that "he shall fall seven times." (Prov. 24, 16.)

4. When do we commit mortal sin?

We commit mortal sins when we wilfully violate the Law of God in an important matter.

5. Why are grievous sins also called *mortal* sins?

Because, by grievous sins, the soul loses supernatural life, that is, sanctifying grace, and renders herself guilty of eternal death, or everlasting damnation.

"Sin, when it is completed, begetteth death." (James 1, 15.) —"I know thy works, that thou hast the name of being alive, and thou art dead." (Apoc. 3, 1.)

6. When do we commit venial sin?

We commit venial sin when we transgress the Law of God in an unimportant matter only, or not quite voluntarily.

7. When is the transgression not quite voluntary?

When, with our understanding, we do not sufficiently perceive the evil, or, with our will, we do not fully consent to it.

8. Why are lesser sins also called *venial* sins?

Because they can be forgiven more easily, and even without Confession.

9. Should we dread only grievous sins?

No; we should dread, and carefully avoid any sin, whether it be grievous or venial, as the greatest evil on earth.

"How can I do this wicked thing, and sin against my God?" (Gen. 39, 9.)

10. What should deter us from committing sin?

The consideration of its malice and evil consequences.

11. In what does the malice of mortal sin principally consist?

In this, that mortal sin is—

1. A grievous offence against God, our Supreme Lord, and the most criminal disobedience to His holy will;

2. The most shameful ingratitude to God, our greatest Benefactor and best Father;

3. Detestable infidelity to our most amiable Redeemer, and contempt of His graces and merits.

1. "Thou hast broken My yoke, and thou saidst: I will not serve." (Jerem. 2, 20.)—2. "Hear, O ye heavens, and give ear, O earth, for the Lord hath spoken; I have brought up children and exalted them; but they have despised Me." (Isai. 1, 2.)—3. Of those, "who were once illuminated, have tasted also the heavenly gift, and were made partakers of the Holy Ghost, and are fallen away (from God by mortal sin)," St. Paul says, "that they crucify again to themselves the Son of God, and make Him a mockery." (Heb. 6, 4—6.) "If any man love not our Lord Jesus Christ, let him be anathema." (1. Cor. 16, 22.)

12. Can we comprehend the full malice of an offence against God?

We cannot, because we do not comprehend the infinite greatness and goodness of the Lord our God, who is offended by sin.

13. What most of all shows us the malice and guilt of an offence against God?

1. The grievous punishment of the wicked angels, and of our first parents; 2. The everlasting punishment in Hell, which every mortal sin deserves; and 3. The most bitter Passion and Death which the Only Son of God suffered for our sins.

14. What are the consequences of mortal sin?

Mortal sin 1. Separates us from God, and deprives us of His love and friendship; 2. It disfigures in us the image of God, and disturbs the peace of our conscience; 3. It robs us of all merits, and of our heirship to Heaven; and 4. It draws upon us the judgments of God, and lastly, eternal damnation.

"They that commit sin and iniquity, are enemies of their own soul." (Tob. 12, 10.)—Examples: Cain, Antiochus, Judas. Parable of the rich man.

15. Why should we also carefully avoid venial sin?

1. Because venial sin also is an offence against God, and is, therefore, after mortal sin, the greatest of all evils;

2. Because it weakens the life of the soul, and hinders many graces which God intends to give us; and

3. Because it also brings many punishments of God upon us, and leads us by degrees to grievous sins.

"He that is unjust in that which is little, is unjust also in that which is greater." (Luke 16, 10.)—"Behold how small a fire what a great wood it kindleth!" (James 3, 5.)

Application.—"My Son, all the days of thy life have God in thy mind, and take heed thou never consent to sin. . . . . We lead, indeed, a poor life; but we shall have many good things, if we fear God, and depart from all sin, and do that which is good." (Tob. 4, 6. 23.)

§. 2. *On the different Kinds of Sin.*

16. What particular kinds of sin are there?

1. The Seven Capital or Deadly Sins; 2. the Six Sins against the Holy Ghost; 3. The Four Sins crying to Heaven for Vengeance; and 4. The Nine Ways of being accessary to another Person's Sins.

17. Which are the Seven Capital Sins?

1. Pride; 2. Covetousness; 3. Lust; 4. Anger; 5. Gluttony; 6. Envy; and 7. Sloth.

18. Are these sins always grievous?

They are grievous sins, as often as a weighty duty either to God, our neighbour, or ourselves, is violated by them.

19. Why are they called Capital Sins?
Because they are so many main sources from which all other sins take their rise.

20. When do we sin by *Pride*?
When we think too much of ourselves, do not give God the honour due to Him, and despise our neighbour.

From Pride spring especially: Vanity, ambition, hypocrisy, disobedience, and resistance to Superiors; coldness and hard-heartedness towards Inferiors; an inordinate desire of ruling; quarrel and strife; ingratitude, envy, cruelty, infidelity and heresy, hatred of God. Examples: Lucifer, Nabuchodonosor, Holofernes, Aman, Herod, the Pharisee, &c. —" Pride is hateful before God and men. It is the beginning of all sin: he that holdeth it shall be filled with maledictions, and it shall ruin him in the end." (Ecclus 10, 7. 15.)

21. When do we sin by *Covetousness*?
When we inordinately seek and love money or other worldly goods, and are hard-hearted towards those who are in distress.

Covetousness, or Avarice, leads people to an excessive care for earthly things, to hardness of heart, lying, perjury, theft, fraud, usury, simony, treachery, superstitious seeking after hidden treasures, to manslaughter and murder.—Examples: Achan, Achab, Giezi, Judas, Ananias and Saphira.—"There is not a more wicked thing than to love money; for such a one setteth even his own soul to sale." (Ecclus 10, 10.)— "They that will become rich, fall into temptation, and into the snare of the devil, and into many unprofitable and hurtful desires, which drown men into destruction and perdition." (1 Tim. 6, 9.)

22. How do we sin by *Lust*?
By indulging in immodest, or impure, thoughts, desires, words, or actions.

The ordinary effects of Lust, or Impurity, are: Aversion to prayer and to all that is good; excessive fondness for amusement and dissipation; neglect of the duties of our state of life; great desire of attracting notice; insensibility and cruelty; all sorts of shameless excesses and of unnatural crimes; seduction of innocence; false promises and oaths; theft, ruin of health and of domestic happiness; enmity, duels, suicide or self-murder; and likewise: atheism, sacrilege, worship of the devil, madness, and despair. (See the Sixth Commandment of God.)

23. When do we sin by *Anger?*
When we are exasperated at that which displeases us, fly into a passion, and suffer ourselves to be carried away by a violent desire of revenge.

Anger leads to hatred, enmity, quarrelling, cursing, blaspheming, reviling, and to all the sins and crimes against the Fifth Commandment of God. Examples: Esau, whilst in anger, designs to kill his brother Jacob; Absolon kills his brother Amnon.—" Let all bitterness, and anger, and indignation, and clamour, and blasphemy, be put away from you, with all malice." (Ephes. 4, 31.)

24. When do we sin by *Gluttony?*
When we eat and drink too much, or when, out of time and in an inordinate manner, we long for eating and drinking.

From this vice proceed: Daintiness, profusion, idleness, drunkenness, destruction of domestic peace and comfort, indecent jests and buffooneries, lewdness, adultery, debauchery, impenitence; and likewise, cursing, railing, striking, and murdering. Examples: The rich man (Luke 16, 19. &c.); King Baltassar.—" Take heed to yourselves, lest perhaps your hearts be overcharged with surfeiting and drunkenness, and that day (of judgment) come upon you suddenly." (Luke 21, 34.)—" Their (the intemperate) God is their belly." (Philip. 3, 19.)

25. When do we sin by *Envy?*
When we repine at our neighbour's good, and are sad, when he is in possession of temporal or spiritual blessings, but rejoice when he is deprived of them.

Envy produces: Ingratitude and murmuring against God, blasphemy, blindness, whispering and calumny; hatred, desire of revenge, deceit and knavery, persecution and murder. Examples: Satan, Cain, the Brothers of Joseph, Saul, the Pharisees.—" By the envy of the devil death came into the world: and they follow him that are of his side." (Wisd. 2, 24, 25.)

26. When do we sin by *Sloth*?
When we give way to our natural repugnance to labour and exertion, and thus neglect our duties.

27. What sort of sloth is particularly hateful to God?
Lukewarmness, or laziness in whatsoever concerns the service of God, or the salvation of our soul. Therefore God says: " I would thou wert cold, or hot. But because thou art *lukewarm*, and neither cold, nor hot, I will begin to vomit thee out of My mouth." (Apoc. 3, 15. 16.)

The effects of *sloth in general* are: Neglect of the duties of our calling, ruin of property, lying, deceit, effeminacy, and a great many sins against the Sixth and Seventh Commandments.—" Idleness hath taught much evil." (Ecclus. 33, 29.) —" Go to the ant, O sluggard, and consider her ways, and learn wisdom." (Prov. 6, 6.)—The effects of *Spiritual Sloth, or Lukewarmness*, are: Aversion to all religious exercises, contempt of the word of God and of all means of grace, irritation at salutary admonitions, love of the world, pusillanimity, impenitence, infidelity.—Examples: The slothful servant; the foolish virgins. (Matt. 25.)

28. What benefit should we reap from the doctrine of the Capital Sins?
We should carefully avoid them as the sources of all evil, and most earnestly endeavour to acquire the opposite Virtues.

Application.—Every morning, when you get up, resolve to guard most carefully during the day against your chief fault. At night, examine your conscience on it; and if you have failed, repent, and purpose to confess it as soon as possible.

The Different Kinds of Sin (Continued).

29. Which are the Six Sins against the Holy Ghost?

1. Presumption of God's mercy; 2. Despair; 3. Resisting the known Christian truth; 4. Envy at another's spiritual good; 5. Obstinacy in sin; and 6. Final impenitence.

Examples: Cain, Pharao, the Pharisees, Elymas the magician. (Acts 13.)

30. Why are they called Sins against the Holy Ghost?

Because by them we resist, in an especial manner, the Holy Ghost, since we knowingly and willingly despise, reject, or abuse His grace.

"You stiffnecked and uncircumcised in heart and ears, you always resist the Holy Ghost: as your fathers did, so do you also." (Acts 7, 51.)

31. Why should we particularly avoid these sins?

Because they obstruct the entrance of God's grace into the heart, and, therefore, hinder its conversion, or render it very difficult.

Speaking of these sins, Jesus Christ says: "That they shall not be forgiven neither in this world, nor in the world to come;" (Matt. 12, 32.) that is to say, that they are hardly ever forgiven, because it is very, very seldom that people truly repent of them.

32. Which are the Four Sins crying to Heaven for Vengeance?

1. Wilful murder; 2. Sodomy; 3. Oppression of the poor, of widows and orphans; 4. Defrauding labourers of their wages.

1. "The voice of thy brother's blood *crieth to Me* from the earth." (Gen. 4, 10.)—2. "The *cry of Sodom* and Gomorrha is multiplied, and their sin is become exceedingly grievous. We will destroy this place, because *their cry is grown loud before the Lord.*" (Gen. 18, 20. and 19, 13.)—3. "Do not the widow's tears run down the cheek, and her *cry* against him that causeth them to fall? From the cheek *they go up even to Heaven.*" (Ecclus. 35, 18. 19.)—4. Behold the hire of the labourers, which by fraud has been kept back by you, *crieth*, and the *cry* of them hath entered into the ears of the Lord of sabaoth." (James 5, 4.)

33. Why are they called Sins crying to Heaven for Vengeance?

Because, on account of their heinous malice, they *cry*, as it were, for vengeance, and challenge the Divine Justice to punish them.

34. In how many ways may we become accessory to another Person's Sin, and answerable for it?

In these nine ways: 1. By counsel; 2. By command; 3. By consent; 4. By provocation; 5. By praise or flattery; 6. By silence;† 7. By connivance;‡ 8. By partaking; 9. By defence of the ill done.

† When we could and should prevent another's sin either by kindly admonishing him, or by giving information to his parents, his Pastor, &c.—"If thou declare it not to the wicked, that he may be converted from his wicked way, and live: the same wicked man shall die in his iniquity, but I will require his blood at thy hand." (Ezec. 3, 18.) ‡ When we could and should punish the sinner. Thus Heli sinned; "because he knew that his sons did wickedly, and did not chastise them." (1 Kings 3, 13.)

35. Why are we answerable for the sin which another commits?

Because, in any of the above ways, we are either the cause of his sin, or co-operate with him in it, and thus are as guilty before God, as if we had committed it ourselves, or even more so.

"Not only they that do such things, are worthy of death, but they also that consent to them that do them." (Rom. 1, 32.)

Application.—Always receive wholesome admonitions willingly and gratefully. Never participate in the sins of others; on the contrary, endeavour, to the utmost of your power, to hinder them; and when, for that reason, you are to reveal them, do not say: "I do not like to denounce others, because I should not like them to denounce me." Would you then be sorry, if some one were to snatch from your hands the knife with which you were about to kill yourself?

ON VIRTUE AND CHRISTIAN PERFECTION.

1. Should we be contented with avoiding grievous sins and crimes?

No; we should also diligently endeavour to become more and more virtuous, and to attain the Perfection suitable to our condition.

"He that is just, let him be justified still; and he that is holy, let him be sanctified still." (Apoc. 22, 11.) "Be not afraid to be justified even to death." (Ecclus. 18, 22.)— Example of St. Paul: "Not as though I had already attained, or were already perfect; but I follow after, . . . One thing I do: forgetting the things that are behind, and stretching forth myself to those that are before." (Philip. 3, 12. 13.)

§. 1. *On Virtue*.

2. Why should we endeavour to become more and more virtuous?

Because man is only good, and pleasing to God, inasmuch as he is virtuous.

3. In what does Christian Virtue consist?

Christian Virtue, in general, consists in the perseverance of the will, and in its constant exertions, to do what is acceptable to God.

4. How is Christian virtue divided with regard to its origin?

Into *infused* and *acquired* virtue.

5. What is infused virtue?

Virtue is called *infused*, inasmuch as it is a gift of God, which together with sanctifying grace is imparted to the soul, in order to qualify and dispose her for the practice of *supernatural* virtues, *i.e.* for the performance of such pious actions as are worthy of life everlasting. (Rom. 5, 5.)

6. Which virtues are chiefly infused into the soul?

The three *Theological* Virtues: Faith, Hope, and Charity.

7. Why are they called "*Theological Virtues?*"
Because they come directly from, and directly relate to God.

8. When should we make Acts of Faith, Hope, and Charity?
We should make them frequently, but especially, 1. In great temptations against these virtues; 2. When we receive the Holy Sacraments; and 3. When we are in danger of losing our life, or on our death-bed.

9. How may we make Acts of Faith, Hope, and Charity?
We may make them in this manner:

AN ACT OF FAITH.

O my God, I firmly believe all the sacred truths which Thy holy Catholic Church believes and teaches, because thou hast revealed them, who neither canst deceive nor be deceived.

AN ACT OF HOPE.

O my God, relying on Thy almighty power, and Thy infinite mercy and goodness, and because Thou art faithful to Thy promises, I hope to obtain the pardon of my sins, the assistance of Thy grace, and life everlasting, through the merits of Jesus Christ, our Lord and Saviour.

AN ACT OF CHARITY.

O my God, I love Thee above all things with my whole heart and soul, purely because Thou art infinitely perfect and deserving of all love. I also love my neighbour as myself for the love of Thee. I forgive all who have injured me, and ask pardon of all whom I have injured. Amen.

10. What is acquired virtue?
Virtue is called *acquired*, inasmuch as it is a facility which, with the assistance of God, we acquire by constant practice.

11. What do we generally call those virtues, which can be acquired by practice?

We call them "*Moral Virtues*," because they regulate our moral conduct according to the will of God.

12. Which among them are the four "*Cardinal*"† or "*Principal Virtues*," in which all the others are included?

1. Prudence; 2. Justice; 3. Fortitude; and 4. Temperance. (Wisd. 8, 7.)

† They are called *Cardinal* virtues, because they are, as it were, the *hinges* (cardines) by which the whole moral life of a Christian is supported, and on which it must constantly move. [The Transl.]

13. What is *Prudence*?

Prudence is a virtue which makes us discern what is truly good and agreeable to God, from what only appears to be so, and thus prevents our being seduced to evil.

"Be not conformed to this world, but be reformed in the newness of your mind, that you may prove what is the good, and the acceptable, and the perfect will of God." (Rom. 12, 2.) "Beware of false prophets." (Matt. 7, 15.) Examples: The imprudent Josaphat (2 Paral. 19, 2.); the wise Virgins (Matt. 25.)

14. What is *Justice*?

Justice is a virtue by which we are always determined to do what is right, and, therefore, always disposed to give every one his due.

"Render to Cesar the things that are Cesar's; and to God, the things that are God's." (Matt. 22, 21.)—Ex.: Tobias (Tob. 2, 21.)

15. What is *Fortitude*?

Fortitude is a virtue which enables us to endure any hardship, or persecution, rather than abandon our duty.

Examples: The seven Machabees and their mother, who "esteemed the torments as nothing." (2 Mac. 7, 12.)

16. What is *Temperance*?

Temperance is a virtue which restrains our sensual

inclinations and desires, that they may not allure us from virtue.

"Refrain yourselves from carnal desires which war against the soul." (1 Pet. 2, 11.) Ex.: Esther (Esth. 14, 15—18.)

17. What virtues are especially opposite to the seven Capital Sins?
1. Humility; 2. Liberality; 3. Chastity; 4. Meekness; 5. Temperance in eating and drinking; 6. Brotherly love; and 7. Diligence.

18. What is *Humility*?
Humility is a virtue which teaches us to acknowledge our own meanness, weakness, and sinfulness, and to look upon all good as coming from God.

Examples: Abraham (Gen. 18, 27.)—The Publican (Luke 18, 13.)—St. Paul (1 Cor. 15, 8. 9.)—"Unless you become as little children, you shall not enter into the kingdom of Heaven." (Matt. 18, 3.)

19. What is *Liberality*?
Liberality is a virtue which inclines us to use our property for the relief of the needy, or for other laudable purposes.

Examples: Tobias (Tob. 1, 19. 20.)—Solomon (3 Kings, 5—8.)—The first Christians (Acts 2, 45.)—"Give, and it shall be given to you." (Luke 6, 38.)

20. What is *Chastity*?
Chastity is a virtue which subdues all impure inclinations and desires, by which modesty is violated.

Examples: Joseph, Susanna, and, above all, the Blessed Virgin Mary.—"They that are Christ's, have crucified their flesh, with the vices and concupiscences." (Gal. 5, 24.)

21. What is *Meekness*?
Meekness is a virtue which suppresses all desire of revenge, and any motion of unjust anger and displeasure.

Examples: David (1 Kings 24 and 26.)—St. Stephen (Acts 7, 58.)—"Learn of Me, because I am meek, and humble of heart." (Matt. 11, 29.)

22. What is *Temperance in eating and drinking*?
Temperance in eating and drinking is a virtue by which we control ourselves, especially our appetite for eating and drinking.

Examples: Daniel, Ananias, Misael, and Azarias; (Dan. 1.)—John the Baptist. (Matt. 3, 4.)—"Let us walk honestly, not in rioting and drunkenness." (Rom. 13, 13.)

23. What is *Brotherly Love*?
Brotherly Love is a virtue by which we wish every one well, and sincerely rejoice and condole with our neighbour.

Examples: The history of Ruth and Tobias.—"Love one another with the charity of brotherhood. Rejoice with them that rejoice; weep with them that weep." (Rom. 12, 10. 15.)

24. What is *Diligence*?
Diligence is a virtue which enables us to serve God readily and cheerfully, to promote His honour as much as lies in our power, and faithfully to perform all our duties.

Examples: Mathathias (1 Mac. 2.)—St. Paul (Philip. 3, 13. 14.)—"In carefulness (be) not slothful; in spirit fervent; serving the Lord." (Rom. 12, 11.)

Application.— Unless you perseveringly struggle with your wicked inclinations, you will never acquire the Christian Virtues; therefore, fight faithfully until death, and God will give you the crown of life. (Apoc. 2, 10.)

§. 2. *On Christian Perfection.*

25. Why should we all endeavour to attain the Perfection suitable to our condition?
1. Because our Lord and Saviour says to all: "Be you perfect, as also your Heavenly Father is perfect;" (Matt. 5, 48.)
2. Because we are commanded to love God with our whole heart, and with our whole soul, and with our whole mind, and with our whole strength; (Mark 12, 30.)

3. Because the more holy our life is upon earth, the greater will be our happiness in Heaven; and

4. Because we easily fall into grievous sin, and finally run into eternal perdition, if we do not continually endeavour to increase in virtue. (Matt. 25, 29.)

26. In what does Christian Perfection consist?
Christian Perfection consists in this, that, free from all inordinate love of the world and of ourselves, we love God above all, and all in God.

" What have I in Heaven? and besides Thee what do I desire upon earth? Thou art the God of my heart, and the God that is my portion for ever." (Ps. 72, 25. 26.)

27. Which is in general the way to Perfection?
The imitation of Jesus Christ.

" If thou wilt be perfect, ... and come follow Me." (Matt. 19, 21.)

28. What particular means of attaining Perfection have been recommended by Jesus Christ?
Chiefly those which are called "*Evangelical Counsels.*"

29. Which are the Evangelical Counsels?
1. Voluntary Poverty; 2. Perpetual Chastity; and 3. Entire Obedience to a Spiritual Superior.

30. What is *Voluntary Poverty*?
It is a free renunciation of all temporal things, in order to be less distracted in striving for those that are eternal.

" If thou wilt be perfect, go sell what thou hast, and give to the poor, and thou shalt have treasure in Heaven: and come follow Me." (Matt. 19, 21.)

31. What is *Perpetual Chastity*?
It is a free and perpetual renunciation, not only of all impure pleasure, but even of marriage, in order that we may render undivided service to God.

See Matt. 19, 10—12.—" Now concerning virgins, I have no commandment of the Lord, but I give counsel: . . . . . He that giveth his virgin in marriage, doth well; and he that giveth her not, doth better." (1 Cor. 7, 25. 38.)—" If any one shall say that the marriage state is to be preferred to the state of virginity, or of celibacy, and that it is not better and more blessed to remain in virginity, or in celibacy, than to be united in matrimony; let him be anathema." (Counc. of Trent, Sess. 24. Can. 10.)

32. What is *Entire Obedience*?

It is a renunciation of one's own will, in order to do the Divine will more surely under a Superior who represents God. (Matt. 16, 24.)

33.* Why are the Evangelical Counsels special means of Perfection?

1. Because by them the chief obstacles to Christian Perfection are removed; namely, the inordinate love and desire of earthly goods, sensual pleasures, and independence; and 2. Because by them man sacrifices to the Lord his God, all that he has and is: his exterior goods, by the vow of poverty; his body, by the vow of chastity; and his soul, or his will, by the vow of obedience.

Of these Evangelical Counsels our Divine Redeemer meant to speak, when He said: "All men take not this word, but they to whom it is given." (Matt. 19, 11.)

34. Who are obliged to observe the Evangelical Counsels?

All Religious, and all those who have bound themselves by vow to keep them.

The Secular Clergy also, when they receive the Greater Orders, bind themselves to Perpetual Chastity, in order to be able to devote themselves entirely, and with an undivided heart, to the service of God and of their neighbour. "He that is without a wife, is solicitous for the things that belong to the Lord, how he may please God. But he that is with a wife, is solicitous for the things of the world, how he may please his wife; and he is *divided*." (1 Cor. 7, 32. 33.)

35. Can people in the world also lead a perfect life?

Yes, if they do not live according to the spirit of the world, but according to the spirit of Jesus Christ.

"If any man love the world, the charity of the Father is not in him; for all that is in the world, is the concupiscence of the flesh, and the concupiscence of the eyes, and the pride of life." (1 John 2, 15. 16.) "Whosoever will be a friend of this world, becometh an enemy of God." (James 4, 4.)—"If any man have not the Spirit of Christ, he is none of His." (Rom. 8, 9.)

36. Is then the spirit of the world at variance with the Spirit of Christ?

Most certainly it is, as we distinctly see from those sentences of Jesus, which are called the "*Eight Beatitudes.*"

37. Which are the Eight Beatitudes?

1. "Blessed are the poor in spirit; for theirs is the kingdom of Heaven.
2. "Blessed are the meek; for they shall possess the land.
3. "Blessed are they that mourn; for they shall be comforted.
4. "Blessed are they that hunger and thirst after justice; for they shall have their fill.
5. "Blessed are the merciful; for they shall obtain mercy.
6. "Blessed are the clean of heart; for they shall see God.
7. "Blessed are the peace-makers; for they shall be called the children of God.
8. "Blessed are they that suffer persecution for justice sake; for theirs is the kingdom of Heaven." (Matt. 5, 3—10.)

38. How do we know from the Eight Beatitudes, that the spirit of the world is at variance with the Spirit of Christ?

We know it from this, that the world esteems those very persons miserable and foolish, whom Christ our Lord calls blessed.

The world is accustomed to set forth riches, reputation, honours, and sensual pleasures, as the sources of happiness;

Jesus Christ, on the contrary, teaches us in the Eight Beatitudes, to seek our happiness in God and in His holy service, and, therefore, willingly and cheerfully to endure poverty, persecution, and any hardships that may fall to our lot.

39. What means must a Christian use, let his condition be what it may, in order to attain to Perfection?

He must 1. Delight in prayer, diligently hear the word of God, and often receive the Holy Sacraments; 2. He must steadily subdue and deny himself; and 3. He must perform his daily actions in the state of grace, and in a manner acceptable to God.

1. "They were persevering in the doctrine of the Apostles, and in the communication of the breaking of bread, and in prayers." (Acts 2, 42.)—2. "If any man will come after Me, let him deny himself, and take up his cross, and follow Me." (Matt. 16, 24.)—3. "Whether you eat or drink, or whatsoever else you do, do all to the glory of God." (1 Cor. 10, 31.)

40. How should we deny ourselves?

We should refuse ourselves many things that are dear and agreeable to us, and should also deprive ourselves of lawful things, that we may the more easily abstain from unlawful ones.

41. How may we most easily perform our daily actions in a manner acceptable to God?

By representing to ourselves how Jesus Christ performed them, and by striving to imitate Him for His sake.

42. How should we do our daily work after the example of Christ?

We should do it diligently, patiently, and with a view to please God. Therefore, we should form a good intention at the beginning, and renew it sometimes, when the work is of long continuance.

43. What should we do when we take our meals?

We should before and after meals say grace, with our hands joined together, and be temperate and modest at table.

44. May we also be allowed to take recreation?

Yes; for nothing forbids our taking proper recreation in due time; we should, however, sanctify it by a good intention and by the remembrance of God, and keep within the bounds of modesty?

45. What should our intercourse with our neighbour be?

It should be, 1. Kind, that we may not offend any one; and 2. Prudent, that we may not in any manner be seduced to evil.

46. How should we act in our afflictions?

We should convince ourselves that they come from God, should offer them up to Him, and beg of Him the grace necessary to make a good use of them.

Application.—Think that these words, which God spoke to Abraham, are also addressed to you: "Walk before Me, and be perfect." (Gen. 17, 1.) Strive earnestly to become daily more pious and virtuous. Let this be every morning your resolution, and every night examine your conscience upon it. "My Son, serve God with a perfect heart, and a willing mind; for the Lord searcheth all hearts, and understandeth all the thoughts of minds. If thou seek Him, thou shalt find Him; but if thou forsake Him, He will cast thee off for ever." (1. Par. 28, 9.)

PART III.

ON THE MEANS OF GRACE.

On Grace in General.

1. Can we, by our own natural strength, keep the Commandments, and be saved?

No; we cannot, without the grace of God.

"Without Me you can do nothing," says Christ. (John 15, 5.)—"I will put My Spirit in the midst of you, and I will cause you to walk in My commandments." (Ez. 36, 27.)

2. What do we understand by the grace of God?

By the grace of God we understand here an internal, supernatural help or gift, which God communicates to us, through the merits of Jesus Christ, for our eternal salvation.

3. How many kinds of this supernatural help and gift, or of *Grace* properly so called, are there?

There are two kinds, 1. The *grace of assistance*, called also *actual* or *transient* grace; and 2. The *grace of sanctification* or *justification*, called also *sanctifying* or *habitual* grace.

The grace of assistance is called *actual* and *transient*, because it *acts transiently* upon the soul, whereas the grace of sanctification or justification *remains habitually* in the soul, beautifies it, and makes it *holy* and *just* in the eyes of God.

§ 1. *On the Grace of Assistance.*

4. In what does Actual Grace, or the Grace of Assistance, consist?

Actual Grace consists in this, that God enlightens our understanding, and inclines our will, to avoid evil, and both to will, and to do, what is good.

"*Give me understanding*, and I will search Thy law, and I will keep it with my whole heart. . . . . *Incline my heart unto Thy testimonies*," etc. (Ps. 118, 34. 36.)

5. How far is the assistance of grace necessary to us?

It is so necessary to us that, without the grace of God, we can neither begin, continue, nor accomplish the least thing towards our salvation.

"For it is God who worketh in you, both to will and to accomplish." (Philip. 2, 13.)

6. Why is grace so indispensable to everything that relates to salvation?

1. Because eternal salvation is a good of a supernatural order, and, consequently, can be obtained only by a supernatural power and help, that is, by grace; 2. Because, by grace alone, we enter into connexion with Christ, and partake of His infinite merits, which are the source of every thing that leads to salvation.

1. "Not that we are sufficient to think anything (conducive to salvation) of ourselves, as of ourselves; but our sufficiency is from God." (2. Cor. 3, 5.)—2. "I cast not away the grace of God; for if justice be by the law, then Christ died in vain;" (Gal. 2, 21.) *i.e.*, if the observance of the law alone, without being united by grace with Christ, did justify us, or lead us to eternal salvation, it would not have been necessary for Christ to die in order to merit salvation for us.

By this, however, it is not meant, that man is naturally quite incapable of performing any action that is morally good, but only, that by such morally good actions, as proceed from his naturally good will, he can neither merit, nor in any way obtain, grace or salvation: by them, he can only prepare himself for grace in so far as he does not, by bad actions, still increase the obstacles of it. "No man can come to Me," says Christ, "unless it be given him by My Father." (John 6, 66.)

7. Does God give His grace to all men?

Yes, God gives to all men sufficient grace to enable them to keep, as they are in duty bound, the Commandments, and to work out their salvation.

"The Son of man is come to save that which was lost."

(Matt. 18, 11.)—"God will have all men to be saved, and to come to the knowledge of the truth." (1. Tim. 2, 4.)—"God is faithful, who will not suffer you to be tempted above that which you are able, but will make also with temptation issue, that you may be able to bear it." (1 Cor. 10, 13.)—"God does not command impossibilities; but, when commanding, He admonishes us to do what we are able, and to pray for what we are not able to do, and aids us, that we may be able." (Counc. of Trent Sess. 6. Ch. 11.)

8. But what must we do on our part, in order that the grace of God may conduce to our salvation?

We must not resist it, but faithfully co-operate with it.

"We exhort you, that you receive not the grace of God *in vain*." (2. Cor. 6, 1.)—God stretches forth his hand to save us; if we really wish to be saved, we must take hold of it, and not reject it. Example of St. Paul: "I have laboured more abundantly than all they; yet not I, but the grace of God with me." (1 Cor. 15, 10.)

9. Is it then also in our power to resist the grace of God?

Most certainly; for God's grace does not force the human will, but leaves it perfectly free.

"Jerusalem, Jerusalem, how often would I have gathered together thy children, as the hen doth gather her chickens under her wings, and thou wouldst not!" (Matt. 23, 37.)—"To-day if you shall hear His voice, harden not your hearts." (Ps. 94, 8.)

Application.—Pray daily to God to give you His grace, and take particular care not to close your heart against it. "Behold, I stand at the gate, and knock. If any man shall hear My voice, and open to Me the door, I will come in to him, and will sup with him, and he with Me." (Apoc. 3, 20.)—In order to make His grace operate the more easily in the human heart, God often connects it with exterior events; as, sudden death, diseases, good and bad fortune. Do not heedlessly disregard such Divine warnings; for nothing is more dangerous than not to know the time of the visitation of God.—Example: Jerusalem. (Luke 19, 44.)

§. 2. *On the Grace of Sanctification or Justification*.

10. What is Sanctifying Grace?

Sanctifying Grace is a gratuitous supernatural gift, which the Holy Ghost communicates to our souls, and by which from sinners we are made just, children of God, and heirs of Heaven.

Together with Sanctifying grace "the charity of God is poured forth in our hearts by the Holy Ghost, who is given to us." (Rom. 5, 5.)—With it, God enters into our hearts according to the words of Jesus: "If any one love Me, My Father will love him, and We will come to him, and will make our abode with him." (John 14, 23.)— Through it, we are born again children of God, and our soul receives supernatural life: "Behold what manner of charity the Father hath bestowed upon us, that we should be called, and should be the sons of God." (1. John 3, 1.) (Comp. Page 128, 129. Quest. 6. 7. 8. 12. 13.)

11. Why is sanctifying grace called "*a gratuitous gift?*"

Because it is an entirely free gift, flowing from the compassionate love of God.

"For all have sinned, and do need the glory of God; being justified freely (*i.e.* without their desert) by His grace, through the redemption, that is in Christ Jesus." (Rom. 3, 23. 24.)

12. Why is sanctifying grace also called "*Grace of Justification?*"

Because, by sanctifying grace, man is justified, that is, passes from the state of sin to the state of righteousness and holiness.

13. What then does the justification of the sinner include?

Justification includes, 1. Cleanness from all grievous sins, at least, together with the remission of eternal punishment; and 2. The sanctification and renewal of the interior man.

"You are washed, you are sanctified, you are justified in the name of our Lord Jesus Christ, and the Spirit of our God." (1. Cor. 6, 11.)

14. What first gives rise to the justification of the sinner?

Preventing grace, which enlightens the sinner, and excites him to turn to God.

15. What must the sinner do on his part, in order to attain to justification.

He must, with the assistance of grace, voluntarily turn to God, and believe all that God has revealed, especially, that we are justified by Jesus Christ.

16. What effect has this belief on the sinner?

1. The sinner is struck with a wholesome fear of the justice of God, but hopes to obtain pardon from His mercy.

2. Then, he begins to love God, is sorry for his sins, resolves to lead a new life, agreeable to God, and receives the Sacrament of Baptism, or, if he is baptized, the Sacrament of Penance.

17. What does the sinner receive in the Sacrament of Baptism, or Penance?

He receives sanctifying grace, and together with it the remission of his sins, and interior sanctification, by which he is really made just, acceptable to God, a child of God, and heir of Heaven. (Council of Trent Sess. 6.)

18. How long does sanctifying grace remain in the soul of the justified man?

As long as he does not commit mortal sin.

19. What fruits does the justified man produce by the help of grace?

He produces good, *i.e. meritorious* works; for "every good tree bringeth forth good fruit." (Matt. 7, 17.)

20. Cannot a man who is in mortal sin do good?

He can do good, but without any merit for Heaven. (John 15, 4. 5.)

21. Is then the good done in mortal sin useless?

No; it is, on the contrary, very useful to obtain from the Divine mercy the grace of conversion,† sometimes also, the averting of temporal punishment.‡

† "Redeem thou thy sins with alms, and thy iniquities with works of mercy to the poor: perhaps He will forgive thy offences." (Dan. 4, 24.) Examples: Manasses, (2. Paral. 33, 12)—‡ Achab, (3. Kings 21, 29.) the Ninivites.

22. What do we merit by the good works which we perform in the state of grace?

We merit 1. An increase of sanctifying grace, and 2. Eternal salvation. (2 Tim. 4, 8.)

"If any one shall say, that the justified man, by the good works which he performs through the grace of God and the merit of Jesus Christ, whose living member he is, does not truly merit increase of grace and eternal life; let him be anathema." (Council of Trent Sess 6. Can. 32.)

23. Whence do such good works derive their intrinsic value or meritoriousness?

From the infinite merits of Jesus Christ whose living members we are through sanctifying grace.

"I am the vine, you the branches: he that abideth in Me, and I in him, the same beareth much fruit; for without Me you can do nothing." (John 15, 5. Comp. Counc. of Trent Sess. 6. Ch. 16.)

24. Is every Christian bound to do good works?

Yes; for "Every tree that doth not yield good fruit, shall be cut down, and cast into the fire." (Matt. 3, 10.)

25. What good works should we perform before all others?

1. Those, the performance of which is commanded to all Christians by the Commandments of God and of the Church; and 2. Those which are necessary, or useful, to fulfil the duties of our state of life.

26. What other good works are especially recommended to us in Holy Scripture?

Prayer, Fasting, and Alms; by which in general are understood the works of devotion, mortification, and charity.

"Prayer is good with fasting and alms, more than to lay up treasures of gold." (Tob. 12, 8.)

27. What does God especially regard in our good works?

Our good intention, by which we may obtain from God great reward even for small works.

"Whosoever shall give to drink to one of these little ones a cup of cold water only in the name of a disciple, amen I say to you, he shall not lose his reward. (Matt. 10, 42.)—Example of the Poor Widow. (Mark 12, 41—44.)

28. What is a good intention?

The purpose or good will to serve God, and to honour Him.

29. How may we make a good intention?

We may say, for instance, thus: "O my God, I offer up to Thee all my thoughts, words, and deeds, for Thy honour and glory." Or: "My Lord and my God, all for Thy honour."

30. When should we make a good intention?

It is very useful to make it several times a day, and especially every morning.

31. What means must we particularly use in order to obtain grace?

The Holy Sacraments, and Prayer.

32. Do both these means give us grace in the same manner, and in the same measure?

No; for 1. The Sacraments produce grace in us; Prayer impetrates it for us; 2. Through the Sacraments, we obtain those graces only, for which they were instituted; but, through Prayer, we receive all sorts of graces, except those which can only be obtained by the Sacraments.

Application.—Strive most carefully, to preserve sanctifying grace continually in your heart by avoiding sin and performing good works. "A man making void the law of Moses, dieth without any mercy under two or three witnesses: how much more, do you think he deserveth worse punishments, who hath trodden under foot the Son of God, and hath esteemed the blood of the testament unclean, by which he was sanctified, and hath offered an affront to the Spirit of grace?" (Hebr. 10, 28. 29.)

On the Sacraments.

1. What is a Sacrament?

A Sacrament is a visible sign, instituted by Jesus Christ, by which invisible grace, and inward sanctification, is communicated to our souls.

2. How many things are necessary to constitute a Sacrament?

These three: 1. A visible sign; 2. An invisible grace; and 3. The institution by Jesus Christ.

3. Why has Christ instituted visible signs for imparting his grace to us?

1. That we may have a visible pledge of the inward invisible grace; and 2. That, by participating in these visible means of grace, we may manifest our Communion with the one Church of Christ.

Thus Christ sometimes made use of certain signs, when He conferred spiritual and corporal blessings on people; for instance, when He breathed on His disciples, and said: "Receive ye the Holy Ghost;" (John 20, 22.)—when "He spat on the ground, and made clay of the spittle, and spread the clay upon the eyes of the man born blind;" (John 9, 6.)—when "He put his fingers into the ears of the man deaf and dumb, and spitting, He touched his tongue, and looking up to Heaven, He groaned, and said to him: *Ephpheta*, which is, *Be thou opened.*" (Mark 7, 33. 34.)

4. Do these signs only signify grace?

No; they also effect or produce the grace which

they signify, unless we, on our part, put an obstacle to it; therefore, they are also called *efficacious* signs.

5. What grace do the Sacraments effect?
1. They communicate, or increase, sanctifying grace;
2. Each Sacrament communicates other peculiar graces according to the end for which it has been instituted.

6. How must we receive the Sacraments, in order that they may produce these graces in us?
We must prepare ourselves well for them, and then receive them worthily.

7. What sin does he commit who receives a Sacrament unworthily?
He commits a very grievous sin—a sacrilege.

8. Does not the efficacy of the Sacraments also depend on the worthiness, or unworthiness, of those who administer them?
No; for the Sacraments have their efficacy, not from him who administers them, but from the merits of Jesus Christ by whom they were instituted.

The Sacraments are, as it were, channels through which flow to us the graces which Jesus has merited for us by His bitter passion and death.

9. Were *all* the Sacraments instituted by Christ?
Yes; for God alone can give to outward signs the power of producing grace and sanctification.

10. How many Sacraments has Christ instituted?
These seven: 1. Baptism; 2. Confirmation; 3. Holy Eucharist; 4. Penance; 5. Extreme Unction; 6. Holy Order; and 7. Matrimony.

Our Lord Jesus Christ has instituted just as many Sacraments, as are necessary and conducive to the *supernatural* life of man. For as he is first born into this natural life, then grows up and acquires strength, is frequently supplied with nourishing food, in order to preserve life and to increase his strength, &c.; so also he is 1. Born in *Baptism* to the supernatural life; gains then

2. In *Confirmation* strength and growth; receives 3. In the *Holy Eucharist* a Divine nourishment; finds 4. In *Penance* a remedy to heal all the diseases of his soul, and to restore him to the state of grace; and gets 5. In *Extreme Unction* assistance and strength against despair and the last assaults of the devil. 6. In *Holy Order* the powers of administering the means of grace necessary to the supernatural life, are propagated; and 7. In *Matrimony* the union between husband and wife is blessed, that, being sanctified themselves, they may also bring up their children to a holy, and consequently, to eternal life.

11. How do we know that there are seven Sacraments?

We know it because the Church, "which is the pillar and ground of the truth," (1 Tim. 8, 15.) has at all times taught so.

Not only the Catholics of all ages, but also the modern Greeks, the Russians, and all those Sects who in the first centuries separated themselves from the Catholic Church, have seven Sacraments; which evidently proves that the doctrine of *seven* Sacraments is as old as the Church itself.

12. How are the Sacraments divided?

They are divided 1. Into Sacraments of the *living*, and Sacraments of the *dead;* and 2. Into such as can be received only *once*, and such as can be received *more than once.*

13. Which are the Sacraments of the living?

The Sacraments of the *living* are, 1. Confirmation; 2. Holy Eucharist; 3. Extreme Unction; 4. Holy Order; and 5. Matrimony.

14. Why are they called Sacraments of the *living*?

Because, in order to receive them, we must have supernatural life, that is, sanctifying grace.

15. Which are the Sacraments of the dead?

The Sacraments of the *dead* are these two: Baptism and Penance.

16. Why are they called Sacraments of the *dead*?

Because, when we receive them, we either have not, or, at least, are not obliged to have, the life of grace.

17. Which Sacraments can be received only *once*?
Baptism, Confirmation, and Holy Order.

18. Why can they be received but *once*?
Because they imprint upon the soul an indelible character, or spiritual mark, which consecrates and dedicates him who receives it, in a special manner to the service of God, remains for ever, and will add either to his glory in Heaven, or to his misery in Hell.

19. Whence have we received those ceremonies which, in the administration of the Sacraments, are used together with the signs instituted by Christ?
From the Church which, under the assistance of the Holy Ghost, has ordained them for the increase of our devotion and reverence.

Application.—Esteem the Holy Sacraments as most precious means of grace instituted by Christ; give fervent thanks to God for them, and beware of profaning them by imprecations, or by unworthily receiving them.

On Baptism.

1. Which is the first and most necessary Sacrament?
The first and most necessary Sacrament is Baptism.

2. Why is Baptism the first Sacrament?
Because before Baptism no other Sacrament can be validly received.

3. Why is Baptism the most necessary Sacrament?
Because without Baptism no one can be saved.

"Unless a man be born again of water and the Holy Ghost, he cannot enter into the Kingdom of God." (John 3, 5.)

God has not revealed to us what becomes of those children who die without Baptism. All we know is, that they are not admitted to enjoy the sight of God, nor are punished like those who have sinned of their own free will. However, it is to be supposed that life is also to them a benefit of God.

4. What is Baptism?
Baptism is a Sacrament in which, by water and the word of God, we are cleansed from all sin, and regenerated and sanctified in Christ to life everlasting.

5. Why do you say that we are baptized "*by water and the word of God?*"
Because Baptism is administered whilst water is poured over the head or over the body of him who is baptized, and whilst, at the same time, these words are pronounced: "I baptize thee in the name of the Father, and of the Son, and of the Holy Ghost."

6. Why do you say that, "*in Baptism we are cleansed from all sin?*"
Because in Baptism original sin, and all the sins committed before Baptism, are forgiven?

7. Is also the punishment due to sin remitted?
Yes, the temporal, as well as the eternal punishment is remitted in Baptism.

8. Why then are we, even after Baptism, still subject to some effects of original sin; as, death, concupiscence, and many tribulations and infirmities?
1. That we ourselves may experience how punishable and pernicious sin is, and hate it so much the more; and 2. That we may increase our merits for Heaven by our combats and sufferings.

9. Why do you further say, that we are "*regenerated and sanctified to life everlasting?*"
Because in Baptism we are not only cleansed from all sin, but are also transformed in a spiritual manner, made holy, children of God, and heirs of Heaven.

"He saved us by the laver of regeneration, and renovation of the Holy Ghost, whom He hath poured forth upon us abundantly, through Jesus Christ our Saviour; that, being justified by His grace, we may be heirs, according to hope, of life everlasting." (Tit. 3, 5—7.)

10. By what is this spiritual regeneration and sanctification effected?

It is effected by the sanctifying grace which, together with the Theological Virtues, the Holy Ghost infuses into the soul.

"The charity of God is poured forth in our hearts by the Holy Ghost, who is given to us." (Rom. 5, 5.)

11. And why do you say, that we are regenerated and sanctified "*in Christ?*"

To signify that we receive all these graces, because by Baptism we are united with Christ, and incorporated into His Church.

"There is now, therefore, no condemnation to them that are in Christ Jesus." (Rom. 8, 1.)

12. When did Christ give the Commandment to baptize?

Before His Ascension, when He said to His Apostles: "Going therefore, teach ye all nations; baptizing them in the name of the Father, and of the Son, and of the Holy Ghost." (Matt. 28, 19.)

13. Who can validly baptize?

Any person; but, except in cases of necessity, only Priests who have care of souls are allowed to baptize.

14. Is the Baptism given by non-Catholics also valid?

Yes; it is valid, if they strictly observe in it all that is necessary for Baptism.

15. What sort of water should be used in Baptism?

Any natural water will do for the validity of Baptism. However, when possible, baptismal water, or water blessed for that purpose, should be used.

16. What intention must he have who baptizes?

He must have the intention to baptize *indeed*, that is, to do what the Church does, or what Christ has ordained.

17. What name should be given to the child in Baptism?

The name of some Saint, in whom the child may have an intercessor with God, and an example for his imitation.

18. Why must the person to be baptized renounce Satan, all his works, and all his pomps, before Baptism?

Because no one can belong to Christ, unless he renounce not only *Satan*, but also his *works*, *i.e.* sin—and his *pomps*, *i.e.* the spirit and the vanities of the world, by which Satan blinds men, and entices them to sin. (Matt. 4, 8. 9.)

In Baptism we promise to believe, to avoid sin, and to lead a new life, agreeable to God. On the other hand, God promises us His grace and eternal salvation. These mutual promises are called the *Covenant of Baptism*.

19. Why does the Priest place a white linen cloth upon our head in Baptism?

To remind us that we should preserve the innocence we have received, pure and spotless until death; therefore, when he puts it on us, he says: "Receive this white garment, and see thou carry it without stain before the Judgment-seat of our Lord Jesus Christ, that thou mayest have eternal life."

20. What does the lighted candle, which is put into the child's hand after he is baptized, signify?

That a Christian ought to shine by his faith and virtuous life before the whole world.

"So let your light shine before men, that they may see your good works, and glorify your Father who is in Heaven." (Matt. 5, 16.)

The other ceremonies of Baptism are also very ancient, and have all a deep meaning. 1. The child, or party to be baptized, remains without the Church, because only Baptism gives him entrance into it.—2. The Priest breathes three times in his face, to signify the new and spiritual life he receives by the grace of the Holy Ghost.

(Gen. 2, 7. and John 20, 22.)—3. The sign of the cross made upon his forehead and upon his breast, denotes that he is becoming the property of his Crucified Redeemer, whose doctrine he is to carry in his heart, and to profess openly.—4. The blessed salt, which is put into his mouth, is an emblem of Christian wisdom, and of preservation from the corruption of sin.—5. By the exorcisms, which are repeated several times, the power of the devil, "who has the empire of death" (Heb. 2, 14.), is broken in the name of the Blessed Trinity.—6. The laying of the Priest's hand upon the person to be baptized, signifies the protection of God; and the stole, laid upon him, and by which he is led into the Church, is a sign of the ecclesiastical power, in virtue of which the Priest admits him into the Church.—7. The touching of the child's ears and nostrils with spittle in imitation of our Saviour (Mark 7, 33.), signifies that, by the grace of this Sacrament, his spiritual senses are opened to the doctrine of Christ.—8. After having renounced the devil, and all his works, and all his pomps, he is anointed with holy oil on the breast and between the shoulders, because, as a champion of Christ, he has now manfully to fight against the devil and the world.— 9. After Baptism, the crown of his head is anointed with chrism, to intimate that he is now a Christian, *i.e.* an Anointed of God, etc.

21.* What should Sponsors, or Godfathers and Godmothers, be particularly mindful of?

Sponsors should bear in mind that they become, as it were, the Spiritual Parents of the infant that is baptized, and make in his name the profession of faith, and the baptismal vows; that, therefore,

1. They should be good Catholics themselves;
2. They should take care that the child be instructed in the Catholic religion, and well educated, if his natural Parents should neglect their duty in this respect, or be prevented from performing it; and
3. That they cannot marry their Godchild, or his Parents.

22.* How many Godfathers and Godmothers does the Church admit?

The Church generally admits but one Godfather for

a boy, and one Godmother for a girl; or, at most, one Godfather and one Godmother for one person to be baptized. The others who may be admitted besides, are only to be considered as witnesses of his Baptism, and, consequently, contract no spiritual relationship.

23. Can the Baptism of water never be supplied?

When it is impossible to have it, it may be supplied by the Baptism of desire, or by the Baptism of blood.

24. What is the Baptism of desire?

An earnest wish, and a determined will to receive Baptism, or to do all that God has ordained for our salvation, accompanied with a perfect contrition, or a pure love of God.

"Every one that loveth, is born of God, and knoweth God." (1. John 4, 7.)

25. What is the Baptism of blood?

Martyrdom for the sake of Christ.

"He that shall lose his life for Me, shall find it." (Matt. 10, 39.)

Application.—Never forget what you owe to God for the inestimable grace of Baptism; and often, if possible, every Sunday, renew your Baptismal Vows.

On Confirmation.

1. What is Confirmation?

Confirmation is a Sacrament in which, through the Bishop's imposition of hands, unction, and prayer, those already baptized are strengthened by the Holy Ghost, in order that they may steadfastly profess their faith, and faithfully live up to it.

2. Who teaches us that the Sacrament of Confirmation was instituted by Christ?

The infallible Catholic Church in accordance with the Holy Scripture,† with the doctrine of the Holy Fathers,‡ and with the practice of the most ancient times.§

† The Holy Scripture reckons the doctrine of Confirmation, as well as that of Baptism and Penance, amongst the

fundamental truths of Christianity. (Hebr. 6, 1. 2.) It testifies that Christ promised the Holy Ghost to the faithful, and that the Apostles imparted Him by prayer and imposition of hands. "When the Apostles, who were in Jerusalem, had heard that Samaria had received the word of God, they sent unto them Peter and John. Who, when they were come, prayed for them, that they might receive the Holy Ghost; for He was not as yet come upon any of them, but they were only baptized in the name of the Lord Jesus. Then they laid their hands upon them, and they received the Holy Ghost." (Acts 8, 14—17.)—" They (the disciples of Ephesus) were baptized in the name of the Lord Jesus; and when Paul had imposed his hands on them, the Holy Ghost came upon them, and they spoke with tongues and prophesied." (Acts 19, 5. 6.)—‡ The Holy Fathers designate this Sacrament by various names; as, *Confirmation* (*i.e.* strengthening), *Imposition of hands, Sealing, Unction, Chrism, Mystery of the Holy Ghost.* "The Sacrament of Chrism," says St. Augustine, " is just as holy as Baptism."—§ History attests that even in the earliest days of the Church the Bishops travelled about to lay their hands on those that were baptized, and to call down the Holy Ghost upon them.

3. What are the effects of Confirmation?

1. Confirmation increases sanctifying grace in us; 2. It gives us the Holy Ghost, to enable us to fight against evil, and to grow in virtue; and 3. It imprints on us, as soldiers of Christ, a spiritual mark which can never be effaced.

"He that confirmeth us with you in Christ, and that hath anointed us, is God: who also hath sealed us, and given the pledge of the Spirit in our hearts." (2 Cor. 1, 21. 22.)

4. Who has power to confirm?

The Bishops, as Successors of the Apostles, have power to confirm; in urgent cases, however, the Pope can delegate this power also to a Priest, who is not a Bishop.

5. How does the Bishop give Confirmation?

He extends his hands over all those who are to be confirmed, and prays for them all in general, that the Holy Ghost may come down upon them; then he lays his hand upon each one in particular, and anoints him with holy chrism; and he concludes by giving to all in common the Episcopal Benediction.

6. How does the Bishop anoint those to be confirmed?

He makes the sign of the cross with holy chrism upon the forehead of each one, saying at the same time: "N., I sign thee with the sign of the cross, and I confirm thee with the chrism of salvation in the name of the Father, and of the Son, and of the Holy Ghost."

7. Of what does the chrism, blessed by the Bishop, consist?

Of oil of olives, and balm.

8. What does the oil signify?

The oil signifies the inward strength which we receive for the combat against the enemies of our salvation.

9. Why is fragrant balm mixed with the oil?

To signify, that he who is confirmed receives the grace to preserve himself from the corruption of the world, and to send forth, by a pious life, the sweet odour of virtue.

10. Why does the Bishop make the sign of the cross on the forehead of him whom he confirms?

To intimate that a Christian must never be ashamed of the Cross, but boldly profess his faith in Jesus Crucified.

"I am not ashamed of the Gospel; for it is the power of God unto salvation to every one that believeth." (Rom. 1, 16.)

11. Why does the Bishop, after he has anointed him, give him a slight blow on the cheek?

To remind him, that, being now strengthened, he ought to be prepared to suffer patiently any kind of humiliation for the name of Jesus.

12. Is confirmation necessary to salvation?

Confirmation is not absolutely necessary to salvation; yet, it would be a sin, not to receive it through neglect or indifference.

Whatever has been instituted by God for the sanctification of all, must also ardently be desired, and thankfully accepted, by all.

13. Who is capable of receiving Confirmation?
Every one who is baptized.

14. How is a person to prepare himself for receiving the Sacrament of Confirmation?
1. He must cleanse his conscience from all, at least, grievous sins; 2. He must get himself well instructed in the fundamental truths of our faith, particularly, in those which regard this Sacrament; and 3. He must heartily desire the grace of the Holy Ghost, and, for that purpose, he must fervently pray, and perform good works.

15. How are we to receive Confirmation?
We must 1. Earnestly ask for the Gifts of the Holy Ghost; 2. Promise God, that we will live, and die, as good Christians; and 3. Not leave the church, before the Bishop has given his benediction.

16. What should we do after Confirmation?
We should 1. Give humble thanks to God; 2. Spend that day especially in devotion; and 3. Preserve and increase the grace of the Holy Ghost by perseverance in our struggle against the enemies of salvation, and by an ardent zeal in all that is good.

17. * Why are Sponsors, or Godfathers and Godmothers, required also in Confirmation?
That they may present to the Bishop those who are to be confirmed, and afterwards advise and help them in their spiritual combat for which they are consecrated in this Sacrament?

The Sponsor enters into this engagement by laying his hand on the right shoulder of the person to be confirmed. Thus he becomes his spiritual Parent and Guardian, and has to preserve him from losing the grace of Confirmation; and there arises from it the same spiritual relationship, and, consequently, the same impediment of marriage, as in Baptism.

18. * What qualities does the Church require in the Godfathers and Godmothers of those who are confirmed?

They must be Catholics, must have been confirmed, be blameless in their conduct, and of such age, that they are able to fulfil their duties as Sponsors. Parents cannot be the Sponsors of their children; and the Sponsor in Confirmation is to be different from the Sponsor in Baptism.

Application.—Perform without fear all the duties of a Catholic Christian; and should you have to suffer ignominy and persecution on account of your faith, consider it an honour, and rejoice in it after the example of the Apostles. (Acts 5, 41.)

ON THE HOLY EUCHARIST.

§. 1. *On the Real Presence of Christ in the Blessed Sacrament.*

1. What is the Holy Eucharist?

It is the true Body and the true Blood of our Lord Jesus Christ, who is really and substantially present under the appearances of bread and wine for the nourishment of our souls.

It is called "*Eucharist*" from the Greek word "*Eucharistia*," which means "*Good Grace*," because it contains Christ our Lord, the true grace, and the source of all Heavenly gifts; or "*Thanksgiving*," because, when we offer this most spotless victim, we render to God a homage of infinite value, in return for all the benefits which we have received from His bounty, particularly, for the inestimable treasure of grace bestowed on us in this Sacrament.—It is also called the *Blessed* or *Most Holy Sacrament*, because it contains Jesus Christ Himself, the Author of all the Sacraments, and of all sanctity. The *Sacrament of the Altar*, because it is on the Altar it is offered and reserved. The *Holy Host*, because it contains Jesus

Christ, the true Host or Victim, immolated for us. The *Viaticum* (*i.e.* Provision for a journey), as well because it is the spiritual food by which we are supported during our mortal pilgrimage, as also, because it prepares for us a passage to eternal happiness and everlasting glory. (Catech. of the Counc. of Trent.)

2. Is there in the Holy Eucharist all that is requisite for constituting a Sacrament?

Yes; there is 1. The visible sign, *i.e.* the appearances of bread and wine; 2. The invisible grace, *i.e.* Jesus Christ Himself, the Author and Dispenser of all graces; and 3. The institution by our Lord Jesus Christ.

3. When did Jesus Christ institute this Sacrament?

He instituted it at the Last Supper, the evening before His bitter Passion.

4. How did He institute it?

Jesus took bread, blessed it, and broke and gave it to His Disciples, saying, "*Take ye, and eat: this is My Body.*" After that, in like manner, He took the chalice with wine in it, blessed and gave it to His Disciples, saying, "*Drink ye all of this: this is My Blood.—Do this for a commemoration of Me.*" (Short Hist. of Rel. § 24.)

5. What became of the bread and wine, when Jesus pronounced these words over them: "This is My Body—This is My Blood?"

The bread was, in an invisible manner, changed into the true Body, and the wine, into the true Blood of Jesus Christ.

6. After these words of Christ, what did still remain of bread and wine?

Nothing but their species or appearances.

7. What is understood by the appearances of bread and wine?

All that which of bread and wine is perceived by the senses; as form, colour, taste, smell, &c.

8. How do we know that with these words, "This is My Body, this is My Blood," Christ gave His true Body, and His true Blood, to the Apostles?

We know it,

1. Because Christ had long before promised to His disciples, that He would give them His real flesh to eat, and His real blood to drink,† and because He afterwards, at the Last Supper, expressly declared that that which He then gave them as food and drink, was really His Body and His Blood;‡ and

2. Because the Apostles and the Catholic Church have at all times believed and taught so.‖

† "The bread that I will give, is My flesh, for the life of the world. The Jews therefore strove among themselves, saying: How can this man give us his flesh to eat? Then Jesus said to them: Amen, amen, I say unto you: Except you eat the flesh of the Son of man, and drink His blood, you shall not have life in you. For My flesh is meat indeed, and My blood is drink indeed." (John 6, 52. &c.)

‡ Christ foresaw that the Church would understand His most clear and distinct words in their proper and literal meaning. Had He wished to be understood in a different manner, He would also have spoken differently, that He might not, in such most important matter, give occasion to misunderstanding and error.

‖ The teaching of the Apostles, especially of St. Paul, is evident from 1 Cor. 10, 16. and 11, 23—29; the teaching of the whole Church, from her prayers and rites, relating to the Divine service; from the decrees of her Councils; from the numerous testimonies of the Holy Fathers and ecclesiastical writers. For instance, St. Justin, Martyr, says: "As Jesus Christ took flesh and blood, so also is the food consecrated by His words, flesh and blood of the Incarnate Jesus."—St. Cyril, Bishop of Jerusalem, gives this evidence: "As Christ Himself declared and said, 'This is My Body;' who would dare to doubt it? As He openly protested, saying, 'This is My Blood;' who would hesitate, and think that it is not His Blood? Once He changed water into wine; and should we question, whether He could change wine into blood?" No less plain and precise are the testimonies of St. John Chrysostom, St. Ambrose, St. Augustine, and of many other Fathers, even of the first centuries.—We have also a strong proof of the antiquity of the Catholic doctrine in this, that the Schismatic Greek Church believes and teaches quite the same.

9. Did Christ give also to His Apostles power to change bread and wine into His Sacred Flesh and Blood?

Yes, He gave them that power with these words, "*Do this for a commemoration of Me.*" (Luke 22, 19.)

10. To whom did this power pass from the Apostles?

It passed from the Apostles to the Bishops and Priests.

11. When do the Bishops and Priests exercise this power?

At Mass, when they pronounce over the bread and wine these words, "This is My Body, this is My Blood."

12. Is there then after the consecration no longer bread and wine on the altar?

No; there is then on the altar the true Body and the true Blood of Jesus Christ under the appearances of bread and wine.

This change is properly called "*Transubstantiation*," which means, a real conversion of the whole substance of the bread into the substance of the Body of Christ our Lord, and of the substance of the wine into the substance of His Blood. (Counc. of Trent Sess. 13. Ch. 4. and Can. 2.)

13. How long does Christ remain present with His Sacred Flesh and Blood?

As long as the appearances exist.

14. Is there under the appearance of bread, only the Body, and under the appearance of wine, only the Blood of Christ present?

No; under each appearance, Christ is present entire and undivided, as He is entire and undivided in Heaven.

15 When the Priest breaks or divides the Sacred Host, does he also break the Body of Christ ?

No ; he breaks or divides the appearances only : the Body of Christ itself is present in each part entire and living, in a true, though mysterious manner.

16. What does the Real Presence of Jesus Christ in the Holy Eucharist require us to do ?

To visit Him frequently, and to adore Him with the most profound humility and awe, and with the most ardent love and gratitude.

" Let all the Angels of God adore Him." (Hebr. 1, 6.) —In order to show due honour to the Blessed Sacrament, the Church exposes it for public adoration, gives Benediction with it, carries it reverently about in solemn procession, has established Feasts and Confraternities (of the Most Holy Sacrament, of the Sacred Heart of Jesus.) —As an emblem of adoration and love, a lamp is kept burning day and night before the altar where the Blessed Sacrament is reserved in the tabernacle.

17. Is Christ present in the Holy Eucharist, only that He may be also as Man with us.

He is also present for two other reasons,

1. That He may offer Himself for us in the *Holy Sacrifice of the Mass ;* and

2. That, in *Holy Communion*, He may give Himself to us for the nourishment of our souls.

Application.—Rejoice that our Lord and Saviour is pleased to remain in the Blessed Sacrament amongst us to the end of the world. Thank Him for this exceedingly great favour; love Him, and visit Him often and with devotion. Pour out all your sufferings before this amiable Comforter, and have full confidence in His help; for He Himself invites you, saying: " Come to Me, all you that labour, and are burdened, and I will refresh you." (Matt. 11, 28.)

§ 2. *On the Holy Sacrifice of the Mass.*

18. What is a Sacrifice?

A Sacrifice is in general a visible gift offered to God for the purpose of honouring and adoring Him as the Supreme Lord.

19. Have there been Sacrifices at all times?

Yes, there have been Sacrifices from the beginning of the world, and under the Old Law they were strictly commanded by God Himself.

20. Why were the Sacrifices of the Old Law abolished?

Because they were only figures of the unspotted Sacrifice of the New Law, and were, therefore, not to last longer than the Old Law itself.

"For the law having a shadow of the good things to come, not the very image of the things, by the self-same sacrifices, which they offer continually every year, can never make the comers thereunto perfect; for it is impossible that with the blood of oxen and goats sin should be taken away. Wherefore, when He (Christ) cometh into the world, He saith: *Sacrifice and oblation Thou, (O God,) wouldst not; but a body Thou hast fitted to Me. Then said I: Behold I come: in the head of the book it is written of Me, that I should do Thy will, O God.* . . . . He taketh away the first, that He may establish that which followeth." (Hebr. 10, 1—9.)

21. What is the Sacrifice of the New Law?

The Sacrifice of the New Law is the Son of God Himself, Jesus Christ, who, by His death on the Cross, offered Himself to His Heavenly Father for us. (Heb. 9, 14.)

22. Was all Sacrifice to cease with the death of Christ?

No; there was to be also in the New Law of Grace a *Perpetual Sacrifice*, in order to represent continually that which was once accomplished on the Cross, and to apply the fruits of it to our souls.

23. Was such a Sacrifice also promised to us by God?

Yes, even in the Old Law it was prefigured by the Sacrifice of Melchisedech,† and foretold by the Prophet Malachias.‡

† As Melchisedech offered bread and wine (Gen 14, 18.), so also Christ offers Himself under the species of bread and wine unto the end of the world. Therefore, it is said in Ps. 109.: "*The Lord hath sworn, and He will not repent: Thou art a Priest for ever according to the order of Melchisedech.*"—‡ "*I have no pleasure in you (Jews), saith the Lord of Hosts, and I will not receive a gift of your hand; for from the rising of the sun even to the going down, My name is great among the Gentiles, and in every place there is sacrifice, and there is offered to My name a clean oblation.*" (Mal. 1, 10. 11.)

24. Which is this perpetual Sacrifice, foretold by Malachias?

It is the Sacrifice of the Mass.

25. By whom was the Sacrifice of the Mass instituted?

It was instituted by Jesus Christ, when at the Last Supper He offered Himself up under the appearances of bread and wine to His Heavenly Father, and commanded His Apostles thenceforth to celebrate this His Sacrifice.

26. What then is the Mass?

The Mass is the perpetual Sacrifice of the New Law, in which Christ our Lord offers Himself, by the hands of the Priest, in an unbloody manner, under the appearances of bread and wine, to His Heavenly Father, as He once offered Himself on the Cross in a bloody manner.

27. What is the difference between the Sacrifice of the Mass and the Sacrifice of the Cross?

The Sacrifice of the Mass is essentially the same Sacrifice as that of the Cross; the only difference is in the manner of offering.

28. Why is the Sacrifice of the Mass the same Sacrifice as that of the Cross ?

Because in both it is the same who offers, and who is offered namely, Jesus Christ our Lord.

The Priest is only the minister and visible representative of Christ; therefore, he does not speak in his own name, but in the name of Christ: "This is My Body. . . This is My Blood."

29. How is the manner of offering different in both ?

On the Cross, Christ offered Himself in a bloody manner; but in the Mass, He offers Himself in an unbloody manner, whilst He renews the Sacrifice accomplished on the Cross, without suffering or dying any more.

30. If Christ dies no more, how then can the Sacrifice which He consummated on the Cross, be renewed in the Mass ?

It is renewed, because in the Mass Christ offers Himself really and truly under the emblems of the bloody death which He suffered on the Cross, that is, under the separated appearances of bread and wine.

By virtue of the words which the Priest pronounces, the Body of Christ becomes present under the appearance of bread, and His Blood, under the appearance of wine; and both these appearances being visibly *separated* from each other, the separation of the Blood from the Body, consequently, the bloody death on the Cross is represented in an unbloody, mystical manner. This unbloody renewal is, however, not made in order that we may be redeemed anew, for the Sacrifice of the Cross was sufficient for the redemption of the whole world; but, that we may have a standing memorial, and a lively, though unbloody, representation of the bloody Sacrifice of the Cross, by which God is perfectly honoured, and the abundant fruits of the Redemption are applied to our souls.

31. How do we prove that, from the time of the Apostles, the Mass has always been celebrated ?

We prove this, 1. By the words of St. Paul, which

clearly show that as early as in the times of the Apostles the Christians had an altar of their own;† for where an altar is, there must also be a Sacrifice; and 2. By the undeniable testimonies of the Holy Fathers, the decrees of the Councils, the most ancient prayers of the Mass, and by many other memorials of the Eastern and Western Churches.

† "We (Christians) have an altar, whereof they have no power to eat who serve the tabernacle," *i.e.*, the Jews. (Hebr. 13, 10. Comp. 1 Cor. 10, 18—21.)

32. To whom do we offer the Sacrifice of the Mass?

We offer it to God alone; however, we also celebrate the memory of the Saints in it.

33. How do we celebrate the memory of the Saints in the Mass?

1. By rendering thanks to God for all the graces bestowed upon them in this life, and for the glory they now enjoy in Heaven; and 2. By imploring their intercession for us.

34. What are the ends for which we offer the Mass to God?

We offer it to God,

1. As a *Sacrifice of Praise* for His honour and glory;

2. As a *Sacrifice of Thanksgiving* for all the graces and benefits received from Him;

3. As a *Sacrifice of Propitiation* for the many offences given to Him; and

4. As a *Sacrifice of Petition* for obtaining His assistance in all our necessities of soul and body.

35. What effects has the Mass as a Sacrifice of Propitiation?

It has these effects, that we obtain from the Divine Mercy,

1. Graces of contrition and repentance for the forgiveness of sins; and

2. Remission of temporal punishment deserved for sins.

36. To whom are the fruits of the Mass applied?

The *general* fruits are applied to the whole Church, both the living and the dead;

The *particular* fruits are applied, 1. To the Priest who celebrates the Mass; 2. To those for whom in particular he offers it up; and 3. To all those who assist at it with devotion.

37. Which are the principal parts of the Mass?

The principal parts of the Mass are, 1. *Offertory;* 2. *Consecration;* and 3. *Communion.*

38.* What do you think of the Ceremonies which the Church has added to the Sacrifice of the Mass?

The Ceremonies of the Mass have all been handed down to us from the most ancient times; many from the times of the Apostles themselves, and their sublime and mysterious signification is intended to fill our hearts with devotion and reverence.

1. The Priest prays with heartfelt sorrow, and profoundly inclined, at the foot of the altar; then having ascended the steps, he kisses it reverently, reads the Introit, and prays again in the spirit of humility to God, by reciting alternately with the server the "Kyrie eleison" (Lord, have mercy on us). 2. He intones joyfully the Hymn of the Angels (Gloria), and turns then towards the people, to wish them the Divine Blessing. 3. He prays at the side of the altar, in the name of all who are present, to God for the necessities of all. After that, he reads two portions of the Holy Scripture, the Epistle and the Gospel, the latter, however, at the other side of the altar, to intimate that the Evangelical doctrine, rejected by the Jews, passed over to the Heathens. 4. The Gospel is followed, on certain days, by the Nicene Creed. This is the preparation for the Sacrifice, which was anciently called the *Mass of the Catechumens, i.e.* of those who were still in the first rudiments of Christianity, because they were permitted to assist at it thus far, before they were baptized. Now begins, 5. The *Sacrifice* itself by the *Offertory:* the Priest, united with the people, offers bread and wine, and then washes his hands, to show the purity of heart with which we should assist at

the Holy Sacrifice. 6. He invites all to fervent prayer, and, praising God, he joins with the Choirs of Angels, saying: "Holy, holy, holy," etc. 7. Next follow prayers, said in a low voice, for the Church, her Rulers, and all the faithful, under the invocation of the Blessed Virgin and all the Saints. 8. Then he pronounces the mysterious words of *Consecration*, adores, making a genuflexion, and elevates the Sacred Body and the Sacred Blood above his head. At the ringing of the bell, the people adore on their knees, and strike their breasts in token of repentance for their sins. 9. The Priest begs of God, graciously to accept the Sacrifice, to have mercy on all mankind, also on the souls in Purgatory, and concludes with the Lord's Prayer, which contains the substance of all petitions. 10. After a preparatory prayer, during which, at solemn Masses, the Kiss of Peace is given, follows the Holy *Communion*, of which all those who are present should partake, at least spiritually. 11. The Communion being over, the whole ends with a prayer of thanksgiving, the Blessing of the people, and the reading of the Gospel of St. John

39.* Why is the Mass said in Latin?

1. Because this language comes from Rome, whence we received our faith; 2. Because, being a dead language, it does not change in the course of time like living languages; and 3. Because thereby the *Unity* and *Uniformity* of the Church, even in her public service, is represented and preserved over the entire earth.

40.* Why has the Church assigned particular vestments for the Priest, whilst officiating at the altar?

That we may remember that the Priest does not act at the altar in his own person, but as the representative of Jesus, and that he celebrates a most holy Divine Mystery.

In the Old Testament, God Himself minutely appointed the vestments for the Priests, and said: "Aaron and his sons shall use them when they approach to the altar to minister in the Sanctuary, lest being guilty of iniquity they die." (Exod. 28, 43.)

The different colours of the Priest's vestments have also their meaning. The *White* signifies innocence and spiritual joy; the *Red*, the love of God; the *Green*, the hope of eternal life; the *Violet* or *Purple*, humility and penance; the *Black*, deep mourning.

Application.—Endeavour to assist daily at the Holy Sacrifice of the Mass with sincere devotion and profound reverence; for there is no other act so holy and Divine, so rich in graces and heavenly blessings. At the Offertory, offer yourself with Jesus Christ to your Heavenly Father; at the Consecration, humbly adore your Saviour, and beg His pardon; at the Communion, communicate, at least *spiritually*, that is to say, desire most earnestly to be united with your dearest Lord in this Sacrament of Love.

§. 3. *On Holy Communion.*

41. What is Holy Communion?

Holy Communion is the real receiving of the Body and Blood of Jesus Christ for the nourishment of our souls.

Communion means, Union of the faithful with Christ, and with one another; or, Common participation of the Body and Blood of Christ. (See Page 272, Quest. 46.)—It is also called the *Lord's Supper*, the *Receiving of the Blessed Sacrament—of the Holy Eucharist*, etc.

42. Is it God, or the Church only, that has commanded us to receive Holy Communion?

God also has commanded it to us; for Christ our Lord says expressly: "Amen, Amen, I say unto you: Except you eat the Flesh of the Son of man, and drink His Blood, you shall not have life in you." (John 6, 54.)

43. Must we also drink the chalice, in order to receive the Blood of Christ?

No; for under the appearance of bread, we receive also His Blood, since we receive Him whole and entire, His Humanity and His Divinity.

Therefore, Christ promises eternal life to those also, who receive him under the appearance of bread alone: "If any man eat of this bread, he shall live for ever; and the bread that I will give, is My flesh, for the life of the world." (John 6, 52.)—" This is the bread that came down from Heaven. Not as your fathers did eat manna, and are dead. He that eateth this bread, shall live for ever." (John 6, 59.)

44. But why then did Christ institute the Holy Eucharist in both kinds?

Because He instituted it, not only as a Sacrament, but also as a Sacrifice, for which both kinds are required. (See Page 266, Quest. 30.)

Accordingly, the words of Christ, "Drink ye all of this" (Matt. 26, 27.), imply by no means a command to all the people, but only to the Apostles, and their Successors, the Bishops and Priests, when they celebrate the Holy Sacrifice of the Mass. Therefore, Priests also, when they do not actually celebrate Mass, communicate under one kind only.

45.* Why does the Catholic Church give Holy Communion to the faithful in one kind only, namely, under the form of bread?

1. To prevent the Sacred Blood from being profaned, since, under the appearance of wine, it might easily be spilled, and could not well be reserved;

2. To make it easy for all to receive the Blessed Sacrament, as many feel a disgust at drinking out of a common chalice; and

3. To declare thereby against the Heretics, that Christ is present whole and entire under each kind.

In the very first times of the primitive Church, the sick, prisoners, and all those who communicated at home, received the Blessed Sacrament only under the form of bread. Thus only the breaking of bread is mentioned by St. Luke 24, 30: "Whilst He was at table with them, He took bread, and blessed, and brake, and gave to them;" and in the Acts 2, 42.: "And they were persevering in the doctrine of the Apostles, and in the communication of the breaking of bread, and in prayers." (Comp. Acts 2, 46.)—Subsequently, it is true, Pope Leo and Pope Gelasius commanded the chalice to be received, but only in order to combat the erroneous doctrine of the Manicheans, who detested wine as something diabolical, and to prevent these Heretics from approaching with the Catholics to communion.

46. Why will our Lord communicate Himself to all the faithful as food ?

1. To give us a proof of His tender, superabundant love, and to unite Himself most intimately with us: " He that eateth My Flesh, and drinketh My Blood, abideth in Me, and I in him." (John 6, 57.) and

2. To unite us also most closely together with one another by a bond of love and concord. " For we, being many, are one bread, one body, all that partake of one bread. (1. Cor. 10, 17.)

47. What graces does Holy Communion impart to our souls ?

By uniting us in the most intimate manner with Jesus Christ, the Source of all Divine graces, it imparts to us innumerable graces, especially these :

1. It preserves and increases sanctifying grace ;

2. It weakens our evil inclinations, and gives us a desire and strength to be virtuous ;

3. It cleanses us from venial, and preserves us from mortal sin; and

4. It is to us a pledge of our future resurrection and everlasting happiness. (John 6, 55.)

48. Does every one receive in Holy Communion the graces it is intended to give ?

No ; he who receives Holy Communion unworthily, that is, in the state of mortal sin, brings damnation upon himself.

" Whosoever shall eat this Bread, or drink the Chalice of the Lord unworthily, shall be guilty of the Body and of the Blood of the Lord. But let a man prove himself, and so let him eat of that Bread, and drink of the Chalice; for he that eateth and drinketh unworthily, eateth and drinketh judgment to himself, not discerning the Body of the Lord." (1. Cor. 11, 27—29.)—Comparison with the Ark of the Covenant, which brought happiness and blessing upon the pious Israelites, but misfortune and a curse upon the impious Philistines.

49. What sin does he commit who dares to communicate unworthily ?

1. He commits, like Judas, a horrible sacrilege, because he is guilty of the Body and of the Blood of the Lord (1. Cor. 11, 27.); and

2. He renders himself guilty of the blackest ingratitude, because he treats his Divine Redeemer with the foulest indignity in the very same instant, in which he is favoured by Him with the greatest proof of His immense love. (Ps. 54, 13.)

50. What are frequently the consequences of an unworthy Communion, even in this life?

Blindness and hardness of heart, and sometimes also sudden death, and other temporal punishment.

Example: Miserable end of Judas, of whom our Saviour said: "It were better for him, if that man had not been born." (Matt. 26, 24.) And of such St. Paul says: Therefore (on account of unworthily receiving), are there many infirm, and weak among you, and many sleep" (the sleep of death). (1. Cor. 11, 30.)

51. What then must we do, when we have committed a grievous sin?

We must make a good confession before we receive.

"Let a man prove himself, and so let him eat of that Bread, and drink of the Chalice." (1. Cor. 11, 28.)

52. How must we further prepare ourselves, as to the *soul?*

We must endeavour, 1, To cleanse our heart also from venial sin; and 2. To excite in it sentiments of fervour and devotion.

53. Does venial sin also render our Communions unworthy?

Venial sin does not render them unworthy or sacrilegious, but it diminishes the graces which they otherwise would produce.

54. How can we excite sentiments of fervour and devotion in our heart?

By pious meditations and devout exercises.

55. Which are the best exercises before Holy Communion?

The Acts, 1. Of Faith and Adoration; 2. Of Humility and Contrition; and 3. Of Hope, Love, and an ardent Desire.

56.* How do you make an *Act of Faith?*
O my Jesus, I firmly believe all that Thou hast revealed, but especially, that Thou art really present in this Most Holy Sacrament, because Thou, the eternal and infallible Truth, hast declared it.

57.* How do you make an *Act of Adoration?*
O my Jesus, in union with all the Angels and Saints I adore Thee in this Most Holy Sacrament, in which Thou art concealed for the love of me; I adore Thee as my Lord and my God, my Creator and my Redeemer.

58.* How do you make an *Act of Contrition?*
O my Jesus, I am most heartily sorry for all my sins, because by them I have provoked and offended Thee, my most bountiful God, whom I love above all things.

59.* How do you make an *Act of Humility?*
My Lord and my Saviour, how dare I approach Thee after having so often offended Thee! Indeed, I am not worthy to receive Thee into my heart; but only say the word, and my soul shall be healed.

60.* How do you make an *Act of Hope?*
Yes, my most amiable Jesus, Thy mercy is unbounded! Thou vouchsafest to come to me, and to dwell in my heart; so Thou wilt also, I confidently hope, sanctify me, and replenish me with Thy grace.

61.* How do you make an *Act of Love?*
O my Jesus, Thou hast loved me unto the death of the Cross, and, for the love of me, Thou wilt now become also the food of my soul. Oh! What return can I make for Thy love? For the love of Thee, I will live and die.

62.* How do you make an *Act of Desire?*

Come, O Jesus, come and take possession of my heart; it shall be entirely Thine. Come, my Jesus, come and visit me, and strengthen me with Thy grace.

63. How must we prepare ourselves, as to the *body*?

1. We must be fasting; that is, from twelve o'clock the night before, we must not have taken even the least thing by way of eating or drinking;† and

2. We must be decently dressed.

† The Church commands this under pain of a grievous sin, in order to prevent great abuses that would follow from the disregard of this law.

64. Who are dispensed from this command to receive fasting?

Those who are dangerously ill, and receive the Blessed Sacrament by way of *Viaticum*, *i. e.* as a preparation for their passage into eternity.

65. How should we approach to Holy Communion?

With the greatest reverence, with hands joined and raised, and eyes cast down.

66. What should we do at the time of our receiving the Sacred Host?

We should spread the communion-cloth over our hands, and under our chin, hold the head erect and firm, extend the tongue a little upon the under lip, and then most reverently receive the Sacred Host.

Do not keep the Sacred Host in your mouth until it is quite dissolved; but let it moisten a little upon your tongue, and then swallow it. Should it stick to the roof of your mouth, remove it with your tongue, and not with your finger. In some places, to facilitate the swallowing of the Sacred Particle, wine is given; but there is no obligation to take it, and much less are we to believe that it is the Blood of our Lord.

67. What must we do after receiving Holy Communion?

We must retire with the greatest modesty to our place, and spend some time in devout prayer.

No time is more precious and more favourable for obtaining graces, than that which immediately follows Holy Communion; therefore, we should avail ourselves of it in the best manner we can. It is, indeed, a bad sign, if we cannot, in meditation and prayer, entertain ourselves for half an hour, or at least for fifteen minutes, with our dear Redeemer.

68. What sort of prayers ought we especially to say after Holy Communion?

Those in which we humble ourselves before the Lord, thank Him, offer ourselves up to Him, express our love, and implore His graces.

69.* In what manner may we say these prayers?

We may say them in the following manner:—

AN ACT OF HUMILITY.

O my Jesus, whence is this to me, that Thou, my God, shouldst have vouchsafed to come to me, a poor sinner!

AN ACT OF THANKSGIVING AND OBLATION.

Most amiable Jesus, what return can I make to Thee for all that Thou hast done for me! I offer to Thee my body, and my soul, and all that I possess. All my thoughts, my desires, my words, and all that I do, shall be Thine, shall be for Thee.

AN ACT OF LOVE.

O Jesus, inflame my cold heart with the fire of Thy love, in order that I may love Thee more than all things, more than myself.

AN ACT OF PETITION.

O my Lord and my God, grant me, a poor creature, all the graces I stand in need of; for Thou art, indeed, infinitely rich, and infinitely good.

O most bountiful Jesus, remain within me with Thy grace; strengthen and bless me by the virtue of this Holy Sacrament, now and at the hour of my death. Amen.

70. How should we spend the day of Communion?

We should spend it, as much as possible, in pious

exercises, and avoid wordly recreations and amusements.

Application.—Consider how the Lord pours forth, in the Most Holy Sacrament of the Altar, the treasures of His Divine Love for mankind; and resolve, therefore, to approach to the Holy Table as often as you can with permission, and to receive the Bread of Angels with as much devotion and purity of heart, as you can possibly attain to.

On Penance.

1. What is understood by Penance?

By Penance is understood, 1. The *Virtue*, or disposition of heart, by which man repents of his sins, and is converted to God; 2. The *Punishment*, by which he atones for the sins committed; and 3. The *Sacrament* of Penance.

2. What is the Sacrament of Penance?

It is a Sacrament in which the Priest, in the place of God, forgives sins, when the sinner is heartily sorry for them, sincerely confesses them, and is willing to perform the penance imposed upon him.

3. Does the Priest truly remit the sins, or does he only declare that they are remitted?

The Priest does really and truly remit the sins in virtue of the power given to him by Christ.

4. When did Christ give the power of remitting sins?

When after His Resurrection He breathed on the Apostles, and said to them: "Receive ye the Holy Ghost. Whose sins you shall forgive, they are forgiven them; and whose sins you shall retain, they are retained." (John 20, 22. 23.)

5. Did not Christ impart this power to the Apostles only?

No; He imparted it also to all those who were to succeed the Apostles in the Priesthood, as the Church has always believed and taught. (Comp. Page 135. Quest. 18. 19.)

6. Why was the power of forgiving sins to pass from the Apostles to their Successors also?

Because Christ instituted His means of salvation for all times, and for all men, who stand in need of them.

7. Can all sins be forgiven by the Sacrament of Penance?

Yes, all the sins we have committed after Baptism, can be forgiven, if we confess them with the necessary disposition of repentance.

"If we confess our sins, He is faithful and just, to forgive us our sins, and to cleanse us from all iniquity." (1 John 1, 9.)

Yet not *all* sins can be forgiven by *every* Priest. For 1. In order that a Priest may be able to absolve validly from sins, it is not only required that he should have received this power in Holy Order, but also, that he should have been especially authorized by his Bishop to administer the Sacrament of Penance in his Diocese. 2. According to an ancient, lawful, and salutary practice, the Pope and the Bishops are accustomed to reserve to themselves the absolution from certain very grievous sins, from which, therefore, other Priests can absolve only in virtue of a particular authorization. When, however, there is immediate danger of death, and no Priest, peculiarly authorized to hear Confessions, is present, any other Priest can absolve from *all* sins.

8. But why must we confess our sins in order to have them forgiven?

Because Christ ordained it so, when He instituted the Sacrament of Penance.

9. How do we prove that Christ has ordained Confession?

We prove it, 1. By His own words: "Whose sins you shall forgive," &c.; for unless we declare our sins, and the whole state of our soul, to the Priest, he cannot know whether, in virtue of the judicial power which God has conferred on him, he is to forgive, or to retain them;

2. By the testimony of the Holy Fathers of the Church, who unanimously teach, that we have not to expect from God forgiveness of our sins, if we are ashamed to confess them to the Priest;† and

3. By the custom that has existed at all times and among all nations, of confessing sins; for if Confession had been instituted by human laws, and not by Christ Himself, people would certainly never have generally complied with it.‡

† "Whosoever is ashamed to declare his sins to man, and will not confess them, he shall be confounded in the day of judgment in the face of the whole world." (St. John Chrysostom.)—"If the sick man is ashamed to discover the wounds of his soul to the physician, he cannot be cured." (St. Jerome.)—Thus likewise: Origen, St. Cyprian, St. Basil, St. Pacian, St. John Climacus, St. Gregory the Great, and others.—‡ That Confession was practised as early as in the times of the Apostles, is proved by Tradition; and even the Holy Scripture testifies (Acts 19, 18.) that, when the Apostle St. Paul was at Ephesus, "Many of them that believed, came confessing and declaring their deeds."

10.* But could we not also receive forgiveness of our sins by confessing them to God alone?

By no means; or else the full power which Christ gave to the Priests, of retaining or remitting them according to their judgment, would, indeed, be vain and useless.

"Confess your sins one to another (not then to God alone), that you may be saved." (James 5, 16.)—"Let no one say: I do penance privately before God; God who knows me, sees what is going on in my heart. Was it then said in vain: Whatsoever ye shall loose on earth, it shall be loosed also in Heaven? Were, then, the keys given in vain to the Church of God?" (St. Augustin.)

11. Is then the Sacrament of Penance necessary for salvation to all those who have sinned?

It is necessary for salvation to all those who have committed a grievous sin after Baptism.

12. Can the Sacrament of Penance never be supplied?

When the Sacrament of Penance cannot be received, it can be supplied by a perfect Contrition, and a firm resolution to confess our sins as soon as an opportunity offers.

13. What are the effects of the Sacrament of Penance?

1. It remits the sins committed after Baptism;

2. It remits the eternal, and at least a part of the temporal, punishment due to our sins;

3. It restores, or, if it is not lost, it increases, sanctifying grace; and

4. It also confers other particular graces to enable us to lead a holy life.

14. How many things are required on our part, in order to receive the Sacrament of Penance worthily?

These five: 1. Examination of Conscience; 2. Contrition; 3. Resolution of Amendment; 4. Confession; and 5. Satisfaction.

§. 1. *On the Examination of Conscience.*

15. What is meant by *examining our conscience?*

To examine our conscience means, to meditate seriously upon our sins, in order that we may know them well.

16. How must we begin the Examination of Conscience?

By imploring the assistance of the Holy Ghost, that He may give us the grace, rightly to know, to repent, and to confess, our sins.

17. How do we implore the assistance of the Holy Ghost?

Come, O Holy Ghost, enlighten my understanding, that I may rightly know my sins; move also my heart, that I may properly repent of them, sincerely confess them, and truly amend my life.

18. In what manner should we examine our conscience?

1. We should reflect, when we last made a good Confession, and whether we performed the penance laid upon us; and

2. We should go through the Commandments of God and of the Church, likewise through the obligations of our state of life, and the different kinds of sin, and, at the same time, we should ask ourselves, how we have offended God by thoughts, words, actions, and omissions.

19. Must we also examine ourselves on the number, and the circumstances of our sins?

Yes; at least, when they are mortal.

20. Against what faults are we to guard in the Examination of Conscience?

1. We must not examine ourselves too hastily and superficially; 2. We must not conceal our favourite sins from ourselves; 3. We must not take all that to be trifling which the world considers as such; but we should place ourselves in spirit before the tribunal of God; 4. Nor must we be too scrupulous either.

21. How much time ought we to employ in the Examination of Conscience?

The more carelessly we have lived, and the longer we have staid from Confession, the more time and diligence ought we to employ in examining ourselves.

22. How can we facilitate this examination?

By examining our conscience every day, and by going frequently to Confession.

§. 2. *On Contrition.*

23. What is Contrition?

Contrition is a hearty sorrow for, and a detestation of our sins.

24. What qualities must Contrition have, that our sins may be forgiven?

These three: It must be 1. *Interior*; 2. *Universal*; and 3. *Supernatural*.

25. How must Contrition be *interior*?

We must not merely grieve for our sins in words, but we must also detest them in our heart as the greatest evil, and sincerely wish we had not committed them.

"Rend your hearts, and not your garments." (Joel 2, 13.)—"A sacrifice to God is an afflicted spirit: a contrite and humbled heart, O God, Thou wilt not despise." (Ps. 50, 19.)

26. How must Contrition be *universal*?

We must be sorry for *all* the sins we have committed, or, at least, for all mortal sins.

27. If a penitent has no sorrow for his venial sins, would his Confession nevertheless be valid?

If he has to confess venial sins only, and is not truly sorry for any one of them, his Confession is null.

If since our last Confession we have to accuse ourselves of venial sins only, and, because they do not seem to be grievous, we doubt whether we have sufficient Contrition for them; it is advisable to repent again of some *grievous* sin of our former life, which we have already confessed, and to include it in our Confession, saying at the end of it: " For these, and all my other sins which I cannot at present call to my remembrance, and also for the sins of my past life, especially for . . . . I am heartily sorry," &c. This must also be done when we are not quite certain whether we have committed any sin since the last Confession. (Comp. Page 289. Quest. 65.)

28 How must Contrition be *supernatural*?

The sorrow for our sins must arise not from the consideration of their natural evil consequences, but from supernatural motives; namely, because we have offended God, lost His grace, deserved hell, &c.

**29. Would it not then be sufficient to be sorry for

our sins on account of the temporal loss incurred by them

To be sorry for our sins, only because we have lost by them, for example, our health, property, reputation, &c., is nothing but a natural Contrition, which is of no avail.

Thus the sorrow of King Saul, Antiochus, and others, was a merely natural sorrow; on the contrary, that of King David, Mary Magdalen, Zacheus, the Apostles Peter and Paul, and other Scripture Penitents, was supernatural.

30. What then should we do in order to obtain supernatural Contrition?

We should 1. Earnestly ask God for His grace; and 2. We should seriously call to our mind what Faith teaches us of the malice of sin, and its fatal consequences;* for supernatural Contrition must proceed from grace, and motives of Faith.

31. Why must Contrition proceed from motives of Faith?

1. Because Faith is the foundation and root of all Justification; and 2. Because, otherwise, Contrition does not prompt us to renounce evil entirely, and for ever; but only, inasmuch as we have to dread temporal losses.

32. How many kinds of supernatural Contrition are there?

Two: *Perfect Contrition* and *Imperfect Contrition*, commonly called *Attrition*.

33. When is Contrition *Perfect*?

When it arises from Perfect Love; *i.e.* when we detest sin more than all other evils, for the sole reason that it offends God, the Supreme Good.

Since Perfect Contrition proceeds from Perfect Love, in order to excite ourselves to Perfect Contrition, it is very profitable, previously, or at the same time, to excite ourselves to Perfect Love.

---

* See Page 223, and 224. Quest. 11—15; and Page 129. Quest. 14.

34. When is Contrition *Imperfect*?
When our Love is not Perfect, and when, therefore, the fear of Hell and of the loss of Heaven, or the heinousness of sin itself must excite and determine us, to detest sin above all other evils, and to offend God no more.

Perfect Contrition is, therefore, a sorrow for sin, arising from the Perfect Love of God: *Imperfect Contrition* is, on the contrary, a sorrow for sin, arising from any other motive which, though good and supernatural, is not perfect. In order to excite ourselves to *Perfect Contrition*, let us consider how much God deserves to be loved by us, on account of His infinite goodness, *i.e.* on account of that perfection which He, as the Sovereign Good, possesses; and how, nevertheless, we have despised and insulted Him, our most amiable Father; how we have expelled Him from our heart, and renounced His love and friendship for ever. In order to excite ourselves to *Imperfect Contrition*, let us consider how terrible are the pains of Hell or of Purgatory, which we have deserved; how beautiful Heaven, which we have lost; how detestable sin, which nailed the Son of God to the Cross, has deprived our soul of grace, disfigured her, rendered her ugly and execrable before God and His Angels, &c.; and let us, therefore, repent the offence given to God, by hating it more than all the evils of the world.

35. Must Contrition necessarily be Perfect?
It is not necessary for the remission of sin that we should have Perfect Contrition; we should, however, strive to obtain it.

36. Why should we strive to obtain Perfect Contrition?
Because, the more Perfect our Contrition is, the more is our repentance meritorious and acceptable to God, and the more certainly it obtains our pardon.

37. When should we make an Act of Perfect Contrition, even *without* the Sacrament of Penance?
1. In danger of death; and 2. As often as we have the misfortune to commit a mortal sin, and cannot immediately go to Confession.

38. When must we make the Act of Contrition *in* the Sacrament of Penance?

We must make it before our Confession, or, at least, before the Priest gives us Absolution.

39. Can Contrition ever be supplied in case of necessity?

No; Contrition is so necessary that it cannot be supplied by anything, or in any case.

§. 3. *On the Resolution of Amendment.*

40. What must Contrition necessarily include?

Contrition must necessarily include, 1. Hope of pardon; and 2. Resolution of Amendment.

41. What is a Resolution of Amendment?

A Resolution of Amendment is a sincere will to mend our life, and to sin no more.

42. What must be the qualities of our Resolution of Amendment?

Our Resolution of Amendment must be, like our Contrition, 1. *Interior* or *Sincere;* 2. *Universal;* and 3. *Supernatural.*

43. What must he be determined to do, who has a firm and sincere Resolution of Amendment?

He must be determined,

1. To avoid, at least, all grievous sins, so that he would suffer anything, rather than commit even one;
2. To shun the danger, and especially the proximate occasion of sin;
3. To use the necessary means of amendment;
4. To make due satisfaction for his sins; and
5. To repair whatever injury he may have done to his neighbour.

44. What is meant by the proximate occasion of sin?

By the proximate occasion of sin, is meant a person, a company, an amusement, and such like, by which people usually were, or, if they do not avoid them, probably will be led into sin.

45. Is it a strict duty to shun the proximate occasion ?

Yes, whenever it is possible; for he who will not avoid the occasion of sin, has not a sincere purpose to avoid sin itself.

46. What ought they to consider who will not avoid the proximate occasion, or will not desist from their habitual sins ?

That the Priest's Absolution is of no avail to them, but only aggravates their guilt.

47. How can we make an Act of Imperfect and Perfect Contrition, together with a Resolution of Amendment ?

In this manner:

O my God, from the bottom of my heart I am sorry for all my sins; not only, because by them I have rendered myself unworthy of Thy grace, and liable to Thy just punishment in this life and in the next; but especially, because I have offended Thee, the Sovereign, Most Perfect, and Most Amiable Good, whom I now love above all things. I hate and detest all my sins, and am firmly resolved, never more to offend Thee, my most amiable God, and carefully to avoid the occasion of sin.

§. 4. *On Confession.*

48. What is Confession ?

Confession is a sorrowful declaration of our sins to a Priest, in order to obtain Absolution from him.

49. What are the necessary Qualities of Confession?

Confession must be 1. *Entire;* 2. *Sincere;* and 3. *Clear.*

50. When is Confession *entire* ?

When we confess, at least, all grievous sins which we remember, together with their number and necessary circumstances.

51. But what must we do, if we do not recollect the number rightly ?

We must declare it as well as we are able, and say, for instance: I have committed this sin *about* . . . times a day—week—or month.

52. What sort of circumstances must we confess?

We must 1. Especially confess such circumstances as change the nature, or aggravate the guilt, of our sins; and 2. Mention in general every thing by which the Confessor may be enabled to judge rightly of the state of our conscience, and to put us on our guard against relapsing into sin.

1. Should a person have stolen *Church property*, wished his *parents* dead, coveted his neighbour's *wife*, *injured* some one by telling a lie, &c.; it would not be sufficient for him to confess, that he has stolen, wished some persons dead, had an evil desire, told a lie.—2. Therefore, we must also declare whether we have injured our neighbour much or little, knowingly or unknowingly; whether the occasion of sin still continues; whether we have often before confessed, and never mended, the evil habit, &c.

53. What is to be observed in the declaration of the circumstances?

We must avoid making any person known, who may be concerned in our sins, refrain from all superfluous narrations, and express ourselves in as modest and decent a manner, as the nature of the sin allows.

54. Must we also confess venial sins?

We are not indeed obliged to confess venial sins; yet it is good and wholesome to do so.

55. But if we do not know whether something is a mortal, or a venial sin, what are we to do?

We are to confess it, because many people mistake mortal sins for venial ones.

56. When is Confession *sincere*?

When we accuse ourselves just as we find ourselves guilty before God, without concealing or disguising any thing, or excusing it by vain pretences.

57. What should the penitent consider, if he is ashamed to make a sincere Confession?

He should consider, 1. That a Confession, which is not sincere, procures him neither remission of sins, nor peace of conscience; but that the Confession, as well as the Communion which follows it, is another grievous sin, a Sacrilege, and deserves eternal damnation; and

2. That it is much better for him to confess his sins to one Priest, bound by secrecy, than to live always uneasy in sin, to die unhappy for ever, and to be put to shame at the last day before the whole world.

As the Confessor is bound to suffer even martyrdom, rather than reveal any thing heard in Confession, so is every one else, who may have accidentally overheard any part of a Confession, bound to the strictest secrecy.

58. What must we do, if we have omitted something in Confession, which we were obliged to declare?

1. If we have omitted it without our fault, it is only required to mention it in the next Confession; but

2. If we have omitted it, either because we were ashamed to confess it, or because we did not carefully examine our conscience; we must also say, in how many Confessions we have omitted it through our fault, and repeat them all.

59. When is Confession *clear*?

When we so express ourselves, that the Confessor can understand everything well, and clearly see the state of our conscience.

60. Would our Confession be clear, if we accused ourselves in general only; for example, that we have not loved God, that we have thought or spoken evil?

By no means; we must distinctly name and specify the different sins.

61. What is a *General Confession*?

A General Confession is that in which we repeat all, or some of our former Confessions.

62. When is a General Confession necessary?

As often as our former Confessions were sacrilegious, either through want of sincerity, or of sorrow and resolution, or through a culpable negligence in the examination of our conscience.

63. When principally is a General Confession useful and advisable?

1. As a preparation for first Communion; 2. On entering on a state of life; 3. In dangerous illness; 4. At the time of a Jubilee, a Mission, &c.

64. How do you begin your Confession?

Having made the sign of the Cross, I say: "I, a poor and miserable sinner, accuse myself to God, the Almighty, and to you, my Father, in His stead, that since my last Confession which was . . . , I have committed the following sins." (Here I confess my sins.)

Or in the following manner:

Having arrived at the Confessional, I kneel down, make the Sign of the Cross, and ask the Priest's Blessing by saying: "Bless me, Father, for I have sinned." After receiving his Blessing, I say the first part of the "*Confiteor*" as far as "through my most grievous fault." Then I say how long it is since my last Confession, whether I then received Absolution, and performed my Penance. After this, I confess all the sins I can recollect, beginning with those which I may have forgotten in my last Confession.

65. How do you finish your Confession?

In conclusion I say: "For these, and all the sins of my whole life, I am most heartily sorry, because by them I have offended God, the Supreme and Most Amiable Good. I detest all my sins, and am firmly resolved to mend my life, and to sin no more. I humbly ask Penance and Absolution of you, my Ghostly Father."

Or, I conclude by saying:

"For these, and all my other sins which I cannot

at present call to my remembrance, and also for the sins of my past life, especially for . . . . , (See Page 282. Quest. 27. Note.) I am heartily sorry, purpose amendment for the future, and most humbly ask pardon of God, and Penance and Absolution of you, my Ghostly Father." Here I finish the *Confiteor*: "Therefore, I beseech the Blessed Mary, ever Virgin," &c.

66. What should we do after this?

We should listen with attention to the instruction which the Confessor may think proper to give, and to the Penance he enjoins; and when he asks us questions, we should answer them with sincerity and humility.

Take care not to leave the Confessional before the Priest has given you notice, by saying for instance: "Go in peace;" or, "May God Almighty bless you!" or something similar.

67. What are we to do, if we should not receive Absolution?

We should humbly submit to the decision of the Confessor, and, by true amendment, render ourselves worthy of it.

§ 5. *On Satisfaction.*

68. What is Satisfaction in the Sacrament of Penance?

It is the performance of the Penance enjoined by the Confessor.

69. For what purpose does the Confessor impose a Penance on us?

1. For the expiation of the temporal punishment of sin; and
2. For the amendment of our life.

70. Does not God then, with the sin, remit also all punishment?

God always remits, with the sin, the eternal, but not always the temporal punishment; therefore, the Prophet Nathan said to David: "The Lord hath taken away thy sin; nevertheless, the child that is born to thee, shall surely die." (2 Kings 12, 13. 14.)

71. What is the temporal punishment due to our sins?

It is that punishment which we have to suffer either here on earth, or in Purgatory.

72.* Why does God not always remit the temporal punishment together with the eternal?

1. Because His *Justice* demands that, by the enduring of the punishment, we should make some reparation for the injury done to Him; and

2. Because in His *Mercy* He will, by the fear of such punishment, render us more cautious, and guard us against relapsing into sin.

73.* Has not Christ then made full satisfaction for our sins?

Yes, Christ has abundantly satisfied for our sins; nevertheless He requires that we also, in union with Him, should make satisfaction: just as He has prayed for us, and nevertheless requires that we also should pray, in order to be saved.

"I fill up those things that are wanting of the sufferings of Christ." (Col. 1, 24.)—"If we suffer with Him, we shall be also glorified with Him." (Rom. 8, 17.)

74. From whom has the Priest the power to impose works of Penance?

From Jesus Christ who gave to His Church the power, not only to loose, but also to bind. (Matt. 18, 18.)

75. Is the Confession invalid, if the penitent does not perform the Penance enjoined?

If after Confession he does not perform the Penance which in Confession he was willing to perform, the Confession is not invalid; but he commits a sin, and deprives himself of many graces.

76. When should we comply with the Penance enjoined?

If the Confessor has fixed no time for it, the best way is to comply with it directly, and before we have fallen again into any grievous sin.

77.* What should we do, if the Penance seems to be too severe?

We should consider how light the present Penances are in comparison with the ancient Canonical Penances, and with the eternal punishment we have deserved; but if we should really be unable to do the Penance, we should respectfully mention it to the Confessor.

78. Should we perform that Penance only, which the Confessor lays upon us?

We should also endeavour to satisfy the Divine Justice by other voluntary penitential works, and by patience in our sufferings.

79. What shall we have to expect, if we neglect to make due satisfaction to the Divine Justice?

We shall have so much the more to suffer in Purgatory, and that without any merit for Heaven.

80. Are we, after Confession, under no other obligation than to satisfy the Divine Justice?

We are also obliged,

1. To repair, to the utmost of our power, the scandal we have given, and the injury we have unjustly done to our neighbour; and

2. To employ the means necessary not to relapse into sin, and to amend our life.

1. Example of Zacheus: "Behold, Lord, the half of my goods I give to the poor; and if I have wronged any man of any thing, I restore him four-fold." (Luke 19, 8.)— 2. "Behold thou art made whole: sin no more, lest some worse thing happen to thee." (John 5, 14.)

81. What should they think, who always relapse into their former grievous sins?

That their Confessions are much to be suspected, and that their state is extremely dangerous.

" When the unclean spirit is gone out of a man . . . he goeth and taketh with him seven other spirits more wicked than himself, and entering in they dwell there; and the last state of that man becomes worse than the first." (Luke 11, 26.)

82. What means should we especially use in order that we may not relapse into sin?

We should 1. Strictly follow the instructions and directions of our Confessor; 2. Carefully avoid the occasions of sin; 3. Daily examine our conscience; 4. Be assiduous in praying, in hearing the word of God, and receiving the Sacraments of Penance and of the Holy Eucharist; and 5. We should often meditate on the Four Last Things of man.

Application.—When you have sinned, go to Confession without delay, but never without a diligent Examination of Conscience, a true Contrition, a firm Resolution of Amendment, and a sincere declaration of your sins; that the Sacrament of Penance, so replete with grace, may not become for you a source of eternal perdition.

On Indulgences.

83. By what means does the Church assist us in the discharge of the temporal punishment due to our sins?

By the grant of Indulgences.

84. What is an *Indulgence*?

An Indulgence is a remission, granted out of the Sacrament of Penance, of that temporal punishment which, even after the sin is forgiven, we have yet to undergo either here, or in Purgatory.

85. How does the Church remit the punishment due to our sins?

By making to the Divine Justice compensation for us from the inexhaustible Treasure of the merits of Christ and His Saints.

Indulgences, therefore, derive their value and efficacy from the Spiritual Treasure of the Church, which consists of the superabundant merits and satisfactions of Christ and the Saints. This treasure is to be considered as the common property of the faithful, committed to the administration of the Church, since, by virtue of the *Communion of Saints* by which we are united as members of one body, the abundance of some supplies the want of others.

"In this present time, let your abundance supply their want, that their abundance also may supply your want, that there may be an equality." (2 Cor. 8, 14. Comp. Page 148. §. 4.)

86. What is generally required to gain an Indulgence?

It is required, 1. That we should be in the state of grace, and have already obtained, by true repentance, forgiveness of those sins, the temporal punishment of which is to be remitted by the Indulgence; and 2. That we should exactly perform the good works prescribed for the gaining of the Indulgence.

87. What must we believe with regard to Indulgences?

We must believe,

1. That the Catholic Church has power to grant Indulgences; and

2. That the use of them is very salutary to us. (Counc. of Trent, Sess. 25.)

88. From whom has the Catholic Church the power of granting Indulgences?

From Jesus Christ, who made no exception when He said: "Whatsoever thou shalt loose on earth, it shall be loosed also in Heaven." (Matt. 16, 19. & 18, 18.)

That the Catholic Church has also at all times exercised this full power, is evident even from 2 Cor. 2, 10.

89. Who has a right to grant Indulgences?

This right belongs especially to our Most Holy Father, the Pope, who, being the Successor of St.

Peter, has received from Christ the keys of the kingdom of Heaven; the Bishops, however, have also the power of granting some Partial Indulgences.

90. For what reasons are Indulgences very salutary to us?

For these:

1. They discharge our debt of temporal punishment;

2. They encourage us to make our peace with God, by substituting for the fearful Canonical Penances easier exercises of piety;

3. They incite us to true repentance and amendment, since without these requisites they cannot be gained at all;

4. They urge us to receive frequently the Sacraments of Penance and of the Holy Eucharist, and to perform good works;

5. They console fervent penitents in their fear of the judgments of God.

To assert that, by an Indulgence, the Church forgives *sins*, past or future, or that she grants Indulgences for *money*, is a gross calumny. It is true that, when granting an Indulgence, she has sometimes, besides the condition of a sincere repentance, prescribed alms-deeds for charitable purposes; for instance, for the building of a Church, or of an hospital; but as this, laudable as it was in the beginning, gave, nevertheless, in the course of time, occasion to abuses, the Council of Trent abolished the abuses, declaring, however, that "The use of Indulgences is very salutary to Christian people, and approved of by the authority of the Sacred Councils." (Sess. 25.)

91.* Is it then not true that the Church, by Indulgences, frees us from the obligation of doing penance?

No; she does not free us from the obligation of doing penance according to our capacity, since, the greater is our penitential zeal and love to God, the more do we participate in the Indulgence; she will only assist us in our inability to expiate all temporal punishment in this life, and thus, by a generous indulgence, effect what, in ancient times, she endeavoured to attain by the rigorous Penitential Canons.

92. How many kinds of Indulgences are there?

There are two kinds: A *Plenary* Indulgence, which is the remission of the whole debt of temporal punishment due to sin; and a *Partial* Indulgence, which is the remission of a part of it only.

93.* What is meant by an Indulgence of forty days, or seven years?

A remission of such a debt of temporal punishment, as a person would discharge, if he did penance for forty days or seven years, according to the ancient Canons of the Church.

94. What is meant by a *Jubilee*?

A Jubilee is a Plenary Indulgence which the Holy Father grants every twenty-fifth year, or upon extraordinary occasions; during which time, in order to increase the fervour of repentance in the faithful, Confessors have a special power to commute private vows into other works of piety, and to absolve in all reserved cases.

95. Can Indulgences also be rendered available to the Souls in Purgatory?

Yes, all those which the Pope has expressly declared to be applicable to them.

Application.—Value and esteem Indulgences, and avail yourself of every opportunity of gaining them worthily for yourself, as well as for the souls of the faithful departed.

On Extreme Unction.

1. What is Extreme Unction?

Extreme Unction is a Sacrament in which the sick, by the anointing with holy oil, and by the prayer of the Priest, receive the grace of God for the good of their souls, and often also of their bodies.

This Sacrament is called *Extreme Unction*, because it is usually the *last* of the holy unctions which are administered by the Church.

2. Whence do we know that the Sacrament of Extreme Unction was instituted by Christ?

We know this, 1. From the Holy Scripture; and 2. From the constant doctrine of the Church.

3. What does Holy Scripture say of the Sacrament of Extreme Unction?

The Apostle St. James says in his Epistle (5, 14. 15.): "Is any man sick among you, let him bring in the Priests of the Church, and let them pray over him, anointing him with oil in the name of the Lord; and the prayer of faith shall save the sick man, and the Lord shall raise him up, and if he be in sins, they shall be forgiven him."

4. Why do we infer from these words, that Christ has instituted Extreme Unction?

Because the anointing with oil could have no Sacramental power of forgiving sins, if Christ had not so ordained it.

5. How is Extreme Unction administered?

The Priest anoints the different senses of the sick person with holy oil, and uses, at each anointing, this form of prayer: "Through this holy unction, and His most tender mercy, may the Lord forgive thee whatever sins thou hast committed by thy sight (by thy hearing, etc.)."

6. What effects does Extreme Unction produce in the soul?

Extreme Unction 1. Increases sanctifying grace; 2. It remits venial sins, and also those mortal sins which the sick person can no more confess; 3. It removes the remains † of sins already forgiven; and 4. It strengthens the soul in her sufferings and temptations, especially in her agony.

† By *remains of sins*, we understand the temporal punishment, the evil inclinations of the heart, and the weakness of the will, which are the consequences of sins committed, and *remain* even after the sins have been forgiven.

7. What effects does Extreme Unction produce in the body?

It often relieves the pains of the sick person, and sometimes restores him even to health, if it be expedient for the salvation of his soul.

8. Who can, and ought to receive Extreme Unction?

Every Catholic who has come to the use of reason, and is in danger of death by sickness; but not such, as in health expose themselves to the danger of death.

9. How are we to receive Extreme Unction?
We are to receive it,

1. In the state of grace; wherefore we must previously, if possible, confess our sins, or, at least, make an Act of Perfect Contrition; and

2. With faith, hope, and charity, and resignation to the will of God.

Acts of these and similar virtues should often be made by the sick person during illness, especially when his end approaches, and all present ought to help him to do so. It may be briefly done in the following words:

> I believe, my God, in Thee,
> I most firmly hope in Thee,

And I love most truly Thee,
And all men are dear to me.
All my sins are grieving me,
Which, I beg Thee, pardon me.
I resign myself to Thee,
Thank for good and evil Thee,
Nay, I'll live and die for Thee.
                    Amen.

10. When should we receive Extreme Unction?

We should receive it, if possible, whilst we are still in our senses, and after having received the Viaticum.

11. How often can Extreme Unction be received?

In each dangerous illness it can be received once; it can, however, be repeated on relapse into danger that had passed.

12.* Is it not unreasonable for a person, from fear of death, to defer, or even neglect, the receiving of Extreme Unction?

Certainly; for

1. Extreme Unction has been instituted even for the health of the body;

2. The sick person will recover more probably, if he employs in time the remedy ordained by God, than if he waits until he cannot recover except by a miracle; and

3. If his sickness be mortal, what can he wish better, than to die happy, to which end this Holy Sacrament gives him grace.

Relatives also, or Attendants of the sick person, sin grievously, if through their fault the last Sacraments are not administered to him in due time. " His sisters, therefore, sent to Him, saying: Lord, behold, he whom Thou lovest is sick." (John 11, 3.)

Application.—When God, in His mercy, visits you with a dangerous illness, be sure not to put off the receiving of the Holy Sacraments to the last moment;

otherwise death may surprise you, when it is no longer possible to have the attendance of a Priest.

On Holy Order.

1. On whom did Christ Himself confer the Priesthood?

On His Apostles.

2. Was the Priesthood to discontinue with the death of the Apostles?

No; no more than the Church was to discontinue with them.

3. How was the Priesthood continued?

By the Sacrament of Holy Order.

4. What is Holy Order?

Holy Order is that Sacrament which communicates to those who receive it, the full power of Priesthood, together with a special grace to discharge their sacred duties well.

5. What are the principal powers of Priesthood?

1. The power to change bread and wine into the Body and Blood of our Lord; and 2. The power to forgive sins.

The power of consecrating bread and wine, Christ gave to His Church at the Last Supper (Comp. Page 262. Quest. 9), and the power of forgiving sins, after His Resurrection. (Comp. Page 277. Quest. 4.)

6. Is there in Holy Order also a visible sign which indicates the communicating of the invisible power and grace?

Yes, there are several; as, the imposition of hands and the prayer of the Bishop, the delivery of the chalice with wine, and of the paten with bread.

The imposition of hands and prayer are also mentioned in Holy Scripture: " I admonish thee, that thou stir up the grace of God, which is in thee by the imposition of my hands." Thus wrote St. Paul to Bishop Timothy, 2 Tim. 1, 6., and in a similar manner 1. Tim. 4, 14.—By Prayer and imposition of hands, Paul and Barnabas were also ordained: "Then they, fasting and praying, and imposing their hands upon them, sent them away." (Acts 13, 3.)

7.* But are not *all* Christians true Priests by their Baptism?

No; as the true Priesthood of the Old Law was propagated by natural descent from Aaron, so it is also in the New Law propagated by a spiritual descent from the Apostles, that is, by ordination.

8.* Why then does St. Peter say that all Christians are "*a kingly Priesthood?*" (1. Pet. 2, 9.)

Because all, by their Baptism, are obliged to offer up to God internal or *spiritual sacrifices* (1. Pet. 2, 5.) of faith, hope and charity, of prayer and mortification.

From this passage, it can no more be inferred that all Christians are true *Priests*, than that all are true *Kings*. In the Old Law also, God said to the Israelites: "You shall be to Me a *priestly kingdom*" (2 Kings 19, 6); nevertheless, there was a particular Priesthood, which alone was authorized to offer Sacrifices.—Punishment of King Ozias. (2 Paral. 26.)

9. Who can validly administer the Sacrament of Holy Order?

Bishops only, who have received this power by a particular Consecration.

As no one can be made a Priest except by the Sacrament of Holy Order, which can validly be administered only by a Bishop, who again has received the power of administering it, from another Bishop lawfully consecrated; it is evident that, by an uninterrupted succession of Bishops lawfully ordained and consecrated, the Priesthood ascends to the Apostles on whom Christ Himself conferred the Priestly and Episcopal Powers both for themselves and for their Successors.

10. Cannot also Civil Authorities, or Christian Communities, confer spiritual powers?

No, they cannot confer spiritual powers on others, because they have none themselves.

Hence the Council of Trent decrees (Sess. 23. Ch. 4), "That all those who, being only called and instituted by the people, or by the civil power and magistrate, ascend to the exercise of these ministrations, and those who of their own rashness assume them to themselves, are not to be looked upon as ministers of the Church, but as *thieves and robbers, who have not entered by the door.*" (John 10, 1. 8.)

11. Can a Priest be deprived of his Ordination?

No; he can as little be deprived of Ordination as of Baptism, because it imprints an indelible character upon the soul.

A Priest, therefore, or a Bishop, cannot be deprived of the powers which he has received in his Ordination or Consecration, to change bread and wine into the Body and Blood of Jesus Christ, and to offer up the Holy Sacrifice of the Mass, to administer Confirmation, Extreme Unction, and Holy Order; but the power of remitting sins by Sacramental Absolution, can be taken from him, because the valid administration of the Sacrament of Penance is also dependent on *Jurisdiction*, that is to say, on his mission or authorization by a lawful spiritual Superior. (Comp. Page 278. Note to Quest. 7.) For this very reason, the Priests and Bishops of the Schismatical Greek Church, and all those who ever have fallen away from the Catholic Church, retain the powers of their Ordination and Consecration, which originally they received from the Catholic Church; but all other spiritual power, which depends on the Apostolical Mission, and comes from the Head of the Catholic Church, expires with their separation from the Church.

12. Are there any other Orders besides those of Priest and Bishop?

Yes, there are others which are preparatory degrees to the Priesthood.

13. Which are these other Orders?

1. The *Four Minor* Orders, by which those who receive them are qualified for various offices connected with the Divine Service;

2. The Order of *Subdeacon*, who has to assist the Deacon when serving at the altar; and

3. The Order of *Deacon*, who immediately assists the Priest at the altar, and helps him also in baptizing, preaching, and giving Holy Communion.

14. Who can, and ought to embrace the Ecclesiastical State?

He only, who is called to it by God.

Parents who, actuated by temporal interests, force their children to take Holy Orders, sin most grievously, and are responsible for all the evil consequences resulting from it.

15. What should the faithful do in order to obtain worthy Priests and Pastors?

They should often and fervently pray to God for that grace, and render themselves worthy of it by their love of the Church, and respect for the Priesthood.

" Pray ye, therefore, the Lord of the harvest, that He send forth Labourers into His harvest." (Matt. 9, 38.)

Application.—Always show due respect and submission to Priests, as the Representatives of God, and the Dispensers of His Holy Mysteries; and should you happen to perceive in any of them human failings and infirmities, do not be scandalized, but " Whatsoever they shall say to you, observe and do; but according to their works do ye not." (Matt. 23, 3.)

On *Matrimony*.

1. By whom was Matrimony instituted?

Matrimony was instituted by God Himself, when He gave to Adam in Paradise Eve for his wife, that they both might lead a godly life, and live together in faithful and indissoluble love.

2. Was the sanctity of Matrimony always respected according to its original institution?

No; when by sin the entire human race had fallen away from God, the contract of marriage was no longer kept so holy, until our Saviour came, and not only restored Matrimony as God had originally instituted it, but even elevated it to the dignity of a Sacrament.

3. How did Christ restore Matrimony to its original institution?

He ordained that Marriage should again, as it was from the beginning, subsist between one man and one woman only, and that unto the death of either of them; and He proposed, therefore, His spiritual union with the Church as an example to married people. (Ephes. 5.)

"Moses by reason of the hardness of your heart permitted you to put away your wives; but from the beginning it was not so. And I say to you, that whosoever shall put away his wife, and shall marry another, committeth adultery; and he that shall marry her that is put away, committeth adultery." (Matt. 19, 8. 9. and Luke 16, 18. Mark 10, 11. 12.)

4. Can then the bond of marriage never be dissolved?

Spiritual Superiors can, indeed, for important reasons, allow a husband and wife to live separated from each other; but, nevertheless, they continue married people, and neither of them can validly contract a second marriage, whilst the other party is living.

"To them that are married, not I, but the Lord commandeth that the wife depart not from her husband. And if she depart, that she remain unmarried, or be reconciled to her husband. And let not the husband put away his wife." (1 Cor. 7, 10. 11.)

5. How do we know that Matrimony is a Sacrament?

1. St. Paul teaches so, who calls Matrimony in the Church "*a great Sacrament* ;"† (Ephes. 5, 32.)

2. The Church has, at all times, believed and taught so, as is evident, not only from the Holy Fathers, but also from the teaching of those Sects, who in the first ages separated themselves from us.

† St. Paul teaches that husbands and wives should be united with each other, as Christ and His Church are united. Now, the union that subsists between Christ and His Church, is *supernatural*, and *replete with graces;* consequently, Matrimony is a sign to which invisible grace is attached, and, therefore, a Sacrament.

6. What then is Matrimony in the Church of Christ ?

Matrimony is a Sacrament by which two single persons, man and woman, are married to each other, and receive grace from God, to discharge the duties of their state faithfully until death.

7. How is this Sacrament received ?

The bridegroom and the bride declare before their Pastor and two witnesses, that they take each other for wife and husband, whereupon the Priest blesses their union.

Another Priest can only unite them in Matrimony, when commissioned by the Pastor of the parties, or by the Bishop, for that purpose.

8. What are the duties of married persons ?

1. They should take the mutual love of Christ and His Church for their model, and live with each other in peace and conjugal fidelity, until death separates them ;

2. They should edify each other by leading a holy life ;†

3. They should concur together in bringing up their children in the fear of God, and suffer no ser-

vants to be in their house, who might endanger their innocence.

4. The husband should treat his wife with kindness, support and cherish her; the wife should obey her husband in all that is just and honourable, and conscientiously manage the domestic concerns.‡

† "Marriage honourable in all, and the bed undefiled; for fornicators and adulterers God will judge." (Hebr. 13, 4.)
—‡ "As the Church is subject to Christ, so also let the wives be to their husbands in all things;" *i.e.* that are just and honourable. "Husbands, love your wives, as Christ also loved the Church, and delivered Himself up for it. . . . For no man ever hated his own flesh, but nourisheth and cherisheth it, as also Christ doth the Church." (Ephes. 5, 24—29.)

9.* What should married people consider, when they are tempted to break their conjugal fidelity?

1. That by adultery they break the solemn contract they have made in the presence of God and of the Church;

2. That they break the most sacred bond by which, according to God's disposal, human society is united and kept together;

3. That they disturb domestic peace, hinder the good education of their children, and destroy the happiness of the whole family; and

4. That they expose themselves to the danger of falling into disgrace and misery, and all sorts of sins and vices, and even, of being severely chastised, and ultimately entirely rejected by God Himself.

"He that is an adulterer, shall destroy his own soul; he gathereth to himself shame and dishonour, and his reproach shall not be blotted out." (Prov. 6, 32. 33.)

In the Old Law, adultery was, by God's command, punished with death, and in the primitive Church, with public penance of many years, like manslaughter.—Sin and punishment of King David.

10. What should those people bear in mind, who intend to enter the married state?

1. They should not thoughtlessly espouse each other;

2. They should be properly instructed, and be free from impediments;

3. They should live innocently whilst they are espoused, and not think that, during that time, they are allowed greater liberties, or to live together in the same house;

4. They should enter the married state with a pure and holy intention; and

5. Before they marry, they should make a good Confession, and worthily receive Holy Communion.

" We are the children of saints, and we must not be joined together like heathens that know not God." (Tob. 8, 5.)

Example of Sara who could say to God: "Thou knowest, O Lord, that I never coveted a husband, and have kept my soul clean from all lust. Never have I joined myself with them that play, neither have I made myself partaker with them that walk in lightness. But a husband I consented to take, with Thy fear, not with my lust." (Tob. 3, 16—18.)

11.* Who may be said to espouse each other thoughtlessly?

1. All who neglect to have previous recourse to God, and disregard His will, the advice of their parents, and the salvation of their own soul in the affair; (Prov. 19, 14.)

2. Those who, in their choice, care less for religion and virtue, than for temporal advantages, etc.; and

3. Those who do not first consider whether they will be able to fulfil the weighty duties of the married state.

The husband should be able to maintain his wife and children; he should not be a free-thinker, or addicted to gambling, drinking, quarreling, cursing, etc. The wife should be free from vanity, love of finery, and capriciousness; she should be chaste, pious, modest, industrious, and economical. Both should possess the requisite virtue, intelligence, and learning in religious matters, in order to be able to give their children a Christian education.

12. Are people bound to keep their promise of marriage?

Yes, under pain of grievous sin; unless both parties voluntarily retract it, or either of them, for particular reasons, has a right to retract, which is to be decided by their spiritual superiors.

13. What sin do they commit, who receive the Sacrament of Matrimony with an unholy intention, or in the state of mortal sin?

They render themselves guilty of sacrilege, and, therefore, unworthy of all the Divine graces and blessings.

14. How many kinds of *Impediments* are there?
There are two kinds:

1. Such as render marriage *unlawful;* as, for instance, The forbidden times, the simple vow of chastity, a promise of marriage to another person, etc.;

2. Such as render it also *null;* for instance, Consanguinity and affinity to the fourth degree inclusively; spiritual relationship, a solemn vow of chastity; one of the parties not being a Christian; likewise (in those places where the Council of Trent has been received and published) the marriage not being contracted in the presence of the Pastor, or of a Priest commissioned by him, and of two witnesses at least; and others.

In order to discover whether there are any Impediments of marriage, it is very advisable for the parties to make a sincere General Confession some time before they enter into the contract. For this same reason, the Bans are published in the Church; and any one who knows of an Impediment, is in conscience bound to declare it to the Pastor.

15. What is understood by the *forbidden times*?

1. The time which begins with the first Sunday of Advent, and ends with the Epiphany of our Lord; and 2. That which begins with Ash-Wednesday, and ends with Low Sunday, within which times the Church forbids the *solemnizing of marriage*, because they have been particularly set apart for penance and prayer.

In many Dioceses it has been decreed that within these times no marriage is to be contracted without a special dispensation from the Bishop. But even in case this is granted, the married parties, conformably to a general command of the Church, are forbidden to celebrate their wedding with pageantry, entertainments, and rejoicings; nor is the Priest allowed to say the Mass appointed in the Missal for the Bridegroom and the Bride, or to give them the solemn nuptial Benediction independently of this Mass.

16.* Can the Impediments of Marriage never be dispensed with?

The Church can dispense with some, when there are sufficient reasons, but not with all; on this subject the parties must confer with their Pastor.

Only the Church, in whose power it is to grant or to refuse the dispensation (and not those who ask for it, and are too easily deceived by a blind passion), is competent to decide whether the reasons be sufficient. That these reasons must, at all events, be weighty, is evident from the Decree of the Council of Trent (Sess. 24. Ch. 5), which says that "Impediments of marriage are either never, or but rarely, to be dispensed with." A dispensation got by fraud, though valid before men, is, nevertheless, invalid before God.

17. What should we think of *mixed* marriages, *i.e.* of marriages, which are contracted between Catholics and non-Catholics, especially Protestants?

- That the Church has, at all times, disapproved of

such marriages, and never permits them, except on certain conditions.

18.* Why does the Church disapprove of such marriages?

1. Because the Catholic party is exposed to great danger of either losing, or becoming indifferent to the faith;

2. Because the Catholic education of the children is generally deficient, and not seldom impossible;

3. Because the non-Catholic party does not acknowledge Matrimony either as a Sacrament, or as indissoluble, and can, therefore, according to his or her principles, separate, and marry again, which the Catholic consort is not permitted to do; and

4. Because for that very reason such a marriage never is a true emblem of the most intimate, indissoluble union of Christ with His Church, which, however, every Christian marriage ought to be; in fine

5. Because the happiness of conjugal union depends, above all, on unity of faith.

19. On what conditions does the Church consent to a mixed marriage?

On these: 1. That the Catholic party be allowed the free exercise of religion; 2. That he or she earnestly endeavour to gain by persuasion the non-Catholic consort to the true Church; and 3. That all the children be brought up in the Catholic religion. (Breves of Pius VIII. and Gregory XVI.)

20.* Is the Church obliged to make such conditions?

Yes; otherwise she would either be indifferent to the eternal perdition of her children, or deny, that she alone is the true saving Church.

21. Can then a person never be permitted to contract a mixed marriage, unless the Catholic education of the children be previously secured?

No; for such a marriage would be a grievous sin against the Catholic Church, and the spiritual welfare of the children that may be born; wherefore the Church can in no case give her consent to it.

Parents who consent to such a marriage of their child, render themselves guilty of the same sin as the child, and incur a severe responsibility before God.

Application.—In the choice of a state of life, consult, above all things, God and the salvation of your soul. Should you, after a mature deliberation, think yourself to be called to the married state, prepare yourself for it by prayer, good works, and especially, by a good General Confession, and be careful not to follow those who, by sin and vice, draw the curse of God upon their heads.

On Sacramentals.

1. What do we usually understand by Sacramentals?

By *Sacramentals* we understand,

1. All those things which the Church blesses or consecrates for the Divine service, or for our own pious use; as, Holy Water, Oil, Salt, Bread, Wine, Palms, Altars, Chalices, &c.

2. Also the Exorcisms, Blessings, and Consecrations used by the Church.

2. Why are such things called Sacramentals?

They are called Sacramentals, because they resemble the Sacraments, though they are essentially different from them.

3. What is the difference between the Sacramentals and the Sacraments?

1. The Sacraments were instituted by God, and

operate by the efficacy which God gave them; the Sacramentals, on the contrary, were instituted by the Church, and produce their effects by the prayers and blessings of the Church.

2. The Sacraments have an infallible effect, unless we put an obstacle in their way; but the effect of the Sacramentals depends principally on the pious intention of the person who makes use of them.

3. The Sacraments effect immediately inward sanctification, whereas the Sacramentals, by imparting subordinate graces, only contribute towards it, and protect us also from temporal evils.

4. The Sacraments are in general necessary, and commanded by God; but the Sacramentals are only recommended by the Church as useful and wholesome.

4. Why does the Church consecrate or bless the things belonging to the Divine service?

The Church consecrates or blesses all those things that belong to the Divine service, as, Churches, Altars, Bells, Vestments, etc., 1. In order to sanctify them, and dedicate them peculiarly to the Divine service; and 2. To render them more venerable and salutary to us. (Anniversary of the Dedication of a Church).

"Every creature is sanctified by the word of God and prayer." (1 Tim. 4, 5.)—Thus, even in the Old Law, the altar and all the vessels thereof were sprinkled and anointed, as the Lord had commanded. (Levit. 8, 11.)

5. Why does the Church bless also Bread, Wine, the Fruits of the field, and such like things?

The Church blesses these things,

1. After the example of Jesus Christ, who also blessed loaves and fishes; (Luke 9, 16.)

2. That " to them that love God, all things (may) work together unto good;" (Rom. 8, 28.) and

3. That, as by the sin of Adam the curse of God

extended to all the creatures of the earth (Gen. 8, 17. Rom. 8, 20—22), so also His blessings may be poured out over all.

From our birth to our death, the Church incessantly shows her love and solicitude for us: She prays for us, consoles us, helps us, blesses us; even over our last place of rest—the cemetery and grave—she pronounces her blessing.

6. Why should we especially make a devout use of the Sacramentals?

Because we participate through them in the prayer and blessing of the whole Church, in the name of which the Priest consecrates and blesses.

If in the Old Law the blessing of the Patriarchs was so highly esteemed, how much more should we esteem the blessing of the Church, which Christ has intrusted with the inexhaustible Treasure of His means of grace and salvation!

7. Has then the prayer of the Church a particular efficacy?

Yes, the prayer of the Church has a particular efficacy,

1. Because she is the Body of Christ, animated and guided by His Spirit; and

2. Because her prayer is always united with the prayer of Jesus and His Saints.

8. What does the Church usually pray for, when she consecrates or blesses?

She prays for the averting of the judgments of God, for protection against the devil, for peace, blessing, well-being of the soul and body, etc.

That the Church should use symbolical signs, especially the Sign of the Cross, and blessed things, as, Holy Water, Holy Oils, Agnus Dei's, Palms, etc., in imparting her blessing and the fruits of her prayer, ought not to surprise us more, than that God, both in the Old and New Testament, was pleased to distribute His graces and blessings to the people by means of various signs and things. (See Num. 21, 9.—Tob. 6. 8. & 11.—4 Kings 5. & 13.—Mark 6, 13. etc.)

9. How should we use Holy Water?

A pious Christian sprinkles himself with Holy Water, not only when he enters or leaves the Church, but also in his house, when rising and going to bed, when going out and returning, and on many other occasions; and, at the same time, he begs of God that, through the Blood of Jesus Christ, he may be more and more purified, and be protected in all dangers of soul and body.

10. Why are the people sprinkled with Holy Water before High Mass?

Because we should be pure and holy, when we appear in the presence of God, and pray to Him.

Application.—Beware of being indifferent to the prayers and blessings of the Church, but respect and esteem them, and use all things blessed by the Church, especially Holy Water, with due reverence and devotion.

On Prayer.

1. What is Prayer?

Prayer is the raising up of our minds and hearts to God, either to praise Him, or to thank Him, or to beg His grace; and, therefore, it is divided into *Prayer of Praise, Prayer of Thanksgiving,* and *Prayer of Petition.*

2. What does *to praise God* mean?

To praise God means, to rejoice at His infinite Perfections, and to glorify and adore Him on that account. (Ps. 9, 3.)

Examples: David in his Psalms; the three Children in the fiery furnace (Dan. 3.); the Blessed Virgin. (Luke 1, 46. etc.)

3. Are we obliged to praise God?

Yes, we are; for this, we were created, and this will one day be our eternal occupation in Heaven. (Apoc. 4.)

"My mouth shall speak the praise of the Lord, and let all flesh bless His holy name for ever, yea for ever and ever." (Ps. 144, 21.)—"Be ye filled with the Holy Spirit, speaking to yourselves in psalms, and hymns, and spiritual canticles, singing and making melody in your hearts to the Lord." (Eph. 5, 18. 19.)

4. Must we also *thank* God for His gifts?

Yes; for ingratitude is a detestable vice, whereas gratitude is the best means to obtain new benefits.

"In all things give thanks; for this is the will of God in Christ Jesus." (1. Thess. 5, 18.)

5. Must we also *beg graces* of God?

"Ask," says Jesus Christ Himself, "and it shall be given you; seek, and you shall find; knock, and it shall be opened to you." (Luke 11, 9.)

6. Is Prayer necessary to *all*?

Prayer is necessary for salvation to all who have sufficiently the use of reason.

7. Why is Prayer necessary to all?

Because God has commanded it, and because, without it, we do not receive the graces necessary to persevere to the end.

8. But does not God already know what we stand in need of?

Most certainly; but we do not pray, to tell God what we stand in need of, but to acknowledge Him as the Giver of all good gifts, to testify our dependence on Him, and thereby to render ourselves more worthy of His gifts.

9. What are the principal fruits of Prayer?

Prayer 1. Unites us to God; 2. Makes us heavenly-minded; 3. Strengthens us against evil; 4. Gives us zeal and energy for good; 5. Comforts us in adversity; and 6. Obtains help for us in time of need, and the grace of perseverance unto death.

Examples: Moses (Exod. 17, 11.); Samuel (1. Kings 12, 18.); Judith (Judith 9. etc.); Esther (Esther 14. etc.); the Machabees (2. Mac. 15, 27.); the first Christians, whilst Peter was in prison. (Acts 12, 5. etc.)

10. How must we pray that we may obtain these fruits?

We must pray 1. With devotion; 2. With humility; 3. With confidence; 4. With resignation to the will of God; and 5. With perseverance.

11. When do we pray *with devotion?*

When our prayer comes from the heart, and we avoid all distracting thoughts as much as possible.

"This people honoureth Me with their lips; but their heart is far from Me." (Matt. 15, 8.)

12. Are all the distractions in prayer sinful?

They are sinful, when we ourselves are the cause of them, or wilfully admit or entertain them; but when we struggle against them, they increase our merit.

13. What should we do, in order that we may be less distracted in our prayers?

Before our prayers, we should as far as possible banish all worldly thoughts, and represent the Omnipresent God in a lively manner to our mind.

"Before prayer prepare thy soul, and be not as a man that tempteth God." (Ecclus 18, 23.)

14. When do we pray *with humility?*

When we address our prayers to God with a sincere acknowledgment of our weakness and unworthiness.

"The prayer of him that humbleth himself, shall pierce the

clouds." (Ecclus 35, 21.)—The Pharisee and the Publican. (Luke 18.)

15. When do we pray *with confidence*?

When we firmly hope that God will hear our prayer, inasmuch as it is conducive to His honour and to our salvation.

"Let him ask in faith, nothing wavering; for he that wavereth is like a wave of the sea, which is moved and carried about by the wind. Therefore let not that man think that he shall receive any thing of the Lord." (James 1, 6. 7.)

16. Why may, and ought we to have this firm hope?

Because God *can* give us all good things, and, for the sake of Jesus, *will* also really do so, as our Saviour Himself solemnly assures us, saying: "Amen, amen, I say to you, if you ask the Father any thing in My name, He will give it you." (John 16, 23. Comp. Mark 11, 23. 24.)

17. But why do we not always receive what we ask for?

1. Either because we do not pray as we ought; or
2. Because that which we ask for, is prejudicial to our salvation; or
3. Because we do not persevere in praying; therefore, we must also pray with resignation to the will of God, and perseverance.

18. When do we pray *with resignation to the will of God*?

When we leave it entirely to Him, to hear us when, and how He thinks proper.

"Father, not My will, but Thine be done!" (Luke 22, 42.)

19. When do we pray *with perseverance*?

When we do not desist, although we are not aware of being heard, but continue to pray the more fervently.

Example of the woman of Canaan. (Matt. 15.)—Parable of the friend who asks for three loaves. (Luke 11, 5—10.)

20. Must we always use a set form of words in our prayers?

No; this is done in *Vocal* Prayer only; but there is also an *Interior* or *Mental* Prayer, called *Meditation*.

21. In what does *Meditation* consist?

It consists in reflecting upon the life and sufferings of Jesus, upon the Divine Perfections, or other truths of our religion, in order to excite in our hearts pious sentiments, but especially good and efficacious resolutions.

22. When ought we to pray?

Christ says, "That we ought always to pray, and not to faint." (Luke 18, 1.)

23. How is it possible to pray always?

We pray always, when we frequently raise up our minds and hearts to God, and offer up to Him all our labours, sufferings, and pleasures. Yet, at certain times, we are to pray in an especial manner.

24. When are we thus especially to pray?

1. In time of temptation and other urgent need, and during private and public calamities; 2. In the morning and at night; before and after meals; when the Angelus-bell rings; and when we are in the Church.

25. Why should we particularly pray in the Church?

Because the Church is especially the house of God and of prayer, where all that we see and hear, is intended to raise our minds and hearts to the meditation on Divine things.

26. For whom must we pray?

We must pray for all men: for the living and the

dead; for friends and enemies; especially for our parents, brothers and sisters, benefactors, spiritual and temporal Superiors, and also for heretics and infidels.

"I desire therefore, first of all, that supplications, prayers, intercessions, and thanksgivings be made for all men, for kings, and for all that are in high station, that we may lead a quiet and a peaceable life in all piety and chastity." (1. Tim. 2, 1. 2.)

Application.—Consider how happy you are, that you, a miserable worm of the earth, are allowed to speak to God, the Most High, as a child speaks to his father. Pray, therefore, often and willingly, and always with as much devotion as you possibly can, both at home and in the Church.

§. 1. *On the Lord's Prayer.*

27. Which is the most excellent of all prayers?
The most excellent of all prayers is the *Our Father* or the *Lord's Prayer.*

28. Why is the *Our Father* called the *Lord's Prayer?*
Because Christ our Lord has taught it to us, and commanded us to say it. (Matt. 6, 9—13.)

29. What does the Lord's Prayer contain?
It contains a short *Preface* and *Seven Petitions.*

30. What do you call its *Preface?*
These words: "*Our Father who art in Heaven?*"

31. What does the word *Father* remind us of?
That God is our *Father*, so good and so worthy of veneration that there is no earthly father like Him; and that we, therefore, ought to pray to Him with a childlike reverence, love, and confidence.

32. Why do we say, *our* Father, and not, *my* Father?

Because, God being the Father of *all* men, we are all His children, and should, therefore, love one another as brothers, and pray for one another. (Mal. 2, 10.)

33. Why do we add these words: "*Who art in Heaven?*"

To call to our mind,

1. That God, though He is everywhere, dwells especially in Heaven, where we shall one day see Him face to face. (1 Cor. 13, 12.)

2. That we are but pilgrims upon earth, and that our true country is in Heaven; and

3. That, when we pray, we must detach our hearts from all earthly things, and raise them up to Heaven.

34. What do we ask for in the *First* Petition: "*Hallowed be Thy name?*"

That the name of God may never be profaned or blasphemed, but that God may be rightly known, loved, and honoured by us and by all men.

35. Why is this the *First* Petition?

Because we are to esteem the honour and glory of God more than all things else.

36. What do we ask for in the *Second* Petition: "*Thy kingdom come?*"

1. That the kingdom of God, the Church, may be more and more extended upon earth;

2. That the kingdom of Divine grace and love may now be established in our hearts; in order that

3. After this life, we may all be admitted into the kingdom of Heaven.

37. What is the meaning of the *Third* Petition: "*Thy will be done on Earth as it is in Heaven?*"

1. We ask that we, and all men, may do the will of

God on Earth as faithfully and cheerfully, as the Angels and Saints do in Heaven; and

2. We profess that, in all things, we submit ourselves to the holy will of God.

38. What do we ask for in the *Fourth* Petition: " *Give us this day our daily bread?* "

We ask that God would give us all that is daily necessary for our soul and body.

39. Why does Christ bid us ask for our *daily* bread only?

To teach us, that we should wish only for necessaries, not for riches and abundance.

" Having food, and wherewith to be covered, with these we are content." (1 Tim. 6, 8.)

40. What do we ask for in the *Fifth* Petition: " *Forgive us our trespasses, as we forgive them that trespass against us?* "

That God would so forgive us all our sins, as we forgive others who have offended us.

41. May those who do not forgive, expect forgiveness themselves?

No; on the contrary, they pass judgment upon themselves, as often as they say the *Our Father.*

" Forgive thy neighbour if he hath hurt thee; and then shall thy sins be forgiven to thee when thou prayest." (Ecclus 28, 2.)

42. What do we ask for in the *Sixth* Petition: " *Lead us not into temptation?* "

We ask that God would remove from us all temptations, and all the dangers of sin, or, at least, give us grace sufficient to resist them.

43. By whom are we tempted to sin?

1. By our own Flesh or Concupiscence; " For the flesh lusteth against the spirit;" (Gal. 5, 17.)

2. By the World, *i.e.*, by its vain pomps, bad examples, and wicked maxims; and

3. By the Devil, "Who, as a roaring lion, goeth about seeking whom he may devour." (1 Petr. 5, 8.)

44. Why does God permit us to be tempted?

1. To keep us humble;

2. To try our faithfulness, or to punish our unfaithfulness; and

3. To increase our zeal for virtue, and our merits.

1. "Lest the greatness of the revelations should exalt me, there was given me a sting of my flesh, an angel of Satan, to buffet me." (2 Cor. 12, 7.)—2. "The Lord your God trieth you, that it may appear whether you love Him with all your heart and with all your soul, or no." (Deut. 13, 3.)—3. Blessed is the man that endureth temptation; for when he hath been proved, he shall receive the crown of life, which God hath promised to them that love Him." (James 1, 12.)

45. Is temptation in itself a sin?

Temptation in itself is not a sin; but to expose ourselves heedlessly to temptation, or to yield to it, is a sin.

For our consolation and instruction, Christ Himself allowed the Devil to tempt Him. (Matt. 4.)

46. What must we do in order that we may not yield?

We must especially watch and pray, as Christ our Lord says: "Watch ye, and pray that ye enter not into temptation." (Matt. 26, 41.)

47. What do we ask for in the *Seventh* Petition: "*But deliver us from evil?*"

That God would preserve us from all evil of soul and body, especially from sin, and eternal damnation.

48. Why do we add the word, "*Amen*," or "*So be it?*"

To express by it our ardent desire, and also our confidence, of being heard.

Application.—Always say the Lord's Prayer with reverential attention, remembering that we have received it from our Divine Redeemer Himself.

§. 2. *On the Angelical Salutation.*

49. What prayer do Catholics usually say after the *Our Father?*

The prayer, which is said in honour of the Mother of God, and is called the *Angelical Salutation* or *Hail Mary.*

50. Why do we add the Angelical Salutation to the Lord's Prayer?

That the Most Blessed Mother of God may second our weak prayer by her powerful intercession with her Divine Son.

51. How many parts has the Hail Mary?

Two parts: *A Prayer of Praise* and *a Prayer of Petition.*

52. Of what is the *Prayer of Praise* composed?

1. Of the words of the Archangel Gabriel: "*Hail* (Mary), *full of grace, the Lord is with thee; blessed art thou among women;*" and

2. Of the words of St. Elizabeth: "*And blessed is the fruit of thy womb,*" to which we add the name of *Jesus.*

"*Hail*" is a term of salutation, equivalent to "*Ave*" or "*Salve,*" and means, "*Be well,*" "*Health to thee,*" or "*I salute thee.*" (The Transl.)

53. When did the Archangel Gabriel speak those words?

When he announced to the Blessed Virgin Mary, that she would become the Mother of God. (Luke 1, 28.)

54. When were the above words spoken by St. Elizabeth?

When Mary went into the hill country, and visited her cousin Elizabeth. (Luke 1, 42.)

55. Why do we address Mary by these words: "*Full of grace?*"

1. Because Mary was replenished with grace, even before her birth; 2. Because she always increased in grace; and 3. Because she brought forth the Author of all graces.

56. Why do we say: "*The Lord is with thee?*"

Because God is, in a most particular manner, with the Blessed Virgin, wherefore she is justly called the Chosen Daughter of the Heavenly Father, the True Mother of the Divine Son, and the Immaculate Spouse of the Holy Ghost.

57. What is the meaning of these words of praise: "*Blessed art thou among women?*"

That Mary is the happiest of all the daughters of Eve:

1. Because she was chosen before all, to be the Mother of God;

2. Because she alone is a Mother, and, at the same time, a Virgin; and

3. Because the first woman entailed a curse on the world, Mary, on the other hand, brought us salvation.

58. Why do we add these words: "*Blessed is the fruit of thy womb, Jesus?*"

To show that the veneration of Mary is inseparable from the veneration of Christ, and that we praise the Mother for the sake of the Son.

59. Of what is the *Prayer of Petition* composed?

Of the words which were added by the Church

" *Holy Mary, Mother of God, pray for us sinners, now, and at the hour of our death. Amen.*"

60. Why were these words added by the Church?

1. That we may profess by them before the whole world, that Mary is truly *Mother of God;* and 2. That we may often implore the assistance of her prayers in all our necessities, and especially, for obtaining the grace of a happy death.

61. Why should we often pray for a happy death?

1. Because our eternal salvation depends on the last moments of our life; 2. Because, at that critical time, the temptations are commonly more violent and more dangerous; and 3. Because perseverance to the end of life is a special grace, for which we ought continually to pray. (Counc. of Tr. Sess. 6. Can. 6. 22.)

62. Has the Blessed Virgin great influence with God?

Certainly; for it has never been heard yet, that any one who had recourse to Mary, and with true devotion implored her intercession, has ever been abandoned by God. (St. Bernard.)

63. What prayer do we say when morning, noon, and night the bell is rung for the "*Angelus?*"

We say the following:

The Angel of the Lord declared unto Mary. And she conceived of the Holy Ghost. Hail, Mary, etc.

Behold the handmaid of the Lord. Be it done unto me according to thy word. Hail, Mary, etc.

And the Word was made flesh. And dwelt among us. Hail Mary, etc.

Pray for us, O Holy Mother of God!

That we may be made worthy of the promises of Christ.

Let us pray:

Pour forth, we beseech Thee, O Lord, Thy grace into our hearts, that we, to whom the Incarnation of Christ Thy Son was made known by the message of an Angel, may, by His Passion and Cross, be brought to the glory of His Resurrection, through the same Christ our Lord. Amen.

Though we should live in countries or places, where such public signal is not given, yet, as this pious exercise is strongly recommended by the Church, and several Popes have granted many spiritual favours and Indulgences to those who daily and devoutly practise it, let us be careful to say this prayer with great devotion every day in the morning, at noon, and in the evening. (The Transl.)

64. Why do we say this prayer?

1. To give thanks to God for the Incarnation of Christ; and 2. To honour the Blessed Virgin, and to recommend ourselves to her protection.

65.* What is the *Rosary*?

It is a very useful and easy form of prayer, mental as well as vocal, which was introduced by St. Dominic in the thirteenth century, was approved of by the Church, and has, since then, always been practised and recommended by her.

This form of prayer is called *Rosary*, because it is, as it were, a *chaplet* of the most beautiful prayers and meditations, wherein the principal mysteries of our religion are wreathed like fragrant *roses*. Hence the name. It is divided into three parts, each part consisting of five Mysteries. The first five are called the *Joyful Mysteries;* the next five, the *Dolorous* or *Sorrowful Mysteries;* and the last five, the *Glorious Mysteries*. It is true, that, in the Rosary, the same salutation is often repeated; but this ought not to surprise us more than that, in Psalm 135, the words, "*His mercy endureth for ever,*" are repeated twenty-seven times; or, that the Angels in Heaven incessantly sing: "*Holy, holy, holy.*" Nor ought this practice to appear tedious to us, since the mind is, in the mean time, to be occupied with the contemplation of the Holy Mysteries. (See Pages IX. and X.)

The Titles of honour, which are given to our Blessed Lady in the Litany of Loretto, as, "*Mystical Rose, Tower of David, Morning Star*" etc., are symbolical expressions taken from the Holy Scripture, and are applied to her on account of the eminent privileges and graces conferred on her.

Application.—Honour the Blessed Virgin in a most particular and childlike manner. Implore her assistance in all your necessities and concerns, and strive eagerly to imitate her charity, patience, purity, and her other virtues.

ON RELIGIOUS PRACTICES AND CEREMONIES IN GENERAL; AND ON SOME IN PARTICULAR.

1. What do we understand by *Religious Ceremonies*?

By *Religious Ceremonies* we understand certain significant signs or actions, which the Church has established for the celebration of the Divine Service.

2. Why is the instruction on *Prayer* followed here by the explanation of *Religious Practices and Ceremonies*?

1. Because Religious Ceremonies have been instituted to give praise and glory to God, no less than Prayer itself; and 2. Because they help us to elevate our souls to God and to the contemplation of Divine things, consequently also, to pray with attention and devotion.

3. How do Ceremonies help us to elevate our souls to God and Divine things?

They help us 1. Because they render the Divine Service more solemn, and thereby captivate our attention, and draw it from earthly objects to God; and 2. Because they represent in a visible manner before our eyes, Mysteries invisible in themselves, and thereby render it easier for us to meditate on them.

4.* Are not Ceremonies idle Observances?

Not at all; for 1. God Himself prescribed, under severe penalties, several kinds of Ceremonies to the Jews; 2. Christ our Lord also used various Ceremonies; and 3. He Himself instituted sacramental signs or Ceremonies.

1. See the Book of Leviticus.—2. For instance, when He healed the man that was deaf and dumb (Mark 7.); when He gave sight to the man born blind (John 9.); when He breathed on His Disciples, and imparted to them the Holy Ghost (John 20,).—3. When He instituted the Holy Eucharist, Baptism, etc.

5.* But must we not adore God in spirit and in truth? (John 4, 24.)

By all means; and, therefore, the Church wishes that we should not merely assist at the Ceremonies, but also understand their meaning, and accompany them with prayer, and pious sentiments.

6. Have then all Religious Ceremonies a meaning?

Yes; all things which the Church makes use of for celebrating the Divine Service, have a mystical signification, and are intended to excite our souls to lively sentiments of devotion.

The Ceremonies of Baptism, See Pages 253 & 254;—of Confirmation, Pages 256 & 257;—of the Mass, Pages 268 & 269;—of the Blessing of water, salt, oil, etc. See Page 311, etc.

7. But are there not also Religious Ceremonies and Practices which are useless and superfluous?

No; that which the holy, infallible Church ordains, approves, or practises, cannot but be useful and salutary, because she is always guided by the Holy Ghost.

8. What is then the use of *Incense*?

Incense is an emblem of reverence and of prayer which should ascend to Heaven as a sweet odour before God. (Ps. 140, 2.)

9. What do the *Lighted Candles* signify?

They signify Faith which enlightens, Hope which soars above this world, and Charity which inflames; and they recall also to our mind those times of persecution, when the Christians celebrated the Divine Service in Catacombs or subterranean caverns.

10. What do the Candles blessed on the Feast of the Purification of the Blessed Virgin Mary, especially call to our mind?

The words of Simeon, that Jesus is "a Light to the revelation of the Gentiles,"† and that we also are to walk "as children of the Light." (Luke 2, 32. Ephes. 5, 8.)

† *i.e.*, a Light to be revealed to the Gentiles, or to lighten the Gentiles. (The Transl.)

11. What does the *Paschal Candle* remind us of?

It reminds us of Jesus Christ, risen from the dead, who rescued us from the servitude of Satan, as formerly the pillar of fire led the Children of Israel out of the bondage of the Egyptians. (Exod. 14, 20.)

12. What do the *Ashes* blessed on Ash-Wednesday call to our remembrance?

That we should humble ourselves, and sincerely repent; therefore, the Priest, whilst he puts ashes on our heads, says: "Remember, man, that thou art dust, and into dust thou shalt return." (Gen. 3, 19.)

Ashes were even in the Old Testament an emblem of penance and humility. Examples: The Ninivites, Judith, Esther, etc.

13. What do the *Palms* on Palm-Sunday call to our mind?

The triumphant entrance of our Lord into Jerusalem, and His victory over Hell; and that we also should strive to gain the palm of eternal life.

14. For what end are *Public Supplications* and *Processions* made?

1. To praise God also publicly, to thank Him, to draw down, by our prayers, His protection and blessing upon town and country, and to avert His chastisements;

2. To proclaim the victory and triumph of the Catholic Religion, for which purpose the Cross and Banner precede; and

3. To be reminded, that we are but pilgrims in this world, and that we should constantly walk before God.

We meet with examples of such Public Supplications and Processions as early as in the most ancient times of Christianity.

15. What should we think of *Pilgrimages*?

When they are made according to the intentions of the Church, they are certainly much to be commended; nay, they are even confirmed by the example of the Saints, and the Indulgences of the Church.

It is true that God is, and hears us, everywhere: nevertheless, He may be more disposed to hear us in certain places, as well as at certain times. Moreover, in Places of Pilgrimage there are many things calculated to excite us to pray with greater fervour and confidence, and, therefore, with more chances of being heard. Should abuses intervene, not the Pilgrimages, but the abuses should be condemned.

16. How does the Church wish Pilgrimages to be made?

The Church wishes 1. That we should not neglect for them the urgent duties of our state or profession; 2. That we should have a good intention; 3. That we should well employ the time engaged in them, and patiently endure the hardships which attend them; and 4. That we should pray fervently at the Holy Place, and, if possible, go there to Confession and Communion.

17.* Have Pilgrimages long been in use ?

They were in use even under the Old Law, where we see that, by an express command of God, the Israelites went on a pilgrimage to the Temple of Jerusalem, as did also Jesus and Mary. And the first Christians went frequently to the place where Christ lived and suffered, and to the tombs of the Apostles and holy Martyrs.

18.* What are *Confraternities* ?

They are pious Associations, generally approved of by the Popes, and established for the purposes of mutual prayer, encouragement and assistance in the performance of good works, and the frequentation of the Sacraments.

Since Confraternities conduce much to holiness of life, when the rules, which, however, as such do not bind under pain of any sin, are well kept; the Church has granted them ample Indulgences: yet all are free to apply or not for admittance into them.

Application.—Participate with great devotion in the Religious Practices and Ceremonies of the Church, and never suffer yourself to be diverted from them either by the mockery or example of impious or thoughtless people.

RECAPITULATION.

1. *Our Religion is Divine.*

This is proved by her History from the Creation of the world to the present time; viz.: By her age, her Founder, her propagation, her duration, her blessings and fruits, etc. (See Short History of Religion, Page 3—63.)

II. *This our Divine Religion teaches,*

That we are in this world in order that we may serve God, and be eternally happy with Him in Heaven. (See Full Catech. of the Catholic Religion, Page 65—68.) For this end we must

1. *Believe* all that God has revealed (Page 69—158);

2. Keep all the *Commandments* which God has given us either Himself (Page 159—211), or through His Church (Page 211—221); consequently, also avoid *Sin*, by which the Divine Command is broken (Page 221—229), and strive to lead a *virtuous life* (Page 230—239). But this we cannot do without the *Grace* of God (Page 240—247).

Therefore we must also

3. Make use of the *Means of Grace* which God has ordained; namely, the *Sacraments* (Page 247—314), and *Prayer* (Page 314—331).

THE END.